Infamous Desire

Infamous Desire

Male Homosexuality in Colonial Latin America

EDITED BY PETE SIGAL

THE UNIVERSITY OF CHICAGO PRESS
Chicago and London

The University of Chicago Press, Chicago 60637
The University of Chicago Press, Ltd., London
© 2003 by The University of Chicago
All rights reserved. Published 2003
Printed in the United States of America

12 11 10 09 08 07 06 05 04 03   1 2 3 4 5

ISBN: 0-226-75702-1 (cloth)
ISBN: 0-226-75704-8 (paper)

Chapter 2 also appears as "Gender Subordination and Political Hierarchy in Prehispanic America," in *Religion in Social Context in Europe and America, 1200–1700,* by Richard C. Trexler, MRTS vol. 238 (Tempe, Arizona, 2002), pp. 553–90. Copyright Arizona Board of Regents for Arizona State University.

Chapter 7, by Serge Gruzinksi, first appeared in Spanish as "Las cenizas del deseo: Homosexuales novohispanos a mediados del siglo XVII," in *De la santidad a la perversión o de la porqué no se cumplía la ley de Dios en la sociedad Novohispana,* edited by Sergio Ortega Noriega (Mexico City: Editorial Grijalbo, 1985).

Library of Congress Cataloging-in-Publication Data

Infamous desire : male homosexuality in colonial Latin America / edited by Pete Sigal.
    p. cm.
    Includes bibliographical references and index.
    ISBN 0-226-75702-1 (cloth : alk. paper) — ISBN 0-226-75704-8 (pbk. : alk. paper)
        1. Gay men—Latin America—History.   2. Homosexuality—Latin America—
    History.   3. Lust—History.   4. Power (Social sciences)—Latin America—History.
    5. Sex role—Latin America—History.   I. Sigal, Peter Herman, 1964–

HQ76.2.L29 I54 2003
306.76′62′098—dc21

                                                            2002020499

For the activists . . .
the living and the dead

CONTENTS

(Homo)Sexual Desire and Masculine Power in Colonial Latin America: Notes toward an Integrated Analysis

PETE SIGAL

> Among the serranos and the Yungas the devil has introduced this vice
> under a kind of sanctity, and in each temple . . . they have a man or
> two, or more . . . who go dressed as women from the time they are
> children, and speak like them, and in manner, dress, and everything
> else imitate women. On feast [days] . . . the chiefs[1] and nobles have
> carnal, foul intercourse . . . with these [men]. To those who told me
> of the wickedness that was committed, and of the ugliness of the sin,
> I responded that they were not at fault, because, during their child-
> hoods they had been put in that position by the chiefs for use in that
> bad and nefarious vice, and to be priests and guard the idols' temples.
> So what I deduced from this was that the devil held such sway in this
> land that, not satisfied with making them fall into so great a sin, he
> made them believe that this vice was a kind of holiness and religion.
> —Pedro de Cieza de León, *La crónica del Perú*

When the Spaniards and Portuguese wrote about the conquest of Latin America, they used many descriptions to denigrate the indigenous populations. Probably the three most common and, to Europeans, most extraordinary images in these chronicles of the conquest were human sacrifice, cannibalism, and sodomy. To many Europeans, the connection between these three was obvious: they represented both the abominable degradation of many indigenous peoples and the extent to which the devil had tricked the people into the most horrific and gruesome acts. At the time of the conquest, same-sex eroticism existed in many, perhaps all, of the indigenous societies of Latin America. After the conquest, sodomy would continue to exist

within a somewhat different framework. During the colonial years, indigenous morality changed, partly as a result of contact with the Europeans.[2] In
urban areas in Europe at the time, communities of sodomites had begun to
form,[3] and the same types of communities were created in the colonies.

The quotation from Cieza de León, a chronicler of the conquest in Peru,
presents some of the complex cultural, political, and social realities related to
colonial Latin American same-sex desires and behaviors. Cieza argues that
the people, particularly the leaders, of many indigenous societies, engaged in
extensive sodomy. He also connects such behavior with indigenous religion,
stating that the indigenous people had a spiritual justification for sodomy.
Then Cieza posits that transvestism and effeminacy were central elements of
the ritualized sodomy. Such an analysis relates to the many different goals of
a chronicler like Cieza. He wanted to provide a description of indigenous ritual, justify the conquest, and stress his own expertise related to the people of
Peru. Further, he brought along with him much ideological baggage from
Europe. Cieza supported a theory then popular in Europe, what elsewhere I
have called (drawing from Rudi Bleys's work) the "progressive development"
theory of sodomy.[4] According to this theory, sodomy was rampant in less
"civilized" societies, but less so in more developed groups.

I have begun this book with Cieza's statement because such an analysis
points to the complexity of any discussion of homosexual desire in colonial
Latin America. The message that this quotation gives about the reality of
colonial era homosexuality is by no means simple; rather, it requires significant interpretation. Michael Horswell and Richard Trexler both use Cieza's
work, but the two scholars make diametrically opposed arguments about how
to interpret such statements. As the reader will note, this book is structured
around a series of debates regarding the relationships between male homosexual behaviors and desires and colonial era representations of masculinity,
femininity, and power. Gender, masculinity, femininity, and power are operative in all the colonial texts which discuss sodomy. The authors vary significantly in their analyses of power, some choosing to focus more on the gender systems, others deciding to emphasize the political and social contexts.
The ensuing arguments shed light not just on the ways in which colonial
Latin Americans had sex and organized their sexual lives, but also on current
academic and political controversies regarding the cultural and social constructions of sexual identity.

In most Latin American societies, residents and outside observers alike
believe that an element called *machismo* is a central component, perhaps *the*
central component, of male identity. But scholars rarely have engaged in any
serious analysis of *machismo*.[5] The *machista* is assumed to be the average
Latin American male, and the *maricón* is seen as his opposite, the "fag" of
Spanish-speaking Latin American societies.[6] This *maricón* is defined by his

presence as an opposing force to the *machista*. While some scholars have attempted to analyze this phenomenon, few have attempted to place that analysis within a broad theoretical or historical context.[7] This collection presents the most recent scholarship on the ways in which male "homosexualities" were represented in colonial Latin America.[8] The book shows that societies' definitions of sexual acts between males were based on the operative gender systems of the colonial period.

All of the essays included in this volume relate sodomy to concepts of desire and power. All relate male homosexual behavior to broader gender systems which defined masculinity and femininity. The mixture of the various indigenous, Iberian, and African gender systems produced strong notions of difference between masculine and feminine spheres. The person who practiced male homosexual acts did not always fit comfortably into either of these spheres, but the image of the man practicing sodomy could be used, as in Cieza's statement, to reinforce normative gender roles, and to challenge the imagined gender system of an entire society.[9] Some of the authors in this volume believe the primary operative element that related the gender system to male homosexual desires and acts was power. They see power as a way of creating dependent male-dominant relationships.[10] Other authors focus more extensively on the ways in which the various cultures conceived of desire. Several discuss the possibility of a relationship between male homosexuality and the concept of an indigenous transgender, transsexual, or third-gender subjectivity. Still others focus on the linguistic and social frameworks of male homosexual acts.

The anthology also alters the historiography of colonial Latin America. Though scholars who have studied this period rarely have considered the topic, I argue here that one cannot understand the cultural, political, and social history of early Latin America without studying the ways in which sexual acts and desires were created, manipulated, and altered. The colonial culture created various normative codes directly and indirectly influenced by social understandings of sexual desire. For example, through its traditions and institutions, society developed an understanding of what it meant to be a successful man. The successful man had honor, engaged in sexual activities with at least one woman, and had children. His masculinity was proven through valor in warfare, business, or some similar activity, and through social status. The implied opposite of this position was the man who allowed other men to penetrate him. He was defeated, effeminate, and dishonorable. To understand the role of the successful man, one must also study the construction of his opposite, for one could not exist without the other.[11]

Colonial Latin American societies viewed sodomy from within their own cultural systems. Iberian societies understood the presence of sodomy as an element of an honor code which asserted male domination. As Geoffrey

Spurling has noted, the public discovery of a sodomitical relationship could challenge the honor of the men involved, particularly the man perceived to be playing the "passive" role. Yet, the punishments for such a discovery varied significantly, and often depended on the man's power within the local political system. Thus, a man's honor was negotiable.[12] Most indigenous societies perceived sodomy as part of a gender system which stressed both a warrior ethic that ingrained an ideology of extreme male dominance and a reciprocal structure that valued the work of both men and women.[13] Within the indigenous systems, sodomy and transvestism had institutionalized presences, though most of the societies treated the existence of known "passive" sodomites with great disdain.

In order to contextualize and analyze the role of male homosexualities in colonial Latin America, I have categorized a series of debates under the headings of identity, sexual desire, and gender and power. Instead of engaging in an extensive analysis of the relative merits of each chapter in this volume, I discuss the authors in the context of these three categories of debates.

IDENTITY

The extreme discretion of the texts dealing with sodomy—that utterly confused category—and the nearly universal reticence in talking about it made possible a twofold operation: on the one hand, there was an extreme severity (punishment by fire was meted out well into the eighteenth century . . .), and on the other hand, a tolerance that must have been widespread (which one can deduce indirectly from the infrequency of judicial sentences, and which one glimpses more directly through certain statements concerning societies of men that were thought to exist in the army or in the courts). There is no question that the appearance in [the] nineteenth century . . . of a whole species and subspecies of homosexuality . . . made possible a strong advance of social controls into this area of "perversity"; but it also made possible the formation of a "reverse" discourse: homosexuality began to speak in its own behalf, to demand that its legitimacy or "naturality" be acknowledged.
—Michel Foucault, *The History of Sexuality*

Foucault's theoretical approach has influenced many historical studies of homosexuality.[14] His influence stems from the social constructionist approach emblematic in this quotation. Here Foucault argues that the nineteenth century witnessed a discursive shift in treatments of male homosexual desires and acts. This shift, from a focus on a confusing set of acts defined as "sodomy" to an unchanging identity of "homosexuality," entailed the creation of a new and qualitatively different type of persona. It is here that Foucault argues that sexual identity itself was created.

Some Latin American historians have viewed arguments like the one Foucault is making here as either irrelevant or obfuscationist. They have argued that the terminology used is imprecise and that the cultural/postmodernist methodology delineated ignores the rules of historical evidence.[15] Other scholars have found such approaches useful.[16] Since social constructionist ideas are used throughout this book, here I delineate two of the questions with which historians must deal in order to use such a theory: (1) What does this approach offer the colonial Latin American historian of sexuality? (2) How does the historical evidence from colonial Latin America shed new light on such social constructionist/postmodernist theory?

The social constructionist approach offers the colonial Latin American historian a way of understanding the meanings derived from sexual acts and desires. A scholar influenced by Foucault, for example, may analyze discussions of sodomy to discover the ways in which the category was used by writers, jurists, and politicians. The essentialist scholar, who argues that sexuality is based only in nature, not constructed in any way by society, is limited to finding gay and lesbian people in history.[17] Those of us who study the sixteenth and seventeenth centuries find few people to study.

The quotation from Foucault presents both the benefits and the drawbacks of his approach. I offer two preliminary critiques based on the early Latin American evidence. First, as we will see, there was little "reticence" in talking about sodomy, at least in the documents used in this volume. Perhaps the "sin that dared not utter its name" was already in the early modern period becoming an obsession within many circles. Perhaps this was caused by the extended contact with other cultures. Second, while we often are confused in our readings of the documents, there is little doubt that the political and religious authorities understood what they meant by sodomy, although the boundaries of the term varied from place to place (sometimes including bestiality, anal intercourse between a man and a woman, and/or sexual activity between two women, and sometimes referring exclusively to anal intercourse between two men).

Foucault maintains that a fundamental shift in the nature of sexual identity took place between the eighteenth and nineteenth centuries. At this time, according to Foucault, homosexuality became ingrained within the individual, compared with sodomy, which was something which the individual did. Note that Foucault also states that communities of sodomites existed, something supported by the evidence presented here. The existence of such communities does not weaken Foucault's overall argument, as long as these communities were not based on an identity ingrained in the individual. Indeed, the Latin American evidence seems to support Foucault on this point. The communities which existed in Mexico and Brazil were formed by men who wanted to engage in sexual activity with other men. Many also engaged in sexual activity with women, and nobody, even those who expressed a strong preference for men, suggested a sexual identity that was ingrained in the individual psyche.[18] The only identities supported by the evidence relate to the effeminacy of particular practitioners of sodomy. Yet, if we were to study similar phenomena among contemporary Latin Americans, we would find, as other scholars have, extensive evidence of homosexuality in which particular men believe their identities to be ingrained within their very senses of self.[19] The Latin American evidence thus supports the idea that a homosexual identity was invented only after the period under discussion in this volume.[20]

Most of the essays included in this collection (Luiz Mott's contribution is a notable exception) are written from the social constructionist perspective. Western society, since the nineteenth century, has developed taxonomies, lists designed to categorize what people do sexually and to make people believe that those sexual desires are internal to their senses of being.[21] The peoples of colonial Latin America, and the indigenous people in particular, had no such taxonomic obsessions.[22] The sociohistorical creation of sexuality as an ingrained identity based on a set of shared experiences was a complex process, and the indigenous peoples did not view sexual desire with the same taxonomies as either modern Western people (categorizing people as either homosexual or heterosexual)[23] or early modern Europeans (classifying acts as sinful or non-sinful and, within certain parameters, basing identities on these acts).[24] Although there were many similarities in these understandings, the indigenous peoples and the Iberians approached sexual desire in very different ways because of their different historical experiences.[25]

Richard Trexler argues that homosexuality did not exist in the early modern period. Luiz Mott and Serge Gruzinski, on the contrary, argue that men identified with homosexual acts were a part of the social landscape in colonial Brazil and Mexico. The other authors make it clear that most, probably all, of the various populations in colonial Latin America knew of and practiced sodomy. While all but Mott argue that homosexuality as understood today is a modern phenomenon, they say that it is an important term for analysis of the early modern period. According to this logic, Trexler defines homosexuality as a modern construction of sexual desire: one in which a person's sexual identity is seen as internal to one's notion of self. Similarly, Gruzinski argues that homosexuality as known today could not have existed. He states that, while communities of sodomites formed in Mexico City and Puebla, these groups were not based on an internally coherent identity, but were composed of people thrown together through their marginalization and the repression of their activities.

Mott's argument contradicts these as he formulates the essentialist side of the debate in order to stress his disagreements with Foucault's philosophy. To Mott, the fact that such communities existed in seventeenth-century Portugal and Brazil shows the problems with social constructionist theory. Here he claims that a gay identity had begun to form. Indeed, Mott's earlier work on the Inquisition in Portugal and Brazil certainly suggests the formation of a broader community of sodomites than most social constructionists would have imagined.[26] Further, Mott argues that the homosexual community had various elements of intragroup socialization, which shows that they were in fact a community faced with oppression.

Mott's chapter is vital to this collection because he accomplishes two important goals: he ably uses Inquisition documents to reconstruct a community of sodomites, and he promotes an argument largely rejected by the other scholars represented in this collection. Yet perhaps Mott's evidence could be understood within the context of Foucault's "theater of power."[27] For, in the *History of Sexuality*, Foucault argues that sexual desire from times long before the invention of homosexuality and heterosexuality in the nineteenth century has been formulated through such a theater, an interaction between social norms and regulatory agencies. Federico Garza Carvajal, looking at the relationship between sodomy and masculinity in seventeenth-century Spain and Mexico City, convincingly argues that the state uses its conception of sodomy to pursue colonial goals. In Mexico City the colonizers, in order to promote masculine valor in that emerging society, find it very important to critique effeminacy.[28] Mary Elizabeth Perry, analyzing sodomy prosecutions in sixteenth- and seventeenth-century Seville (Spain), argues that the presence of particular elements of state power warranted a definition of sodomy in which sodomites were punished severely by state authorities because they saw it as a contagious disease.[29] In Seville and elsewhere, both state and church authorities of the early modern period punished sodomites for two reasons: sodomy was seen as a contagious disease and as a transgression of gender norms.[30] Indeed, in the cases of the Inquisition in Brazil, Mott's evidence does seem to show that both models apply. The Inquisition was concerned with contagion and the corruption of youth, and it was concerned with the role of male effeminacy in society. Both concerns show that a "theater of power" had developed in which agents of the state attempted to assert control in order to protect youth and the gender system.

As several chapters show, the Latin American evidence does not support Foucault's conception of a sudden nineteenth-century shift in the discourse regarding homosexuality. The discursive shift was significantly more gradual: communities of sodomites had formed by the seventeenth century in Mexico and Brazil, just as they had formed by the fifteenth century in Florence and Venice.[31] These communities developed particular notions of identity based on shared experiences. The courts primarily prosecuted actives, seen as seducers. The conception of a passive desiring and seducing an active had not entered into the broader cultural imagination. By the eighteenth century, the notion of an ingrained identity, at least among recalcitrant sodomites, had formed in many areas of Europe and the Americas.[32] Thus passive homosexuals were prosecuted more frequently and severely, as they were often seen as seducers. This shift in identity would lead to the medicalization of discourse in the nineteenth century. This more gradual process, based on various cultural and social reconfigurations, belies the more sudden changes described by Foucault, whose own research emphasizes the discourse of the "experts" who studied sexual desire.

Note that none of the authors argue that no form of sexual identity existed in the early modern period. The Latin American evidence presents the figure of the *puto*, the Hispanic "queer."[33] Spaniards, who also found terms in Nahuatl, Quechua, and Yucatec Maya that meant the same thing,[34] used this terminology to refer to a man who was seen as effeminate and who was believed to take the "passive" role in anal intercourse. The *puto*'s public effeminacy was what characterized him as a *puto*, so his was more of a gender identity than one based on a sexual role. However, the connection between the effeminate male's gender and his sexual role was perceived (at least in the Hispanic world) to be clear. There is evidence both that *putos* formed communities with other *putos*, and that other men knew where to go to find *putos* for sex.[35] Thus a form of sexual identity did exist, but this type of sexuality was different from the modern conception: the *puto*'s sexuality was defined not by the fact that he had sex with men, but by his placing himself in a particular gender and sexual position.[36] The societies studied in this volume organized their conceptual universes in a variety of ways, and this led to clashes in meanings regarding homosexualities.

SEXUAL DESIRE

The following testimony comes from an early-seventeenth-century judicial investigation into allegations against a local Spanish official in rural Peru: "And Damián de Morales said to him, 'Antón, let's be friends,' and he put his hand through his breeches' pocket, saying, 'You are plump Antón,' and he moved his hand over his buttocks, feeling him, and then he moved [his hands] to the front to touch what was his."[37] The case, uncovered by Geoffrey Spurling, alleges that this official attempted to seduce, rape, and sodomize an African slave. The tale speaks volumes about Spanish values and laws and various conflicts between official ideology, political intrigue, and popular culture.

What was Morales's desire? This anthology focuses on *sexual* desire, the desire to engage in, discuss, or fantasize about acts which particular societies considered sexual or erotic. Sexual desire is the impetus of individual thoughts and actions related to sexual acts. An analysis of sexual desire can show ways in which these societies and cultures influenced, altered, established, and repressed meanings and feelings related to sexual acts.[38] We can study sexual desire only if we know what sexual desire is. The line between what is sexual and what is not sexual is by no means obvious. Theoretically, it is plausible to have a society where what we see as sexual intercourse is not believed to be sexual at all. However, all societies of which we have knowledge have considered vaginal intercourse to be sexual. All of these societies have known of sodomy (between men, between men and women, between men and other animals). While it is less clear, all appear to have known of oral sex, sexual acts between women, and the concept of rape. All appear to have considered these acts sexual.

All of the societies discussed in this volume knew that vaginal intercourse led to reproduction, and all appear to have built a framework of sexual desire around this knowledge. Sodomy and rape, however, may have been more about power than desire. If the active partner decided to sodomize or rape the passive only because he wanted to emphasize his power over that individual, then his desire was a desire for power, not a desire for sexual fulfillment. If, on the other hand, he decided to engage in such an act both because he wanted power and because he wanted sexual release, then his desire would have had more than one rationale. For the Spanish, the answer, at least when discussing sodomy, appears to be the second one proffered here. The *puto* was envisioned as one who, for one reason or another, desired to be penetrated.[39] The *puto*'s actual desire went unrecorded, but the discourse surrounding sodomy suggested that the *puto* had certain desires. Yet the depiction of these desires changed through the early modern period, and both rape and sodomy were seen as related to domination and power.[40]

The evidence related to colonial Latin America remains somewhat inconclusive. While Trexler at first appears to argue that notions of sodomy were only about power, not about desire, he does leave room for an analysis based on desire, at least on the part of the active partner. The active is shown in Trexler's work most often as a high-level official or a warrior. In both cases, Trexler maintains that sexual fulfillment was one of the goals of the active partner. However, sexual desire on the part of the passive plays no role in Trexler's work. I have found no evidence of sexual desire on the part of the passive in Maya society. My essay in this volume asserts that the desires of the active partner played important roles in a variety of ways, but that the desires of the passives are not present in the documents. Michael Horswell and Ward Stavig both believe that the passive did in fact desire sexual fulfillment on some level. Horswell in particular argues that the notion of femininity in Andean societies validated such desires. Gruzinski and Mott show that desire in seventeenth-century Mexico City and eighteenth-century Brazil, respectively, allowed men to form an extensive community network. David Higgs presents the most extensive evidence of sexual desire. In the cases of the Carmelites engaged in sexual activity, desire appears to be a paramount force. The actors involved in the sexual acts participated in them on a regular basis, and force was rarely an issue. In all cases the authors admit that, in addition to desire, power played a major role in determining ideas about these sexual acts.

GENDER AND POWER

Gender, or the ways in which a society comes to create notions of difference based on perceived traits which distinguish men from women and boys from girls, is intricately interlinked with the ways in which a society determines and maintains power relations. As I have stated elsewhere, power is to be understood as a method of exercising domination over a person or persons. It most often is institutionalized and made a part of "tradition." In a colonial society, power is manipulated and used by the colonizers in an attempt to gain hegemony, but many others also use it to maintain traditional hierarchies.[41] Here I connect gender and power first through an analysis of the debate related to the cross-dressing figure in indigenous societies and then through an examination of the relationship between masculinity, femininity, and sodomy.

The following appears in a letter from a priest in seventeenth-century Yucatan:

> Lord, the perversity of the miserable people reached such a point [that] next to one of their principal temples they had a walled-around large house of very decorous construction solely for the habitation of acquiescents, into which entered all of those who wished to have their sodomitic copulations, especially those who are very young, so that they could learn there, these ministers of the Demon wearing women's skirts and occupying themselves only in making bread for the priests and in their obscenities.[42]

In this citation, embedded within the priest's moralizing, one finds that ritual transvestism existed among the last Maya societies to be conquered. The earlier quotation from Cieza de León also indicates the importance of transvestism to interpretations of homosexual behaviors among the indigenous peoples of the Americas. While most homosexual behavior which took place within preconquest indigenous societies probably did not involve transvestism, the European chroniclers and subsequent investigators found the presence of transvestism to be an easy way to gauge the level of homosexual activity in a given society.

How can scholars understand the apparent contradiction: a seemingly universal presence of the cross dresser among indigenous societies and the apparent distaste for sodomy represented in many texts? For as Trexler himself notes, most preconquest indigenous societies seem to have abhorred "passivity" in males, and they certainly degraded those boys and men who exhibited characteristics perceived to be feminine.[43]

In the field of lesbian and gay studies, the elusive figure of the berdache has become a major focal point of debate. Although nineteenth-century anthropologists were the first to analyze the berdache in any significant way, colonial observers did mention the presence of this person. The conquerors claimed to be shocked by the presence of the transvested figure who they believed was acting as a receptive partner in anal intercourse.[44] By the nineteenth century, anthropologists interested in finding the "other" and developing, out of the indigenous peoples, "noble savages," were intrigued by the status of such a cross dresser.[45] By the late twentieth century, anthropologists and gay studies scholars asserted that the berdache was some sort of gay predecessor. These scholars have perceived that the berdache was treated with great respect.[46] Moreover, Will Roscoe in particular has asserted that the berdache existed in almost every indigenous society.[47] More recently, Ramón Gutiérrez and Trexler have questioned the role of the berdache, Gutiérrez showing that many of them were forced to transvest themselves. Trexler has shown that many indigenous societies despised femininity and passivity in males.[48] In this volume, the debate regarding the berdache is advanced methodologically and theoretically by Trexler and Horswell. Both place the berdache in the context of gendered power in preconquest and colonial Latin America. Trexler focuses on the construction of masculinity in the indigenous societies, while Horswell analyzes the importance of femininity in Andean culture.

Trexler argues that previous scholars have failed even to consider the way in which gendered power was structured in indigenous societies. Indeed, he argues that the idealistic positing of the berdache as a third gender is based on misplaced wishful thinking. Trexler uses new material to support the claims made in his 1995 book, *Sex and Conquest*. Here Trexler focuses more specifically on the relationship between the berdache and power relations in indigenous societies. The berdache was to serve the nobility so that the nobles would not sexually molest women. They also served as feminized men to the community, who could see them as raped and displaced, thus powerless, men. By transvesting a boy or a man, the noble could prevent that person from gaining too much power in a system where masculinity was valued. By forcing other nobles to give him transvested boys, the noble could assert his superior position to these others, while at the same time gaining prestige by increasing the retinue of people directly dependent on him.

Trexler's analysis is based on a particular reading of masculine power. He is able to show that the value of masculinity could be used to stratify relationships among nobles as well as between nobles and their dependents.

Trexler asserts that masculinity was perceived as the assertion of control and superiority over others and was maintained through the exchange of men, women, and boys. Trexler's book has been criticized by several scholars who argue that he lacks the evidence to make his argument.[49] In this volume, Trexler answers his critics by providing more evidence. Additionally, many studies have shown the importance of the warrior ethic to Mesoamerican and Andean societies.

My own essay presents a different type of analysis in which the transsexualization of desire forms a part of the rituals of masculinity. Using a philological analysis of Maya language texts, I show that power, desire, fantasy, and fear were intermixed in colonial Maya ideas of sodomy. Maya traditions developed a role for sodomy in political and religious structures. That role, embedded in a hierarchical system where nobles asserted their own power over all others, was changed by the Spanish conquest. The Maya also had developed a role for a ritualized transsexualization of the noble male and the male god (and perhaps the noble female and/or the goddess)—a role quite different from the one discussed by Trexler: this was no place for the berdache. However, such transsexualization allowed for Maya nobles to gain symbolic power through the sign of the phallus. This transsexuality related closely to the meaning of all types of sacrifice in Maya society. The Maya also asserted a hierarchical symbolic sodomy in the realm of warfare. This realm was similar enough to Spanish ideas of conquest and contamination that it allowed for a hybrid cultural formation to exist throughout the colonial years. Such an argument supports Trexler's assertions regarding dependent relationships. The power related to both sodomy and the transsexualization of desire ultimately was the power of the masculine male warrior.

Michael Horswell's chapter stands as a counterpoint to Trexler's notion of dependency and domination. Horswell asserts that, in the case of Peru's indigenous peoples, a third-gender subjectivity did exist and that this person fit into a gender system that valued femininity. Horswell argues that, by reading the colonial sources, one can find a place for an intermediate gender that was valued in the cultural and sacred structures of pre-Hispanic and early colonial Andean societies. Horswell bases his argument on a series of colonial indigenous and Spanish writers who discussed the prevalence of sodomy and transvestism in ways which, while moralizing against these practices, revealed enough about pre-Hispanic gender norms to show the place of a liminal figure in between the male and the female. This figure was a third gender that had qualities not associated with the other two. Horswell rejects Trexler's focus on masculinity, asserting that the Andean gender system valued femininity in such a way that the third gender may have existed in a system which actually valorized and used this in-between position in a positive manner. Horswell finds a wide variety of levels upon which one can understand the feminine as positive, the third gender as a cosmologically supported subjectivity, and ritualized sodomy as a culturally valued activity. While the type of argument he promotes has traditionally been the work of essentialists and idealists who treat any discussion of power as anathema to Native American sensibilities, Horswell is no essentialist. He treats gender as a performative iteration of cultural values, and he understands that the third-gender subjectivity he is promoting fits into a structure where cultural, political, and social power were developed. For Horswell, power was not a static promotion of masculinity; rather, it was an element which could be performed in a variety of ways, and could in certain cases value femininity. It is clear from reading Horswell's chapter that the value of femininity was being used in a power structure that promoted a social hierarchy from long before the reign of the Inca.

The debate between Horswell and Trexler represents an important element in the history of homosexualities, and in the history of sexuality in general. Trexler believes that gendered power and male domination are the keys to understanding both sodomy and transvestism in indigenous societies. Horswell believes that gender was structured in a different manner: that, at least for Andean societies, female power was an important factor. Indeed, Andean societies as a whole appear to be more structured around reciprocal relationships than do Mesoamerican societies. The warrior ethic is significantly more present in Mesoamerican documents than in the Andean counterparts. Yet, as I have argued elsewhere, the concept of reciprocity was present in Mesoamerican societies, and such reciprocity did not contradict the warrior ethic or the degradation of male femininity. In the history of homosexualities, Trexler's argument is that one needs to look to the past to understand the ways in which gendered power worked to create particular sexual institutions to assert male power. Horswell contrarily argues that the past presents lessons regarding the possibility of a more respected discourse of feminine desire.

The debate regarding the cross-dresser presumes a connection between masculinity, femininity, and power. Indeed, all of the authors in this collection state that these elements are interrelated. Sodomy thus was not just an act; it was an act presumed to have great importance. Recall the quotation from Cieza, in which he used the presence of sodomy to suggest much more about the society. Homosexual desires and acts were written onto the human body in a way that allowed for a broad social critique. The body itself was rewritten and revised during the process of colonization. Physiological organs were not just apparent or natural, but existed in a context of power relations. So sodomy was presented within colonialist discourse as an act which showed a degraded, effeminate nobility. But the question of how power was maintained and manipulated is a complex one, debated by the authors. Some argue that power was an attempt at male domination in which dependent relationships were created. Others argue that colonialist and elite power reversed or repressed the indigenous and popular notions of reality.

Horswell argues that, in Andean society, the gendered structure of power was different from that of the conquerors: among Andeans the feminine sphere was empowered. To Horswell, the power of femininity was based on the notion that Andean society had a "gender parallel" way of understanding the world.[50] He sees power as something that was divided in a different way in the Andean preconquest world than it was in early modern Spain. Thus power was not about actions related to dependency; on the contrary, it was about the ways in which actions to create and maintain the discourse of the cosmos were structured to control Inca and pre-Incaic power in the Andean world. Horswell understands preconquest power as a result of the combination of Inca hegemony with the actions related to feminization and empowerment of the "passive" transvestite.

For Trexler, power in early modern times was manipulated by a nobility determined to gain dependents. Power was measured by the ability to control, and this ability was determined in advance to be both a masculine preserve and a proof of one's masculinity.[51] So for Trexler the sodomitical and transvestic discourses were centrally located in the active/passive divide. The active partner made the passive symbolically, spiritually, and structurally dependent on him. In this way, he asserted his masculine desires, and he gained political, social, and cultural power. A gender system was used to structure power in such a way that the passive necessarily became stereotypically feminine and thus dependent.

I argue that the colonial Maya structured sodomy in such a way as to assert male domination and the power of noblemen and colonizers. These groups asserted themselves by transsexualizing themselves, thus harnessing the feminine, and by symbolically sodomizing, thus feminizing, others. The Maya thus were able to use a gender parallel structure and male domination at the same time. In my view, power was closely linked with colonization and conquest. These actions created both hybrid cultures and hegemonic structures.[52] Power was maintained through a masculinized discourse which asserted the political, social, and cultural control of noblemen over all others (including, to a certain extent, the gods). This sense of masculine power then mixed with the relatively similar Spanish notions.

Stavig begins by discussing the various Spanish and Peruvian chronicles, showing that most sources say that the Incas despised and punished sodomy. Yet virtually all of the sources say that the northern Peruvian coast had endemic sodomy.[53] Stavig argues that an official opposition to homosexual activity does not mean that such activity was not implicitly tolerated as long as it was hidden from public view. This conclusion, similar to ideas presented by Trexler and Michael Rocke for late medieval and early modern Italy and Spain, is applied closely to late colonial Andean peoples.[54] Clearly there was official opposition to such activity but, more important, the criminal case that Stavig cites shows that serious punishment was not forthcoming, at least not unless the proof was overwhelming. Stavig shows what an imaginative historian can do with just one case. He does not attempt to overstate the importance of the case, but he still analyzes some of the level of opposition to sodomy. The involved Spaniard was a local leader of an indigenous community, was married to an indigenous noblewoman, was a legitimate ruler, and had an alleged sexual relationship with an indigenous man. The Spaniard was perceived as the passive partner in the affair, and at first his gender was questioned. Such a case allows scholars to understand the potential of individual criminal cases. A similar methodology has been used by Geoffrey Spurling, who also makes a number of points related to the crossing of cultural boundaries.[55] Stavig, by showing that Incaic and Hispanic laws were not absolute and could not control sexual desires, develops an ideology of power as something flexible. To Stavig, gendered notions of power certainly played a role, but no more so than ethnic assertions of domination. And, as his one legal case shows, many notions of appropriate social power were turned around. So, to Stavig, power in late colonial Andean societies was partially determined by gender and ethnicity, but also was related closely to flexible interpretations of actions.

Higgs studies two cases of clerical sodomy in colonial Brazil. These cases show that the Inquisition as an institution was most concerned with scandal and political intrigue that could weaken the Church's position in Brazil and Portugal. The context of these cases suggests that the Church, as Stavig has pointed out with regard to the broader society, had a rather flexible understanding of sodomy. Friars had substantial access to engage in sexual acts with one another. The Church was more concerned with regulating clergy than they were with the broader moral discourse. These regulations were related to the perceived power of the Church, and not necessarily to the actions of the individual clergy. The Church, rather strong in the seventeenth century, attempts to hide one sodomy case. Under attack in the eighteenth century, the Church pursues another case.

Mott focuses on the relationship between homosexuality and the Inquisition in colonial Brazil. There he finds that the Inquisition did persecute men based on their perceived homosexuality. Mott states that homosexuality was relatively widespread among the various occupations and social classes. The people were able to establish significant communities, and they were able to make the presence of these communities known to interested men. The people in the communities associated with many men (both active and passive partners). Mott shows that, in Brazil, a community formed that was in some ways analogous to modern gay communities. These communities were forced to face the Inquisition, hostile political authorities, and a moralizing public. Mott relates power directly to an institution: the Portuguese Inquisition. For early modern Iberians, the Inquisition certainly was a central manifestation of the power of both Church and state.[56] One can argue, however, that it was precisely the lack of hegemonic power located in the Church and state that made the Inquisition necessary: people's minds were not controlled effectively enough, and the Inquisition instituted the control of Church and State through systematic fear. Mott sees some of this complexity, but also asserts the power of the institution to act on people. For Mott, power primarily was about the ability to control through fear and repression.

Gruzinski, like Stavig, shows what can be done with just one case, although his case involves a large number of men, all of whom lived in, and engaged in homosexual activity in, a Hispanic environment. He places this case in the context of the colonial enterprise, showing the ways in which a discourse of infection was used to describe sodomy, as it was used also to describe idolatry and other such offenses. Gruzinski's work, the Spanish version of which has inspired several scholars, shows the way in which discourses of domination used sodomitical activity to engage in colonial rule. The perception of sodomy as a disease which could spread inspired fear, at least among those writing about the trial Gruzinski discusses. The cultural matrix for sodomy included clear hostility to both active and passive partners, but the passive partner was seen as the most objectionable, the *puto* of the Hispanic world. The penalties did not reflect this divide between views of active and passive partners. The demography of this community shows that homosexual activity allowed for crossing classes: the people charged were relatively representative of the broader population. The community that formed had an established social network, set meeting places, and developed relationships. They had created a system where they could identify each other and become involved with new people in the network. The social power present suggested that a large number of men desired such activity in the confines of what they viewed to be a relatively safe environment. Gruzinski asserts that power was a flexible entity which was dispersed throughout the cultural, political, and social fields. While the courts were a part of the structures of power, the evidence shows that they did not have hegemonic control. As people were able to form extensive social networks which crossed ethnic, class, and occupational lines, they were able to assert their own power through social means. For Gruzinski power was something that went well beyond the institutions and invaded every aspect of social life.

AN INTEGRATED ANALYSIS

Gonzalo Aguirre Beltrán maintains that the indigenous peoples most strongly resisted European interpretation of "sexual sins."[57] Certainly, the indigenous peoples were unlikely to significantly change their interpretations of sexual desire, but it may be overstating the case to suggest that they were so resistant. Most indigenous peoples developed hybrid notions of desire, at least claimed to accept the concept of sin, and changed their systems of marriage, divorce, and cohabitation. Colonial power, Catholic domination, and the role of the nobles in transmitting Spanish cultural values all mandated such a result.

This anthology is an attempt to understand the debates and to develop an integrated analysis of male homosexualities in colonial Latin America. These men acted within the context of their desires and the power of the colonial gender systems. Homosexual desires, acts, and communities formed in colonial Latin America in various ways and in a wide variety of venues. The cultural and social interpretations of these acts were very different from those we currently understand and accept. These essays are an attempt at understanding these cultural and social developments during the colonial period.

NOTES

1. From *cacique*, an Arawak term the Spaniards used to refer to indigenous leaders.

2. See Silverblatt, *Moon, Sun, and Witches;* Burkhart, *Slippery Earth;* Sigal, *Moon Goddesses.*

3. See Carrasco, *Inquisición y represión;* Gerard and Hekma, *The Pursuit of Sodomy,* particularly the articles by Rocke, Perry, and Mott and Assunção.

4. See Sigal, *Moon Goddesses.*

5. One of the few serious works on this subject, in fact, questions the very concept. See Gutmann, *The Meanings of Macho.*

6. *Maricón* appears to be the most popular contemporary derogatory term for a gay man in Spanish Latin America. *Puto* and other terms are still used.

7. This is not to say that no scholarship exists. The point is, rather, that the relationship between the *machista* and the *maricón* is generally ignored. The notable exceptions and the strongest books on the topic also are some of the most popular books in the field, including Foster, *Gay and Lesbian Themes in Latin American Writing;* Parker, *Bodies, Pleasures, and Passions;* Lancaster, *Life Is Hard;* Balderston and Guy, *Sex and Sexuality in Latin America;* Green, *Beyond Carnival.* The academic study of sexualities in modern Latin America is a substantial and growing field.

8. The history of sexuality during the colonial period in Latin America also has been a subject of much interest in the past few years. Some of the most relevant studies include Quezada, "Erotismo en la religión azteca," *Amor y magia amorosa entre los Aztecas,* "Sexualidad y magia en la mujer novohispana: Siglo XVI," "Sexualidad y magia en la mujer novohispana: Siglo XVII," and "Sexualidad y magia en la mujer novohispana: Siglo XVIII"; Alberro, *Seis ensayos sobre el discurso colonial relativo a la comunidad domestica;* López Austin, *Cuerpo humano e ideología;* Gruzinski, "Las cenizas del deseo"; Ortega, *De la santidad a la perversión o de la porqué no se cumplía la ley de Dios en la sociedad Novohispana;* Mott, *Escravidão, homossexualidade e demonología,* and *O sexo proibido;* Clendinnen, "Yucatec Maya Women and the Spanish Conquest," and *Aztecs;* Arrom, *The Women of Mexico City;* Silverblatt, *Moon, Sun, and Witches;* Seed, *To Love, Honor, and*

Obey in Colonial Mexico; Burkhart, *Slippery Earth;* Lavrin, *Sexuality and Marriage in Colonial Latin America;* Klein, "Fighting with Femininity"; Gutiérrez, *When Jesus Came, the Corn Mothers Went Away;* Herren, *La conquista erótica de las Indias;* Barbosa Sánchez, *Sexo y conquista;* Bleys, *Geography of Perversion;* Kellogg, *Law and the Transformation of Aztec Culture;* Restall, "'He Wished It in Vain'"; Stern, *The Secret History of Gender;* Trexler, *Sex and Conquest;* Stepto and Stepto, *Lieutenant Nun;* Schroeder, Wood, and Haskett, *Indian Women of Early Mexico;* Sigal, "Politicization of Pederasty," and *Moon Goddesses;* Johnson and Lipsett-Rivera, eds., *The Faces of Honor;* Twinam, *Public Lives, Private Secrets;* and Garza Carvajal, *Vir.*

9. Cieza used the figure of the sodomite as a trope designed to show that the proper gender system was being subverted by the improper gender role of the sodomites forced to dress as women. Cieza imagined a particular Andean gender system, one in which sodomy was allowed free reign, at least among the elite.

10. For a more extensive discussion of power as it relates to these operations, see below. Also see Trexler, *Sex and Conquest,* and his essay in this volume. On the theoretical framework of power and how power has been used in studies of sexuality, see Foucault, *The History of Sexuality,* and *Power/Knowledge.*

11. Within the binary thought processes of the early modern Spaniard, the honorable man presumed the presence of his opposite. See the various articles in Johnson and Lipsett-Rivera, eds., *The Faces of Honor.*

12. See Spurling, "The Changing Face of Honor," and "Under Investigation for the Abominable Sin."

13. Silverblatt, *Moon, Sun, and Witches;* Schroeder, Wood, and Haskett, *Indian Women of Early Mexico;* Sigal, *Moon Goddesses.*

14. I begin this section with an extensive quotation from Foucault, both to provoke and to critique. Foucault has been pilloried in many sectors of Latin American history, particularly among Latin American historians working in the United States. He often is seen as either irrelevant or as a colonialist European outsider. At a recent meeting of the Conference on Latin American History, a top Latin American historian stated that an article was praiseworthy specifically because it did not mention Foucault. Other scholars have used Foucault to great benefit. Here I provoke my Latin Americanist colleagues to think about the potential importance of using Foucault. I also critique the Foucauldian emphasis in the history of sexuality.

15. See the issue of the *Hispanic American Historical Review* (79, no. 2 [1999]) dedicated to the cultural history debates.

16. See Gruzinski, *Conquest of Mexico;* Mignolo, *The Darker Side of the Renaissance.*

17. Essentialism has led some scholars to obscure or even deny ostensibly bisexual behavior on the part of the people they study. See Garber, *Vice Versa.*

18. As the reader will note, Luiz Mott makes a very different argument in his chapter in this volume.

19. See particularly Murray, *Latin American Male Homosexualities;* Green, *Beyond Carnival.*

20. Note that the title to this introduction begins with the term "(Homo)Sexual." The reason for this rather awkward construction is the theoretical debate, much of which is alluded to in this anthology, over the concept of homosexuality. The "homo" in the parentheses defines a presence that is necessarily there in order for us to understand the topic in question, but which fits in place *only* for our comprehension. The argument here stands: Homosexuality (or heterosexuality) as we understand it today did not exist in colonial Latin America. The parentheses around the "homo" symbolize both the presence of the term and the lack of presence for what it might be assumed to represent.

21. See Weeks, *Coming Out,* and *Sexuality and Its Discontents;* Foucault, *The History of Sexuality;* Faderman, *Surpassing the Love of Men;* Rubin, "Thinking Sex."

22. At least they had no such taxonomic obsessions with regard to sex. Lévi-Strauss (*Structural Anthropology, The Savage Mind*) and other structuralists have developed the idea that it is an inherent human need to categorize and divide in order to understand. Indeed the indigenous

peoples, at least those of Mexico and the Andes, divided things in various ways. They certainly developed ethnic and national divisions (although they did not understand ethnicity in the modern sense—cultural and not necessarily national difference, where one ethnicity can incorporate people from every class), and they did stress differences between various people based on sexual behaviors. Ramón Gutiérrez (*When Jesus Came, the Corn Mothers Went Away*, 3–36) has shown that the Pueblo of Arizona and New Mexico at the time of the Spanish conquest had structured sexual acts, desires, fantasies, and fears based on certain taxonomic rules related to the ethnic and gendered structure of the society, but that these rules were not similar to those of the conquerors.

23. Such taxonomies never have been so simple, and there has been significant slippage between categories throughout the modern period. Psychological theories regarding bisexuality abound. Many theorists have believed that one could be seduced into homosexuality, and that situational homosexuality (e.g., in prison) was "normal." But, as a whole, the categories were intended to be absolute and to divide identities into normalcy and deviance. See Weeks, *Coming Out;* Chauncey, *Gay New York.*

24. The level of identity associated with the sinner and the "sodomite" is under debate, but it is clear that sodomites formed communities of their own kind, which certainly seems to contradict the idea that identity based on sets of sexual behaviors was invented in the nineteenth century. See Gerard and Hekma, *The Pursuit of Sodomy;* Perry, *Gender and Disorder,* 125–27; Bleys, *Geography of Perversion,* 82–99.

25. See Sigal, *Moon Goddesses,* 7.

26. Mott and Assunção, "Love's Labors Lost."

27. Foucault, *The History of Sexuality.*

28. Garza Carvajal, *Vir.*

29. Perry, "The 'Nefarious Sin' in Early Modern Seville."

30. Perry, *Gender and Disorder,* 125–27; Rocke, *Forbidden Friendships;* Gruzinski, chapter 7 in this volume.

31. See Rocke, *Forbidden Friendships.*

32. On Europe, see Carrasco, *Inquisición y represión;* Rey, "Police and Sodomy in Eighteenth-Century Paris"; Tomás y Valiente et al., *Sexo barroco y otras transgresiones premodernas;* Sarrion Mora, *Sexualidad y confesión;* on Latin America, see Spurling, "The Changing Face of Honor"; Garza Carvajal, *Vir;* and the chapters in this volume.

33. *Puto* today translates as "male whore." However, it was more than a statement about a person's occupation; it was used as a derogatory term in the sense described below.

34. They found them also, no doubt, in other indigenous languages.

35. Perry, *Gender and Disorder,* 123–27.

36. See Gruzinski, chapter 7 in this volume.

37. The excerpt is from Spurling, "Under Investigation for the Abominable Sin," 118.

38. Desire was a central element in the power of the colonizer. If the colonized person's desires could be represented in a particular way, the colonizer could more easily dominate the colonized. If, as in the cases of many of the Latin American indigenous groups, the colonized people could express their desires through the Church, then the colonizer effectively had reinscribed the desire of the colonized, allowing the colonizer to continue to rule with the appearance of legitimacy. See Deleuze and Guattari, *Anti-Oedipus;* Pagden, "Identity Formation in Spanish America"; Klor de Alva, "Nahua Colonial Discourse"; Bhabha, *The Location of Culture.*

39. See Perry, *Gender and Disorder,* 123–27.

40. See Bleys, *Geography of Perversion;* Trexler, *Sex and Conquest.*

41. See Sigal, *Moon Goddesses.*

42. The excerpt is from Jones, *The Conquest of the Last Maya Kingdom,* 499, n. 45; his translation.

43. See Trexler, *Sex and Conquest,* and his essay in this volume. Also see my contribution to this volume and Sigal, *Moon Goddesses,* 222–32. The Mexica, as they promoted the warrior ideal, particularly degraded many feminine characteristics. Yet note the point that Burkhart (*Slippery*

Earth, 132–33) makes: the warrior ethic alternated with a Nahua discourse on moderation. Such a discourse emphasized the balance and equilibrium necessary to achieve success in life and beyond. Such an equilibrium likely would have required the Nahua male to balance those elements considered masculine with others considered feminine. But as I have noted for the Maya, such an attempt at equilibrium did not suggest any tolerance for femininity in men. In fact this equilibrium was maintained through such rituals as penis piercing, which were certainly considered masculine ceremonies (see Sigal, *Moon Goddesses,* 161–73).

44. See Guerra, *Precolumbian Mind;* Gutiérrez, "Must We Deracinate Indians to Find Gay Roots?"; Roscoe, "How to Become a Berdache"; Trexler, *Sex and Conquest,* and chapter 2 in this volume; Horswell, chapter 1 in this volume.

45. See Whitehead, "The Bow and the Burden Strap."

46. Williams, *The Spirit and the Flesh;* Roscoe, *Living the Spirit, The Zuni Man-Woman,* and *Changing Ones.*

47. Roscoe does so by simply finding one or more citations to the berdache in a particular society, then listing the names used. Such an analysis seems extremely simplistic. Did all of these figures really play the positive role Roscoe suggests? Did their roles change through history, or were they as static as he makes them out to be?

48. Gutiérrez, "Must We Deracinate Indians to Find Gay Roots?"; Trexler, *Sex and Conquest.*

49. For a particularly strident review, see Roscoe, *Changing Ones,* 189–200.

50. Here he follows Silverblatt, *Moon, Sun, and Witches;* Harrison, "The Theology of Concupiscence."

51. Trexler arrived at this from his studies in medieval and early modern European history (see Trexler, *Public Life in Renaissance Florence*). For a similar view of gendered power in colonial Mexico, see Stern, *The Secret History of Gender.*

52. Here I partially follow Farriss, *Maya Society;* Clendinnen, *Ambivalent Conquests;* and Gruzinski, *Conquest of Mexico.*

53. This discourse certainly reminds one of the important conclusions of Rudi Bleys in his book (*The Geography of Perversion*). There Bleys shows that at certain points various European discourses demanded that sodomy be present most strongly in the least civilized societies, whereas all advanced societies abhorred and punished homosexual activity.

54. See Trexler, *Sex and Conquest;* Rocke, *Forbidden Friendships.*

55. Spurling, "Under Investigation for the Abominable Sin."

56. The literature on the Inquisition in Latin America is vast. For references to a few of the most relevant books on this particular topic, see Mott, *Escravidão, homossexualidade e demonología,* and *O sexo proibido;* Perry and Cruz, *Cultural Encounters.*

57. Aguirre Beltrán, *Medicina y magia,* 169.

WORKS CITED

Aguirre Beltrán, Gonzalo. *Medicina y magia: El proceso de aculturación en la estructura colonial.* Mexico City: Instituto Nacional Indigenista, 1963.

Alberro, Solange, et al. *Seis ensayos sobre el discurso colonial relativo a la comunidad domestica: matrimonio, familia y sexualidad a través de los cronistas del siglo XVI, el Nuevo Testamento y el santo oficio de la Inquisición.* Mexico City: Instituto Nacional de Antropología e Historia, 1980.

Arrom, Silvia. *The Women of Mexico City, 1790–1857.* Stanford, CA: Stanford University Press, 1985.

Balderston, Daniel, and Donna J. Guy. *Sex and Sexuality in Latin America.* New York: New York University Press, 1997.

Barbosa Sánchez, Araceli. *Sexo y conquista.* Mexico City: Universidad Nacional Autónoma de México, 1994.

Bhabha, Homi K. *The Location of Culture.* New York: Routledge, 1994.

Bleys, Rudi C. *The Geography of Perversion: Male-to-Male Sexual Behavior Outside the West and the Ethnographic Imagination, 1750–1918.* New York: New York University Press, 1995.

Burkhart, Louise M. *The Slippery Earth: Nahua-Christian Moral Dialogue in Sixteenth-Century Mexico.* Tucson: University of Arizona Press, 1989.

Carrasco, Rafael. *Inquisición y represión sexual en Valencia: Historia de los sodomitas (1565–1785).* Barcelona: Laertes, 1985.

Chauncey, George. *Gay New York: Gender, Urban Culture, and the Making of the Gay Male World, 1890–1940.* New York: Basic Books, 1994.

Cieza de León, Pedro de. *La crónica del Perú.* Madrid: Historia 16, 1984.

Clendinnen, Inga. *Ambivalent Conquests: Maya and Spaniard in Yucatan, 1517–1570.* Cambridge: Cambridge University Press, 1987.

———. *Aztecs: An Interpretation.* Cambridge: Cambridge University Press, 1991.

———. "Yucatec Maya Women and the Spanish Conquest: Role and Ritual in Historical Reconstruction." *Journal of Social History* 15 (1982): 427–42.

Deleuze, Gilles, and Félix Guattari. *Anti-Oedipus: Capitalism and Schizophrenia.* Minneapolis: University of Minnesota Press, 1983.

Faderman, Lillian. *Surpassing the Love of Men.* New York: William Morrow, 1981.

Farriss, Nancy M. *Maya Society under Colonial Rule: The Collective Enterprise of Survival.* Princeton, NJ: Princeton University Press, 1984.

Foster, David William. *Gay and Lesbian Themes in Latin American Writing.* Austin: University of Texas Press, 1991.

Foucault, Michel. *The History of Sexuality.* Vol. 1. *An Introduction.* New York: Vintage Books, 1978.

———. *Power/Knowledge: Selected Interviews and Other Writings, 1972–1977.* New York: Pantheon Books, 1980.

Garber, Marjorie. *Vice Versa: Bisexuality and the Eroticism of Everyday Life.* New York: Simon & Schuster, 1995.

Garza Carvajal, Federico. *Vir: Conceptions of Manliness in Andalucía and México, 1561–1699.* Amsterdam: Amsterdamse Historische Reeks, 2000.

Gerard, Kent, and Gert Hekma, eds. *The Pursuit of Sodomy: Male Homosexuality in Renaissance and Enlightenment Europe.* New York: Harrington Park Press, 1989.

Green, James N. *Beyond Carnival: Male Homosexuality in Twentieth-Century Brazil.* Chicago: University of Chicago Press, 1999.

Gruzinski, Serge. "Las cenizas del deseo: Homosexuales novohispanos a mediados del siglo XVII." In *De la santidad a la perversión o de la porqué no se cumplía la ley de Dios en la sociedad Novohispana,* ed. Sergio Ortega. Mexico City: Editorial Grijalbo, 1985.

———. *The Conquest of Mexico: The Incorporation of Indian Societies into the Western World, Sixteenth–Eighteenth Centuries.* Cambridge, U.K.: Polity Press, 1993.

Guerra, Francisco. *The Precolumbian Mind.* New York: Seminar Press, 1970.

Gutiérrez, Ramón A. "Must We Deracinate Indians to Find Gay Roots?" *Out/Look* 1 (1989): 61–67.

———. *When Jesus Came, the Corn Mothers Went Away: Marriage, Sexuality, and Power in New Mexico, 1500–1846.* Stanford, CA: Stanford University Press, 1991.

Gutmann, Matthew C. *The Meanings of Macho: Being a Man in Mexico City.* Berkeley and Los Angeles: University of California Press, 1996.

Harrison, Regina. "The Theology of Concupiscence: Spanish-Quechua Confessional Manuals in the Andes." In *Coded Encounters: Writing, Gender, and Ethnicity in Colonial Latin America,* ed. Francisco Javier Cevallos-Candau, Jeffrey A. Cole, Nina M. Scott, and Nicomedes Suárez-Araúz. Amherst: University of Massachusetts Press, 1994.

Herren, Ricardo. *La conquista erótica de las Indias.* Barcelona: Planeta, 1991.

Johnson, Lyman L., and Sonya Lipsett-Rivera, eds. *The Faces of Honor: Sex, Shame, and Violence in Colonial Latin America.* Albuquerque: University of New Mexico Press, 1998.

Jones, Grant D. *The Conquest of the Last Maya Kingdom.* Stanford, CA: Stanford University Press, 1998.

Kellogg, Susan. *Law and the Transformation of Aztec Culture, 1500–1700.* Norman: University of Oklahoma Press, 1995.

Klein, Cecelia. "Fighting with Femininity: Gender and War in Aztec Mexico." In *Gendered Rhetorics: Postures of Dominance and Submission in History,* ed. Richard C. Trexler. Binghamton, NY: Medieval and Renaissance Texts and Studies, 1994.

Klor de Alva, J. Jorge. "Nahua Colonial Discourse and the Appropriation of the (European) Other." *Archives de Sciences Sociales des Religions* 77 (January–March 1992): 15–35.

Lancaster, Roger. *Life Is Hard: Machismo, Danger, and the Intimacy of Power in Nicaragua.* Berkeley and Los Angeles: University of California Press, 1992.

Lavrin, Asunción, ed. *Sexuality and Marriage in Colonial Latin America.* Lincoln: University of Nebraska Press, 1989.

Lévi-Strauss, Claude. *The Savage Mind.* Chicago: University of Chicago Press, 1966.

———. *Structural Anthropology.* New York: Basic Books, 1963.

López Austin, Alfredo. *Cuerpo humano e ideología.* 2 vols. Mexico: Universidad Nacional Autónoma de México, 1980.

Mignolo, Walter D. *The Darker Side of the Renaissance: Literacy, Territoriality, and Colonization.* Ann Arbor: University of Michigan Press, 1995.

Mott, Luiz. *Escravidão, homossexualidade e demonología.* São Paulo: Icone, 1988.

———. *O sexo proibido: Virgens, gays e escravos nas garras da Inquisição.* Campinas: Papirus Editora, 1989.

Mott, Luiz, and Aroldo Assunção. "Love's Labors Lost: Five Letters from a Seventeenth-Century Portuguese Sodomite." In *The Pursuit of Sodomy: Male Homosexuality in Renaissance and Enlightenment Europe,* ed. Kent Gerard and Gert Hekma. New York: Harrington Park Press, 1989.

Murray, Stephen O. *Latin American Male Homosexualities.* Albuquerque: University of New Mexico Press, 1995.

Ortega, Sergio, ed. *De la santidad a la perversión o de la porqué no se cumplía la ley de Dios en la sociedad Novohispana.* Mexico City: Editorial Grijalbo, 1985.

Pagden, Anthony. "Identity Formation in Spanish America." In *Colonial Identity in the Atlantic World, 1500–1800,* ed. Nicholas Canny and Anthony Pagden. Princeton, NJ: Princeton University Press, 1987.

Parker, Richard. *Bodies, Pleasures, and Passions: Sexual Culture in Contemporary Brazil.* Boston: Beacon Press, 1991.

Perry, Mary Elizabeth. *Gender and Disorder in Early Modern Seville.* Princeton, NJ: Princeton University Press, 1990.

———. "The 'Nefarious Sin' in Early Modern Seville." In *The Pursuit of Sodomy: Male Homosexuality in Renaissance and Enlightenment Europe,* ed. Kent Gerard and Gert Hekma. New York: Harrington Park Press, 1989.

Perry, Mary Elizabeth, and Anne J. Cruz, eds. *Cultural Encounters: The Impact of the Inquisition in Spain and the New World.* Berkeley and Los Angeles: University of California Press, 1991.

Quezada, Noemí. *Amor y magia amorosa entre los Aztecas: Supervivencia en el México colonial.* Mexico City: Universidad Nacional Autónoma de México, 1975.

———. "Erotismo en la religión azteca." *Revista de la Universidad de México* 28 (1974): 6–19.

———. "Sexualidad y magia en la mujer novohispana: Siglo XVI." *Anales de Antropología* 24 (1987): 263–87.

———. "Sexualidad y magia en la mujer novohispana: Siglo XVII." *Anales de Antropología* 25 (1988): 329–69.

———. "Sexualidad y magia en la mujer novohispana: Siglo XVIII." *Anales de Antropología* 26 (1990): 261–95.

Restall, Matthew. "'He Wished It in Vain': Subordination and Resistance among Maya Women in Post-Conquest Yucatan." *Ethnohistory* 42 (1995): 577–95.

Rey, Michel. "Police and Sodomy in Eighteenth-Century Paris: From Sin to Disorder." In *The Pursuit of Sodomy: Male Homosexuality in Renaissance and Enlightenment Europe*, ed. Kent Gerard and Gert Hekma. New York: Harrington Park Press, 1989.

Rocke. Michael. *Forbidden Friendships: Homosexuality and Male Culture in Renaissance Florence.* New York: Oxford University Press, 1996.

Roscoe, Will. *Changing Ones: Third and Fourth Genders in Native North America.* New York: St. Martin's Press, 1998.

———. "How to Become a Berdache: Toward a Unified Analysis of Gender Diversity." In *Third Sex, Third Gender: Beyond Sexual Dimorphism in Culture and History*, ed. Gilbert Herdt. New York: Zone Books, 1994.

———, ed. *Living the Spirit: A Gay American Indian Anthology.* New York: St. Martin's Press, 1988.

———. *The Zuni Man-Woman.* Albuquerque: University of New Mexico Press, 1991.

Rubin, Gayle. "Thinking Sex: Notes for a Radical Theory of the Politics of Sexuality." In *Pleasure and Danger*, ed. Carol S. Vance. Boston: Routledge, 1984.

Sarrion Mora, Adelina. *Sexualidad y confesión: La solicitación ante el Tribunal del Santo Oficio, siglos XVI–XIX.* Madrid: Alianza Universidad, 1994.

Schroeder, Susan, Stephanie Wood, and Robert Haskett, eds. *Indian Women of Early Mexico.* Norman: University of Oklahoma Press, 1997.

Seed, Patricia. *To Love, Honor, and Obey in Colonial Mexico: Conflicts over Marriage Choice, 1574–1821.* Stanford, CA: Stanford University Press, 1988.

Sigal, Pete. *From Moon Goddesses to Virgins: The Colonization of Yucatecan Maya Sexual Desire.* Austin: University of Texas Press, 2000.

———. "The Politicization of Pederasty among the Colonial Yucatecan Maya." *Journal of the History of Sexuality* 8 (1997): 1–24.

Silverblatt, Irene. *Moon, Sun, and Witches: Gender Ideologies and Class in Inca and Colonial Peru.* Princeton, NJ: Princeton University Press, 1987.

Spurling, Geoffrey. "The Changing Face of Honor." In *The Faces of Honor: Sex, Shame, and Violence in Colonial Latin America*, ed. Lyman L. Johnson and Sonya Lipsett-Rivera. Albuquerque: University of New Mexico Press,1998.

———. "Under Investigation for the Abominable Sin: Damián de Morales Stands Accused of Attempting to Seduce Antón de Tierra de Congo." In *Colonial Lives: Documents on Latin American History, 1550–1850*, ed. Richard Boyer and Geoffrey Spurling. New York: Oxford University Press, 2000.

Stepto, Michele, and Gabriel Stepto, eds. *Lieutenant Nun: Memoir of a Basque Transvestite in the New World, Catalina de Erauso.* Boston: Beacon Press, 1996.

Stern, Steve J. *The Secret History of Gender: Women, Men, and Power in Late Colonial Mexico.* Chapel Hill: University of North Carolina Press, 1995.

Tomás y Valiente, F., et al. *Sexo barroco y otras transgresiones premodernas.* Madrid: Alianza Universidad, 1990.

Trexler, Richard C. *Public Life in Renaissance Florence.* New York: Academic Press, 1980.

———. *Sex and Conquest: Gendered Violence, Political Order, and the European Conquest of the Americas.* Ithaca, NY: Cornell University Press, 1995.

Twinam, Ann. *Public Lives, Private Secrets: Gender, Honor, Sexuality, and Illegitimacy in Colonial Spanish America.* Stanford, CA: Stanford University Press, 1999.

Weeks, Jeffrey. *Coming Out: Homosexual Politics in Britain from the Nineteenth Century to the Present.* London: Quartet Books, 1977.

———. *Sexuality and Its Discontents.* New York: Routledge, 1985.

Whitehead, Harriet. "The Bow and the Burden Strap: A New Look at Institutionalized Homosexuality in Native North America." In *Sexual Meanings: The Cultural Construction of Gender and Sexuality*, ed. Sherry B. Ortner and Harriet Whitehead. Cambridge: Cambridge University Press, 1981.

Williams, Walter L. *The Spirit and The Flesh: Sexual Diversity in American Indian Culture.* Boston: Beacon Press, 1986.

CHAPTER ONE

Toward an Andean Theory of Ritual Same-Sex Sexuality and Third-Gender Subjectivity

MICHAEL J. HORSWELL

The study of indigenous gender culture in pre-Hispanic and colonial Latin America is plagued by transculturating tropes of sexuality that claim to represent the "other's" gendered practices in the language of European hegemony. Nevertheless, scholars have made great strides in recognizing the dilemma and have begun deconstructing the walls of the "lettered city" that informs colonial historiography, opening doors to new interpretations of what might have existed before and soon after the contact between American and European cultures. Most recently, the issues of same-sex sexuality and cross-gendered subjects have captured the attention of the readers of this corpus of texts.[1] Who were the "sodomites" often depicted in chronicles and histories of Latin America? How can we characterize the cross-gendered peoples often referred to as hermaphrodites or berdache in the literature? What roles did transgendering play in indigenous societies? Can we differentiate between sacred and profane practices of same-sex sexuality?

In this chapter I address the above-mentioned issues in the specific context of the Andean region,[2] where theoretical approaches to the subject of gender and sexuality have been limited to essentialist, and more recently, constructionist models of interpretation. Most prominent in recent scholarship has been Richard Trexler's *Sex and Conquest*, the most sustained analysis on the Latin American gender-crossing, same-sex practicing subject traditionally referred to as the berdache. Trexler's chapter in this volume summarizes his book's thesis that the pan-American berdache was a product of a pre-Hispanic gender ideology that sexually objectified defeated or otherwise subjugated males in ways that magnified masculine power. These cultural patterns, he argues, remarkably approximated the early modern European treat-

ment of same-sex behavior and effeminized dependency. While this characterization may hold true for other parts of the Americas Trexler analyzes,
I argue here that the Andean versions of this historical subjectivity had culturally distinct meanings that transcended European notions of effeminacy as
dependency and degeneracy. Moreover, I explore different methods to theo-
rize the same-sex sexuality associated with cross-gendering subjects in the
Andes. I read through the transculturating tropes of sexuality embedded
in the colonial discourse in order to reinterpret the references to same-sex
sexuality and cross-gendering as performative iterations of a pre-Hispanic
ritual subjectivity associated with notions of mediation between Andean
masculinity and femininity. Judith Butler's concept of performativity as a
model for gendered identity informs my reconsideration of the berdache
as a "third-gender" subjectivity, to be defined below.[3] The approach privileges
the native people's agency in the representation of their own gender and
sexual culture, even though such representations are mediated by colonial
discourse.[4]

My approach to third gender in the pre-Colombian and colonial Andes
is to underscore the performativity of the subjectivity within a context of
transculturation.[5] Butler's conception of gender "performativity" suggests that
discursive subjectivities are agents of their gendered selves, agents that reit-
erate culturally constructed imitations of an imagined original gender (*Gender Trouble*, 147). Any substance to a gendered identity, that is, its essence,
is actually a phantasm, a mere appearance of substance that has acquired the
illusion of essence through its repetitions in discourse. Individuals imitate
the phantasms in "performances" that pass as gendered identities. Butler has
clarified her position in *Bodies That Matter* by emphasizing the discursive
nature of the human body, which is as much a cultural construct as gender
itself. Therefore, the body is "sexed" through cultural norms.[6] In the Andes, we will see how the body of the third-gender subject signifies culturally
meaningful relationships that are brought into discourse through ritual repetitions. What we might know of third-gender subjects comes from the colonial record of their "performances" of ritual expressions of gender and sexuality.

This limitation to our knowledge of the cultural meaning of third-gender
subjectivities requires a subtle reading of the colonial record. As Butler has
asserted, "[T]he subject is constituted through the force of exclusion and ab-
jection, one which produces a constitutive outside to the subject, an abjected
outside, which is, after all, "inside" the subject as its own founding repudiation" (*Bodies That Matter*, 3). The challenge to reading through transculturating tropes is recognizing that notions of the feminine and third-gender
subjectivities are figured as "abjected outsiders" to performative masculine,
idealized subjects of Spanish colonial discourse. These "abjected outsiders,"

therefore, are left marginalized to dominant subjectivities in the discourse, transformed from earlier performative subjects with different values and meanings. Therefore, we must read third gender as performed subjectivities who have passed through a process of transculturation in the highly contested, colonial contact zone.[7] Third gender is acculturated and deculturated; the subjectivity acquires European notions of degeneracy associated with the sodomy trope while it loses part of its sacred, integrated identity associated with feminine rituality.[8] Neoculturations appear in the discourse as mere phantasms of earlier iterations of ritual subjectivity. This chapter concentrates on reconstructing the pre-transculturated meanings of ritual same-sex sexuality and cross-gendering. To do so requires an understanding of current third-gender theory.

THIRD GENDER

As Gilbert Herdt has argued in his introduction to *Third Sex, Third Gender: Beyond Sexual Dimorphism in Culture and History*,[9] to speak of third genders is not to say there are three genders instead of two; it is to break with the sex and gender bipolarity that has, until recently, dominated Western popular and scientific thought. Herdt follows sociologist George Simmel in viewing the presence of just two categories as creating an intrinsic relationship of potential oppositional conflict. Therefore, Herdt claims "third" as "emblematic of other possible combinations that transcend dimorphism" (20). The essays in Herdt's volume strive to unravel the multiple discourses that construct gender identities around human propensities to "categorize things into twos, threes, or other structures of the mind" (20). Theorizing beyond sexual dimorphism is a gesture toward thinking about infinite rather than finite numbers of gender categories. "Third gender," then, becomes a metonymic signifier for those gendered subjectivities that fall outside the classic dimorphic gender categories but whose intelligibility depends on cultural specificity. Therefore, each third-gender subject can only be meaningfully discussed within the context of his or her gender culture.

Will Roscoe's articles, "How to Become a Berdache" and "Gender Diversity in Native North America: Notes toward a Unified Analysis," and his new recent book, *Changing Ones*, work toward establishing that what the traditional ethnographic literature has long identified as a berdache is in many cases the manifestation of a third-gender designation within specific native cultures.[10] His work also gives an extensive review of "berdache" studies.[11] As Roscoe explains, *berdache* is the term anthropology adopted from colonial discourse in the Americas to refer to men who dress like and adopt the roles of women in native societies. Male berdache have been documented in nearly one hundred and fifty North American societies, while female berdache (females who take on the lifeways of males) appear in half as many groups

("How to Become a Berdache," 330). Because the Western colonial chroniclers, nineteenth-century ethnographers, and, later, anthropologists had neither linguistic nor cultural categories that corresponded to the berdache subjectivity, naming it became a problem and usually resulted in misnomers such as the term *berdache* itself, which was originally a Persian and Arabic term for the younger male partner in a same-sex erotic relationship (331). In the different discourses alluded to above, these subjectivities have been variously named "hermaphrodite," "sodomite," "effeminate," and more recently, "homosexual" and "transsexual."[12] Each of these terms misrepresents the berdache in its own way, some expressing bodily confusions, others inscribing the native subject in Christian or psychosexual discourses, and all ignoring the often sacred roles that these subjects performed.[13]

COMPLEMENTARITY AND LIMINALITY IN ANDEAN GENDER CULTURE

It has become a commonplace in Andean studies to recognize the complementary relationship between men and women in the Andes.[14] Analysis of colonial historiography, archival records, and more recent anthropology and ethnography reveals deeply ingrained daily practices as well as frequent sacred rituals that reinforce the dual nature of gender relations. As several anthropologists have learned from their indigenous informants, all creation is gendered, from the "male" *inti* (sun) and "female" *killa* (moon) to the *pachatata* (earth-father) and the *pachamama* (earth-mother). Men and women seek to fit into this dual vision of the world by negotiating each other's strengths and weaknesses in the reproduction of their culture. Women since pre-Colombian times have had access to and control of material resources and supernatural power. By studying the tradition of parallel inheritance that afforded women property rights within the kinship-based *ayllu* system,[15] the complementary roles of males and females in the basic family unit, the corresponding gender duality of Andean deities, and the religious institutions run by women, Irene Silverblatt concludes that prior to the Inca ethnic group's political ascension in the region, "women and men in the Andean *ayllu* apprehended a world criss-crossed by bonds of gender" (39). Men, while invested with more political power, negotiated with women, dominant over the domestic sphere, to culturally re-create the gendered duality that marked their lives. This segregation of gender roles should not be understood as absolute, since men worked in domestic roles and women in public ones as well. Rather than understand women's roles in the Andes as occupying positions of dependency, as Trexler suggests in his contribution to this volume and his book *Sex and Conquest*, we must read the textual markers of gender relations as performative iterations of the negotiation between men

and women, genders equally endowed with cultural significance. This negotiation is further explored below.

The Inca, as they increased their political power in the region, took ad-
vantage of these complementary linkages between men and women to reproduce ideologically the *ayllu* structure on a larger, interethnic scale. As a
result, Silverblatt argues, women rose parallel to men in the emerging "conquest politics" of the Incas' regional expansion. Integral to these politics
was the re-creation of pre-Inca, gendered "prestige hierarchies" based on relationships established between outsiders conceptualized as male and original inhabitants conceptualized as female (68). These local prestige hierarchies served the purpose of ordering and classifying within the *ayllus*, and the
"conquered" did not lose access to productive resources, nor were they subjugated by force (72). The Incas would later repeat the symbolic patterns in
order to incorporate other ethnic groups into Tawantinsuyu. The new political order established by the Incas, in which Inca rulers were figured as stand-
ins for the male Sun deity, created alliances with newly incorporated territories by taking local chieftains' virgin daughters as *acllas*, or wives of the
Sun/Inca (87). The sexual control with which the Incas treated these young
women, maintaining their virginity and endowing them with semi-divine
status, was one of the primary means by which Tawantinsuyu was governed
(107).

The scholarship summarized above suggests that the Andean cultures
were structured on the basis of a dimorphic gender system in which gender
complementarity was the fundamental basis for human interaction and cultural reproduction. This structure does not, however, account for the third-
gender subjectivities that reportedly populated the Andes alongside the *acllas*,
Incas, and other Andean peoples. If cultural reproduction was linked to
expanding kinship alliances through an ideology of gender complementarity, then where and how does same-sex sexuality and cross-gendering play
a role in Andean culture? Trexler answers that the berdache, as defeated ad-
versary in interethnic politics, becomes a sign for the victorious chieftain's
masculine status, but I ask, Is there a way to consider the performance of
third gender outside the constructionist framework of power relations? My
first task, therefore, is to suggest where a third gender might have fit in the
pre-Hispanic and colonial culture of gender complementarities.

To understand the conceptual place a third gender might have inhabited
in the highly symmetrical cosmology of the Andeans, I turn to Tristan Platt's
"Mirrors and Maize: the Concept of *Yanantin* among the Macha of Bolivia,"
an explanation of the symbolic structure of Andean gender symmetry known
as *yanantin*. This discussion will also flesh out the complex system of gender
complementarity referenced above, underscoring the performative nature of

gender relations in the Andes. This dualistic symmetry is achieved through complex ritual performances such as *tinku,* an Andean practice that affirmed social relations by bringing opposites into harmony, which was (and is) expressed ritually and symbolically in both the Quechua and Aymara cultures.[16] Platt explains how ritual "battles" are performed within the context of a four-part symmetrical division of cultural space. In this division, ecology plays an important structural role, as do kinship relations. Ecologically, Andean space is divided between the *puna* and the valley, with the dividing line being a liminal area known as *chawparani,* whereas each of these divisions is subdivided between two principal *ayllus* known as *hanan* and *hurin* (232). *Hanan* is symbolically gendered masculine, and *hurin* is symbolically gendered feminine. The members of the immediate family and of the patrilocal group maintain exogamous relations while ideally forming matrimonial relations exogamously between the *hanan* and *hurin ayllus* and between the *puna* and valley divisions (235). This structure forms part of what John Murra has called the ecological verticality that creates regional interdependence in the Andes.[17] For our purposes, it is important to understand that *tinku* occurs between the two halves, *hanan* and *hurin,* in a ritual in which the men from the *hanan ayllu* oppose the men from the *hurin ayllu* and the women from *hanan* oppose the women from *hurin* (239–40). This symmetrical pairing of men and women is also repeated in other ritual contexts, such as the "ritual plowing" (240–41) and the "house building" (238–39).

This opposition between same-sex groups in the *tinku* ritual battles presents an interesting question for Platt in his study of *yanantin:* "Why do men battle with men and women with women during the *tinku,* if I am right in seeing the encounter as in part a ritual copulation between male and female moieties?" (246). Platt offers an explanation of the sexual nature of *tinku* by noting the relationship between food and copulation and between fighting and copulation. Catherine Allen also notes the sexual nature of *tinku* during contemporary *puqllay,* or "carnival," in the Peruvian highland *ayllu* of Sonqo.[18] A passage in the indigenous chronicle of Felipe Guaman Poma de Ayala confirms that in his time, the late sixteenth century, *tinku,* or *tinquichi,*[19] as he spells it, did indeed implicate sexuality as the metaphor for conflict resolution between the sexes. Guaman Poma's reference to *tinquichi* is found in his description of *hechiceros* (shamans): "[T]he Indian shamans used to perform tinquichi: they join man to woman so that they fall in love and make the men wear-out."[20] This passage is very suggestive of the inherently conflictive nature of Andean opposite-sex relations, for the joining of the man and woman, according to Guaman Poma, leads to the woman potentially consuming or destroying the man. In this case, the *hechicero* becomes the mediator in the ritual pairing of the *quariwarmi* (man-woman), a potentially dangerous relationship for the man. Union required a ritual or magical impulse so that the opposites could form a complementary relationship. If the heterosexual relationship implied conflict of opposites, how do same-sex relationships fit into the Andean cosmology?

Platt's partial answer to this question provides a symbolic structure from which to address more profoundly same-sex sexuality in the pre-Hispanic Andes. For Platt, the key to understanding Andean gender relations and sexuality is the mirror. The mirror is a potent symbolic tool for the Machas; it is used, for example, in two most important liminal contexts: during the marriage ceremony and at death (32). Platt observes the symmetry that results from a reflected image in a mirror. For example, a right hand reflects back a left hand in the mirror, which would represent perfectly the concept of *yanantin*, the expression for perfect, dualistic, gendered symmetry. What, then, happens when human bodies are reflected in the mirror? The human body represents perfect symmetry of the left and right sides, yet the reflection of a man in the mirror is not that of a woman but of another man, as is the case in which a woman's reflection is but that of another woman. Remembering that the goal of *yanantin* in this context is to unite the man and woman for social and human reproduction, we can understand the importance of the predicament.[21] To understand how the union is symbolically achieved, we must take a closer look at the mirror effect.

If we consider all four possible pairings of man and woman, and their respective reflections within the *yanantin* model, we have, in Platt's words, "male men, male women, female men, and female women" (247–48). This four-part construction of relationships corresponds to the four-part construction of the Andean cosmos, and the four-part division of the Inca empire, Tawantinsuyu, which in colonial Quechua meant "All of Peru, or the four parts, which are *Antesuyu, Collasuyu, Contisuyu, Chinchaysuyu*" (González Holguín 336) The first two pairings of same-sex couples reflect the gendered groupings involved in the *tinku* ritual battles, the house building and ritual plowing ceremonies. The pairing of the groups from *hanan* with the groups from *hurin* is achieved through the symbolic reflection of perfect symmetry represented in the same-sex pairing. The man from *hanan* is reflected back to the man from *hurin*. The woman from the *puna* is reflected back to the woman from the valley. Platt concludes that the two figures of the same-sex pairings create a certain ambiguity that leads to the union of the gender opposites: "The very ambiguity of the middle two elements allows them to be presented, not illogically, by men and women respectively. And we can now understand the ideality of such an arrangement: Two actors of the same sex can affirm the relationship of mirrored symmetry that *should* pertain, in real life, to the conjugal pair" (248).

Platt clarifies and corroborates this hypothesis by comparing an analysis of the Quechua word *yana*'s semantic field with that of related root words, namely *pampa* (a flat place, a thing in common, a common and universal thing); *cuzcachani* and *pactachani* (synonyms: to join two unequal things); and *chulla* (antonym: a thing without a mate, unequal images). After considering these terms and concepts within the context of his previous discussion, Platt concludes that the commonality of the terms is found in the pairing of opposites, just as we have seen *yanantin* function above in the context of gender relations (249–52). To bring these opposites together, in each of the concepts discussed, implied the elimination of inconsistencies and disproportionate halves. In the *tinku* ritual the goal was to reaffirm borders between *ayllus,* so that each side reflected symmetrically the other. In the marriage of man and wife, the ritual aimed at uniting two opposite genders so that each complemented the other in daily interdependence. For this symmetrical pairing to occur, the things to be paired must share limits or borders.

Exegesis of a Quechua synonym for *yanantin, pactachani,* helps us to understand the full meaning of the ritual union of opposites and its corresponding geometrical symbolism. Santo Tomás translates the term as "to pair up unequal things" (Platt, 249). One of its other synonyms, *cuzcachani,* has as its root *cuzca,* or "something flat," leading Platt to conclude that this concept of uniting unequal things has a geometrical attribute, a symbolic character that signified for the Andean a commonality between the notion of flatness and equality (250–51). "The elements to be paired must first be 'pared' to achieve the 'perfect fit.' Here, the crucial notion is that of the *sharing of boundaries* in order to create a harmonious coexistence" (251). Again we see the importance of duality and borders in Andean cultural production. The *chawparani* divides the ecological zones; the *kaypacha* separates the cosmological worlds, *hanaqpacha* and *ukhupacha;* and in the *tinku* ritual, competing *ayllus* share borders marked by stones. What was the *quariwarmi*'s border?

'We have already noted that *yanantin* signified giving assistance to others and the symmetrical pairing of things. But the colonial dictionaries offer other meanings that help explain what might be considered a "border" in the symmetrical pair *quariwarmi.* Domingo de Santo Tomás's 1560 *Lexicon o vocabulario de la lengua general del Perú* recorded the word *yanachani* and its meaning, "one woman embraces another naked."[22] González Holguín's 1608 *Vocabulario de la lengua general de todo el Perú llamado Quichua o del Inca* included the word *yanachacuni* and its definition: "one man to make use of another, or the devil, or the sin of man."[23] These entries reflect what I argue in fuller detail elsewhere: that same-sex sexuality would undergo a process of transculturation, as the colonial discourse matured.[24] Ideology aside, the entries imply that, symbolically, same-sex praxis was related to the *yanantin* concept. To clarify, Platt returns to the mirror images and reminds us that the ideal partner, in order to create the symmetrical reflection, is the same-sex partner (252). And the border? The liminal space between the ideal, same-sex pair seems to be symbolically represented by the sexual act, the moment the two bodies come together physically, thus reflecting the perfect symmetry of same-sex bodies. Through this symbolic union, the opposite genders, each with his or her own autonomous power, can hope to achieve *yanantin*, symmetrical harmony, that is, to live together as helpmates and reproduce both Andean people and culture.

This conceptualization suggests that Andeans conceived of nonprocreative sexuality, at least symbolically, as culture-building at the thresholds of time and space in community rituals. However, does this conceptualization provide for a temporal or even an ongoing subject position in the culture? Thinking from an Andean paradigm in which both male and female genders struggle for harmonious union, achieved through symbolic, ritual same-sex pairing, leads us to explore third-gender subjectivity in the pre-Hispanic and colonial record from a perspective that considers the performance of feminine characteristics and passive same-sex sexuality in positive, culture-producing terms. We are now better prepared to read the discursive fragments of third-gender subjectivity as iterations of an originary ritual subject.

THE MOCHE

This idealization of same-sex praxis may have deep roots in Andean culture. The Moche, whose iconography and material artifacts are increasingly revealing the important place of the feminine in the ideology of the sacrifice ceremony and other rituals, also represented same-sex sexuality in ritual contexts.[25] The Moche culture flourished between A.D. 100 and A.D. 750 on the north coast of present-day Peru, between the Piura valley in the north and the Huarmey valley in the south.[26] The physical environment of the north coast was an important determinant in the region's cultural development and contributes to many explanations of the mythological tradition represented by Moche iconography. While the Moche peoples depended primarily on the Pacific ocean for their sustenance, fishing from reed and balsa boats, the valleys created from the highland rivers' drainage were important oases in the coastal desert plain that runs the length of the Peruvian coast. As these valley centers expanded into larger, more powerful complexes, the Moche began to trade with more distant neighbors, with the "Ecuadoreans" of the north and the offshore Pacific islands (50–51). Also integrated into the Moche society were important contacts with the Yunga, highlands, and Amazonia. Not only did these three eastern regions provide commercial and ritual products to the Moche, they also figured prominently in Moche cultural production through their iconography and art, which reflect the integral relationship the Moche had with the natural environment.

Manuel Arboleda was the first Andean scholar to seriously treat the theme of what he calls "homosexuality" in the erotic ceramics of the Moche.

While others have mentioned it in passing or denied that there was actually such evidence, the most prominent attention devoted to the topic before Arboleda explained the scenes in terms of Moche morality.²⁷ Rafael Larco Hoyle, one of Peru's pioneering archeologists and material culture preservationists, was captive to the homophobia of his times when it came to reading the Moche depictions of same-sex sexuality. Both the Larco Hoyle museum and his book dedicated to the subject of pre-Hispanic erotic art, *Checan*, project colonial and twentieth-century morality onto the Moche ceramic narratives.²⁸ Arboleda has undertaken a more precise study of the material culture related to erotic Moche art, analyzing seven hundred erotic and nonerotic pieces. Arboleda paid close attention to details other than the sexual positions; he observed the vestments and other articles present in the scenes and *guacos* (ceramic vessels) in order to establish the gender of the different characters represented in the art. He has established that one of the *guacos* described by Larco Hoyle as a moralizing depiction of sexual excess that may or may not be of same-sex partners, is of two male subjects. The skeletal figure's male genitals are showing, and the "sleeping" human figure is dressed in typical masculine attire, including a male headdress and tunic (103). Another *guaco* from his sample, also housed at the Larco Hoyle museum, is a pair of skeletal figures, whose genitals are not shown, but whose vestments indicate male gender. This pair is not involved in anal sex, but the reclining figures are kissing and embracing each other (103).

Arboleda's survey of Moche erotic art also included analysis of what he names "mythic-religious" figures and focused on the iconography represented in the *"Tema de la preparación,"* or "Preparation Theme." This scene suggests that the same-sex sodomy represented by the Moche may have had religious significance, for the sexual act at the center of the series of iconographic scenes is highly ritualized. The series begins with a group of three male anthropomorphic figures preparing a liquid substance, which in the following scene is poured over the genital area of two copulating figures. Arboleda speculates that the substance was a hallucinogen, and adds that John Rowe has suggested that it might have been injected into the anus of the passive figure by means of an enema, which would have been an efficient and quick entry of the drug into the blood stream (102). The scene represented to the right of the copulation scene is of an iguana-faced, anthropomorphic figure that mirrors a doglike figure to his left in a prayerful position. Jürgen Golte reads these postures in Moche iconography as gestures of respect.²⁹ In the sequences that Golte has analyzed, the iguana-faced figure, which he calls Figure J, is associated with different ritual contexts, including sacrifices and divinations (58–59). To Figure J's right there is also a winged figure, possibly symbolizing shamanic dream flight. Further toward the right of the copulation scene is a pair of female figures less elaborately dressed than the central figures.

The copulation scene takes place in a structure whose architecture is common in Moche iconography, often represented on top of platforms and pyramids, and whose material remains have been excavated by archeologists.[30] Depicting actions as taking place in these covered venues generally indicates that they are important activities, such as presentation of prisoners, sacrifice ceremonies, and, in this case, ritual copulation. In this sequence, the kneeling figure's genitals are not visible in the copulation scene; however, Arboleda has noted that the headdress and breechcloth worn by the figure, as well as the *rodillera* (knee pads), are usually seen on male figures in Moche art, and he has also noted their association with supernatural beings. The reclining, face-up figure has no supernatural characteristics. However, the figure is wearing *trenzas* (braids) and a breechcloth, that is, both feminine and masculine markers of gender. Arboleda points out the rarity of finding a mixture of gender markers in the same figure in Moche iconography and suggests that "perhaps the presence of these characteristics in one single individual represents an ancient tradition of representing 'berdache,' that is, male individuals who assume and perform the role of the opposite gender."[31] This reading of the iconography as a representation of a third gender (what Arboleda calls "berdache") is a great advancement in the treatment of the same-sex sexuality motif in Moche art. Trexler also agrees that these scenes depict same-sex acts, relating these images to colonial reports on the Pachacamac prayer postures.[32] He proposes that the sexual act is carried out between male rulers and "berdache," concluding that these ceramics represent hierarchical sexual posturing that expresses "dominion of Moche rulers over their male subjects" (114). As I continue to develop my reading of these rituals below, I propose we move away from this interpretation of the ceramic representation to one which reflects the cumulative performances of third-gender ritual sexuality that I piece together in this chapter. Indeed, the context in which these figures appear suggests that they played a ritual role in Moche society. The temple architecture, the ritual attendants (the iguana-faced figure, the winged figure, and the praying dog), and the libations poured on the genital area all indicate the sacred nature of the sexual act being represented. While Arboleda affirms that the ritual most likely was not associated with fertility rites, due to the nonprocreative nature of the sexual acts represented, he goes no further in speculating on a possible meaning of same-sex copulation in Moche culture and makes no attempt at placing the scenes described above in relation to other iconographic representations in Moche art.

Anne Marie Hocquenghem, in her thorough study, *Iconografía Mochica,* has gone a step further in offering an explanation for some sodomy rituals. She has established a relationship between the representations of nonprocreative sexuality, such as heterosexual sodomy and masturbation, and rituals associated with death. Theorizing death as an inversion of life, she posits that sodomy and masturbation reflect inverted sexual practices that may have been employed to affect the transition from this world to the "other world" after death, which might explain the presence of skeletal figures in the copulation scenes. Hocquenghem's principal argument is based on her reading of death and mourning rituals described in Guaman Poma's *El primer nueva corónica y buen gobierno* of 1615. Guaman Poma discussed three periods of death rituals: the funeral, the mourning, and reorganization and replacement of the dead in the community.[33] As part of the mourning process, women cut their hair short and spun thread in the opposite direction than they normally would have. Hocquenghem considers these two practices symbolic of the inversion of daily reality; that is, women inverted the normal order of things. Though her analysis brings us closer to an understanding of the iconography as representation of liminal moments in the Moche ritual calendar, and her interpretation might explain heterosexual sodomy and masturbation, her approach does not interpret third-gender presence in the ritual sex acts depicted in Moche iconography.

The theoretical problem with Hocquenghem's interpretation centers on how we identify the genders of the participants in the ritual represented in the Moche iconography. If we agree that the reclining figure is a third gender, that is, a transvested male who lives as a woman but whose status and roles differ from those of women and men, then to speak of the act of sodomy as an inversion is problematic. Same-sex sodomy as an inversion would depend on a binary gender system in which opposite-sex practices were the norm. Two gendered males copulating would then be the inverse of a heterosexual act and vice versa. In a gender culture in which there exists a third gender, what does same-sex sodomy between a male and a third gender signify? Perhaps a jump forward in time might help us answer the question, for we need to piece together a few more fragments of third-gender performances before a hypothesis can be fully formed.

THIRD-GENDER "PERFORMANCE" IN RECENT ETHNOGRAPHY

Instead of explaining the sexual ritual depicted in the Moche ceramics as signs of power relations between chiefs and subjects, it is more suggestive to explore the commonalities between the Moche representations of third-gender subjectivities and others in colonial historiography and the more recent anthropological record. After examining how third-gender subjectivity is performed in agricultural and *ayllu* boundary-marking rituals, as depicted in recent ethnography, we can return to the colonial record and reconsider other manifestations of third gender.

Billie Jean Isbell, in her ethnography of a small, south-central Andean village, based on fieldwork from the late 1960s and early 1970s, discusses an August corn-planting ritual, *chacrayupay*, in which

> a man dresses as a woman, blackens his face, and "plants" the plaza with the remains left in the bottoms of the brewing pots used to prepare corn beer. This is a reverse portrayal of actual planting. The plaza is planted instead of fields; a transvestite with a reverse-colored face performs the task using "that which is thrown away" as seed.[34]

Isbell offers a provocative interpretation of this ritual, one that suggests a symbolic connection between agriculture and the power of the female gender, which might help us understand third gender's ritual participation in Andean culture.[35] Isbell explains that it was the woman's role to place corn seeds in the ground while men covered them with earth using the native *lampa* hoe (57). Guaman Poma visually represents this tradition in his chronicle as well, in his Edenic depiction of the first generation of Andeans after Viracocha (f48: 43) and in his representation of *chacrayupay*, the ritual Isbell witnessed some 450 years later (f250: 185; see figure 1). As Guaman Poma informs us in the accompanying text, this is the time, August, of sacrifices, celebration, dance, and song (f251: 186). Guaman Poma's drawing clearly delineates the gendered space of the ritual. The men open the ground with their phallic *lampa*, while women place the seeds in the earth. The gender symmetry is highlighted by the presence of the sun and the moon. The only element in the drawing that does not have a counterpart is the figure approaching the planting scene and carrying two tumblers, perhaps *queros* with *chicha*, or other ritual libation. As we will see below, the shawl that the figure is wearing could signify third-gender subjectivity.

Of the transgendering involved in this ritual, Isbell proposes that "men are balancing the scale of procreative power between males and females" (206). In order to maintain social and cosmological equilibrium,[36] the men reverse the order of the planting tradition, thus allaying fears that women's procreative power could create an imbalance. Based on my interpretation of third gender, however, I would modify Isbell's reading of the reversal. The symbolic reversal was not conducted by a man, which would have been the opposite gender of the female protagonist of ritual corn planting, but a cross-dressed man. Instead of invoking the masculine to restore the balance, the Andeans chose to invoke an in-between gender, a third gender. This intervention of a third gender as a mediation between the two opposing genders, between the feminine and the masculine, suggests that the ritual's meaning, which Isbell insightfully explicates, might be the same, only our understand-

Figure 1 The *chacrayupay* ritual (from Felipe Guaman Poma de Ayala, *El primer nueva corónica y buen gobierno*, [1615])

ing of the participating subjects changes. I concluded above that the same-sex sexual act provided the symbolic symmetry necessary for the reproduction of cultural values, such as Platt analyzed in the ritual battles, *tinku*. The third gender is the embodiment of the liminal space between the two sides. Could the feminine attire of the third gender signify the performance of a symbolic border between the ideal reflection that Platt posited as the key to *yanantin*?

Yet another ethnographic report advances my argument and confirms the importance of ritual dress in Andean symbolic acts. Anne Paul's study of Paracas textiles includes an insightful introduction to the symbolic importance of textiles in the Andes from pre-Hispanic to contemporary times. Ethnic dress communicates everyday distinctions of social status as well as messages unique to ritual contexts: "Embedded in items of apparel are visible indicators of such things as ethnic group, *ayllu* affiliation, cosmology, economic status, gender, age, family ties, marital status, and offices held within the community."[37] One such garment invested with ritual symbolism in the Chinchero region (near Cuzco) of the southern Andean highlands is the *llijlla,* or shawl commonly worn by women. The *llijlla* marks a woman's *ayllu* affiliation, while portraying the wearer's personal identity, since each shawl is produced by the wearer. Paul records ethnographers Ed and Christine Franquemont's observations that "during the running of their *ayllu* boundaries, a land-based ritual called *mujonomiento,*" a man cross-dresses by wearing a *llijlla:*

> The *ayllu's* officers bring with them their staffs of office and plant them in the ground, indicating a formal government occasion. The most important officer, the *alcalde,* wears a special red poncho that is different from the standard walnut-dyed brown sheep's wool poncho worn by the other men. A central participant in the celebration is the *waylaka,* a man who recites humorous poems and orations about the history of the stone markers that border the *ayllu,* and dances with a white flag. The *waylaka* dresses as a transvestite, with clothing like that worn by Chinchero women. He wears two *llijllas:* one is held shut with a *tupu* (pin) made of a silver spoon, and the other is draped over one shoulder and under the opposite arm, tied in front. The outer *llijlla* symbolizes a ritual burden, indicating that the wearer has a *cargo* (special responsibility or obligation) for the fiesta. (19–20)

This rich ethnographic account, while not addressing the meaning of the cross-dressing, provides us with more clues as to the ritual context in which such practices occur in the late twentieth century. We can note the differentiation of three distinct gender categories: man, woman, and the transvested *waylaka.* This categorization is marked by the subjects' vestments as well as by their roles in the ceremony. The *waylaka,* performing as a third gender, is invested with the special responsibility of recalling the history of the *ayllus'* borders. The fact that the men and women are separated in distinct groups and the transvested *waylaka* performs a ritual marking borders confirms the relationship suggested above between *tinku* and *yanantin.* Here, the cross-dressed *waylaka's* body is employed in the determination of a community's borders, through dance and song. His feminine attire evokes a memory that might stretch back to pre-Hispanic times and may be related to the figure recorded in Guaman Poma's drawing, who was dressed in a *llijlla*-like shawl with *tupu*, strikingly similar to that of the *waylaka* in the Chinchero ceremony.

Perhaps the transgendered male performed, based on a third-gender phantasmatic original, a liminal subjectivity that mediated between absolute gender opposites. By transforming the body toward the feminine, yet still retaining the sex of a male, he might be seen as that which a mirror's reflection could not achieve. He is the manifestation of the symmetrical opposites doubled over on the other. He is the *quariwarmi*, embodied. I propose, then, that these current ethnographic reports of cross-dressing during festivals represent vestiges of third-gender ritual participation, iterations of subjectivities that might have also performed sexual acts, such as the one depicted in the Moche iconography, as part of their "*cargos.*" The cross-dressing might be considered the performance of an original sacred subject that once mediated between the male and female genders.

Throughout this chapter we observe the performance of different aspects of third-gender subjectivity, including same-sex praxis, cross-dressing, and men "talking like women." As we will continue to see, these iterations of third-gender characteristics often occur in the context of agricultural or other community-building rituals. The *chacrayupay* and the Chinchero *mujonomiento* rituals help us understand the possible relationship between the phantasms of third gender and the mediation between the male and female complements. As the fragments of evidence accumulate, I continue to question whether the reports of ritual, same-sex sodomy are about the expression of power relations between powerful rulers and their degraded subjects.

TEMPLE SODOMY AND THIRD-GENDER SUBJECTIVITY

Our evidence of third-gender rituality is not limited to the ancient Moche or the modern performances of transgendering in agricultural or *tinku* ceremonies. One of the most important artifacts informing our knowledge of third-gender subjectivity comes from the exhaustive work by Pedro de Cieza de León (1508–1560), author of *La crónica del Perú*, whose three volumes were first published between 1553 and his death. Cieza has been regarded as one of the few colonial scribes relatively independent from colonial authorities such as the Church or the Viceroyalty.[38] Though this supposed "objectivity" of the new generation of chroniclers, represented by Cieza, provided more ethnographically sophisticated texts than those of their predecessors, these accounts do not necessarily prove to be "transparent" representations of indigenous cultures. As Sabine MacCormack has pointed out, "[I]n the very process of translating and writing down what they were told, Spaniards inevitably introduced notions of their own that had, strictly speaking, no Andean counterparts" (83). Cieza, like other chroniclers, worked within the sixteenth-century paradigm in which, in the words of Foucault, "to search for a meaning is to bring to light a resemblance."[39]

Cieza seems to struggle with the ethnographic material, wrestling with his Christian conscience while trying to represent the Incas as proto-Christians.[40] His most difficult test might have been whether or not to include what perhaps is the most transgressive of ethnographies in his entire chronicle. The dilemma presents itself as Cieza turns his attention to the Yungas, the people who lived in the *llanos* (plains) located in the valleys along the northern Peruvian coast. Cieza provides detailed information based on his observations and on reports given to him by Domingo de Santo Tomás, a Dominican friar who spent long periods of time in the region and is known for his Quechua grammar and lexicon (*La crónica*, 191), as well as a Quechua language sermon.[41] After dedicating two chapters to the burial customs of the Yungas, Cieza transmits a text that the Dominican friar had given him concerning same-sex temple sodomy and cross-dressing temple attendants. While several critics have referenced this scandalous passage, I underscore Cieza's caution in presenting it to his reader(s) and propose that we carefully analyze various claims in the passage and its colonial context.[42]

Cieza writes an extended preamble to the Santo Tomás text, justifying his inclusion of it in his chronicle: "It is pious that those of us who are Christian have some curiosity: so that by knowing and understanding the bad habits of these people, we can separate them from their habits and make them understand the path of truth, so that they might be saved."[43] Here, curiosity is a Christian virtue, for only through the power of knowing the "others" could the Spanish hope to convert them. Taking into consideration the censorship of the Inquisition and the *Consejo de Indias*, this prelude might have been necessary, for, as Lydia Fossa has pointed out, only Cieza's first volume was allowed to be published; the rest of his chronicles languished in the archives until the twentieth century.[44] Cieza insists in these preparatory remarks that he has only witnessed sodomy in the areas around Puerto Viejo and the island of Puna, claiming that the Incas were "clean" of this sinful vice (*La crónica*, 199). However, Santo Tomás provided Cieza with the following description, which I reproduce in its entirety:

> It is true that as a general thing among the mountaineers and the Yungas the devil has introduced this vice under a kind of cloak of sanctity, and in each important temple or house of worship they have a man or two, or more, depending on the idol, who go dressed in women's attire from the time they are children, and speak like them, and in manner, dress, and everything else imitate women. With these, almost like a

religious rite or ceremony, on feast [days] and holidays, they have carnal, foul intercourse, especially the chiefs and headmen. I know this because I have punished two, one of them of the Indians of the highlands, who was in a temple which they call *huaca*, for this purpose, in the province of the Conchucos, near the city of Huánuco, the other in the province of Chincha, where the Indians are subjects of His Majesty. And when I spoke to them of the evil they were doing, and upbraided them for the repulsiveness of the sin, they answered me that it was not their fault because from childhood they had been put there by the caciques to serve them in this cursed and abominable vice, and to act as priests and guard the temples of their idols. So what I deduced from this was that the devil held such sway in this land that, not satisfied in making them fall into so great sin, he made them believe that this vice was a kind of holiness and religion, to hold more power over them. (*The Incas*, 314)[45]

This detailed account of third-gender ritual subjectivity merits an extended analysis and requires an understanding of a number of Andean cultural concepts.

Santo Tomás contradicts Cieza's assertion that sodomy was not to be found among the Incas, for we learn that two of the third-gender subjects the Dominican disciplined lived in Inca-controlled areas, Huánuco in the northern Peruvian Andes and Chincha to the south of Lima. In fact, we have other evidence that disproves the notion that ritual sodomy was limited to the coastal areas. P. Ludovico Bertonio, a Jesuit linguist who came to Peru in 1578 to work in the missions, began compiling a dictionary of Aymara terms in 1595, which was published eight years later. Bertonio was known for his careful gathering of linguistic material, which he accomplished through working with native informants in Juli, a Jesuit mission in the southern Andes near Lake Titicaca.[46] Among the various entries related to third-gender subjectivities we find this definition: "*Huaussa, Keussa, Ipa:* One (a male) who lives, dresses, speaks, and works as a woman, and is the passive participant in the nefarious sin, just as in old times there used to be many in this land."[47] Here Bertonio has left us a concise image of third-gender subjects as reported to him by native informants and has suggested that the practice was more widespread than Cieza had earlier reported. Actually, Cieza contradicts himself much later in his chronicle when discussing the peoples of Lake Titicaca, who also practiced temple sodomy, at least until they were conquered by the Incas.[48] The similarity between these descriptions, taken from distinct geographical areas by missionaries from different religious orders, suggests that there might have been, before the Spanish arrived, a pan-Andean tradition of third-gender subjectivity. This dangerous text, couched in idolatry discourse by Santo Tomás and bravely included by Cieza, creates an opening for us to understand this subjectivity that was first suggested to us by the Moche iconography and ceramics considered above.

What distinguishes Santo Tomás's text from Cieza's other accounts of sodomy in the Andes is the author's emphasis on the religious use of male same-sex sexuality. This ritual specialization described by Santo Tomás provides us with the cultural meaning of their social relationships. Though Santo Tomás envelops the description of temple sodomy in a discourse of idolatry, the repetition of the sacred nature of the sexual act intimates a desire to communicate the indigenous cultural values informing same-sex praxis.[49] He describes the sodomical act as being carried out in a sacred space, the "temple or place of worship," *huacas* dedicated to certain ritual activities.[50] The sexual rites were performed on special days of the ritual calendar. The act was performed by transgendered specialists, whose number varied according to the "idol" involved. These special attendants are described to be much like the figures observed in the Moche iconography, but here the details are more explicit: they were dressed like women from childhood, they talked like women, and their mannerisms and dress were imitations of women's. As we have seen, Bertonio's definition also included "work like a woman" along with the other gender markers mentioned in Santo Tomás's text.

Their transvesting is consistent with the ritual Moche figure who was depicted with both male and female accoutrements, but Santo Tomás provides information on how they were raised in a transvested state; evidently certain male children were chosen for this ritual role at a young age and trained to fulfill their responsibilities. Trexler reads the reported comments from the third-gender temple attendants whom Santo Tomás punished as evidence that they were forced into their roles (107). I believe, however, we must consider the colonial context in which the Dominican friar is receiving the information from the two third-gender attendants. First, Santo Tomás admonishes them for the sinfulness of their acts, no doubt referring to the Sodom and Gomorrah lesson that was standard evangelical material.[51] Second, an implicit objective of Santo Tomás's report was to glorify the missionary project; his two punished, and perhaps repentant, subjects naturally would blame their "errors" on others, as the Christians blame the idolatries of the indigenous Andeans on the devil. Following this logic, it is risky to say that the youths truly considered themselves "forced" into their sacred roles or that they felt ashamed of their positions. Indeed, feminine status was not demeaned in the way Trexler maintains it was in European culture. Therefore, to take on the passive role and to cross-dress were not necessarily considered inferior activities. In the performative iterations of third-gender subjectivity discussed above in the Chinchero *mujonomiento* ritual, we observed how assuming the third-gender role was considered a special *cargo* within the community. Trexler's reading of the temple sodomites as "debased sexual subordinates" (117) is based on a notion of power in which the female gender and same-sex behavior were devalued as they were in European culture. As I have demonstrated above and elsewhere, and as Silverblatt and Harrison have likewise argued, the feminine was not devalued in the Andes; indeed, it was a vital force to be ritually negotiated.[52] Furthermore, as we will see below, the feminine sphere of culture and same-sex praxis were mythologically sanctioned in Andean religious beliefs.

The practice of young children taking on responsibility, both mundane and sacred, was (and still is) the norm in Andean society. Guaman Poma de Ayala, writing at the beginning of the seventeenth century, records the routine and sacred duties of children. Both boys and girls aged five to nine years worked around their homes (f209: 157 and f230: 171). Boys and girls aged nine to twelve began to serve their communities, at times even working for the deities by killing birds for feathers and gathering flowers for offerings (f205–7: 154–57, and f228: 171). He may be exaggerating the youths' enthusiasm for work as he describes their commitment to their superiors: "All of these activities were done for the love of the Republic and for the magnifying of the Inca's majesty."[53] The historian continues by discussing the Andean concept of reciprocity, *sapsi*, which was the work all members of an *ayllu* contributed to the community. The ethics of reciprocity in Andean communities motivated service, values that the youth learned from an early age.

Ultimately we have too little evidence with which to form a solid hypothesis regarding the third genders' feelings about their role. Silverblatt's discussion of a young female sacrifice in the annual Inca *capacocha* ritual might offer further insights into the participants' feelings in Andean sacred ritual (96–98).[54] Other than the comments offered here, we have only one mention in the Andes of how young men might have felt about adopting these temple roles. Trexler recognizes this passage, which is from Blás Valera, a mestizo Jesuit writing in the Andes at the end of the sixteenth century, but still concludes that the temple sodomites were "sexual subordinates" who served to signify their lords' higher status (117). Blás Valera's description of the indigenous "priests" suggests that they "offered themselves" to serve their deities, even going so far as to castrate themselves or be castrated: "Many of these offered themselves from childhood and lasted, not only in continence until old age, but in virginity. . . . Many of these or others were eunuchs, what they called *corasca*, and either they castrated themselves, in reverence to their gods, or others castrated them when they were children, so that they served in this way of life."[55] Blás Valera is careful to use terms that the European reader could understand; his entire description of Andean religion is one of correspondences between familiar Catholic religious institutions and Andean practices. Therefore his choice of "eunuch" as the name for the castrated temple attendants should not surprise us. What might surprise us are Blás Valera's comments that the people considered the castrated priests sacrosanct: "When they went out into the streets and squares, all the people followed behind, since they regarded them as sacred."[56] That the people of Cuzco, the Inca imperial capital, held these priests in high esteem is further evidence that the effeminized position in ritual contexts was a venerable one. Indeed, Blás Valera goes on to explain how the priests "prayed publicly for the Inca and the people," demonstrating their public religious role and their relationship with the Incas.[57] These comments suggest that the third-gender priests, castrated or transvested, participated in the power structure of Tawantinsuyu and enjoyed a certain status in the society.

The presence of the feminine in the description of third-gender temple attendants also related to their speech. Both Santo Tomás and Bertonio observe that third-gender subjectivities "speak like women," which could refer to the grammatical constructions and idioms they used or to the pitch of their voices.[58] Both meanings are possible and can find support in Andean historiography, but because there are no extant texts that represent the speech of third-gender subjectivities, either in Spanish or in an indigenous language, we will never know for certain. The Quechua (and Aymara) language marks the gender of the speaker, so that an interlocutor would understand the speaker's gender not only by cultural markers like clothing and hair, but also by the way he or she formed his or her words and sentences. For example, a woman refers to her brother as *tura*, while a man refers to his brother as *wawqi*. A man addresses his sister as *pana*, and a woman speaks to her sister as *naña*.[59] Therefore, a third gender speaking as a woman might choose *naña* to address her sister and *tura* to address her brother. This "cross-speaking" would further mark the third gender's identity in ritual, and perhaps even profane, contexts.

There is further evidence, based on kinship relations, that a third gender might indeed abide by the linguistic rules of a woman. Tom Zuidema's study of the Inca *ayllus* and kinship relations explains the way the term *ipa*, seen above as the Aymara name of the third-gender, passive participant in same-sex sodomy, is also the name given to a "father's sister" in Quechua and Aymara.[60] Zuidema relates this signifying of a male in a "female sexual position" as symbolically enabling the male to take a female position in the kinship system; specifically, a younger brother is often gendered female, symbolically a "sister" of his older brother (29–30). Zuidema offers three examples of how this gendering is related to same-sex ritual sexuality. First, he cites Cieza's description of temple sodomy that I am analyzing here. Second, he mentions

Jesuit Pablo José Arriaga's 1621 manual, *Extirpación de la idolatría del Perú,* which, in the context of the extirpation of idolatry that he and others undertook in the first years of the seventeenth century, observed agricultural rituals in which men would speak in a female voice (Zuidema, 31; Arriaga, 207). The "ministers," called "*Parianas*" by Arriaga, who performed these rites were chosen each year from the community and prepared themselves up to two months in advance by fasting and avoiding contact with their wives (Arriaga, 207). Third, a 1621 account relates how younger brothers of a sacrificed older sister "officiated as their sister's priests in time of sowing and harvesting. They exercised these religious functions for their entire lives and transmitted them to their descendants. During the ritual celebrations, these priests spoke in a woman's voice" (Zuidema, 32).[61] While Zuidema and Silverblatt emphasize the pitch or tone of the voice, thus characterizing it as female, the positioning of ritual priests in "female" positions within the kinship system might also imply the use of the gendered semantics mentioned above. Bertonio's dictionary offers us further evidence of this vocal transgendering, recording the following words: "*Cutita chacha: hombre que habla con voz mugeril*" (61), "a man speaking with a woman's voice," which suggests a change in the pitch or tone of the voice. González Holguín's Quechua dictionary does not record a word for the voice change, but there is an enigmatic entry, "*Pau Ola: de hombre a mujer,*"[62] "from man to woman," which might signify transgendering, though we do not know specifically in what context the words would have been used.

There are other performative iterations of third-gender subjectivity related to agriculture found in colonial historiography. Guaman Poma reports that the Andesuyos held a celebration in which one of the dances involved cross-dressing. He presents it along with *fiestas* from other regions, assuring the reader that the ceremonies had nothing to do with witchcraft, idolatry, or enchantments, but were purely for enjoyment. Only the drunkenness of the occasions bothered him, not the cross-dressing dancers (f315: 239). Given that Guaman Poma does not mention transvested people or same-sex practice in the rest of his extensive treatment of Andean customs, and despite his insistence that the *fiestas* were divorced of religious meaning, it is intriguing that he discusses this example. As they danced in a circle holding hands, they sang "in their language," which the author records as "*cayaya caya, cayaya caya,*" an unidentified language of the area (figure 2). They also sang, however, in Quechua, which Guaman Poma includes in his description: "And to the sound of a flute they celebrate, walking in a circle hand-in-hand, they enjoy themselves and celebrate and *they dance the* huarmi auca *all the men dressed as women with their arrows* [my emphasis]; the one who plays the drum: *warmi auca chiauan uaylla uruchapa panascatana anti auca chiuan*

FÍ ESTAS DE LOS ANDISVIOS
CAIACAIAVARMIAVCA

Figure 2 Fiesta of the Andesuyos (from Felipe Guaman Poma de Ayala, *El primer nueva corónica y buen gobierno,* [1615])

uaylla."[63] Cross-dressing for ritual dance seems to have been a public and perhaps common practice, at least common enough to justify a specialized vocabulary. Bertonio includes a word in his Aymara dictionary for a man dressed in women's clothes for use in dances or "when using masks."[64]

Jan Szeminski has translated the dance's name, *huarmi auca,* in this passage from the Quechua as either "*mujer guerrera*" (warrior woman) or "*enemigo de mujeres*" (women's enemy).[65] His translation seems to imply that the men in this ritual dance were paying homage to women warriors, an image of Andean fighting women that appears in other chronicles or, as in the second gloss, that the transgendered men were somehow women's enemies. Although there are reports of tension between women and third-gender subjectivities in the historiography,[66] I believe the second gloss to be nonsensical in the context of this ritual dance, because, in both the text and the accompanying drawing, the cross-dressed men are dancing hand-in-hand with women. Moreover, if we relate the transgendering and the fiesta to a different translation for Guaman Poma's use of the word *auca*, which I propose for our purposes, then the meaning changes completely. To understand the deeper significance of the ritual recorded by Guaman Poma, we must first examine the role played by agriculturally related priests in the Andean mythic tradition.

Henrique Urbano, in his structuralist study of Andean mythology, has identified three principal cycles of myths that survived transcription into the colonial historiography of the southern Andes.[67] In each of the cycles, which he designates Viracocha, Ayar, and Chanca, there are corresponding sociopolitical functions as well as heroes that personify those functions: (1) wisdom, political leadership, and warrior function; (2) the priestly-ritual function; (3) the agricultural and magical-curative function (57–59). I am most interested in the second and third functions in the myths, where I find a link to third-gender ritual subjectivities. The connection is related to the value of the feminine in the spheres of ritual, agriculture, and magic.

In the Viracocha cycle, Urbano found the hero Tocapo's activities to be related to rituals, most explicitly to the production of textiles through weaving (58). Although almost all Andeans at some point in their lives worked in some part of the textile-producing process, we know that certain cloths were destined for ritual use, and these special fabrics were produced under highly regulated conditions in exclusively female spaces, the *acllahuasi,* where the *acllas,* or *mamaconas,* lived in seclusion (Silverblatt, 82). In the Ayar cycle, the ritual function was symbolized by the younger brother known as Ayar Ucho, who, as I analyze in detail below, became identified with one of the most sacred Inca *huacas,* Guanacauri (Urbano, 58). For the Chancas, this purpose was fulfilled by Yanavilca and Teclovilca, who expressed their functions through the ritual use of colors associated with the sun and moon (58). Urbano goes on to outline the symbolism of the third function, that of agriculture and magical-curative practices. In the Viracocha sequence, Imaymana displays knowledge of the specific curative qualities of different plants (59). In the Ayar cycle, Ayar Auca serves a magical-agricultural function in which his role is that of "lord and protector of the agricultural fields."[68] Finally, in the Chanca cycle it is Malma and Irapa who perform the agricultural and curative function, "with markedly feminine activities" (59).

Given this mythic structure of the southern Andean demigods, we can re-consider the Andesuyo, transgendering dance described by Guaman Poma. Could the dance's name, *huarmi auca,* be related to Ayar Auca? The fact that they dance with arrows would suggest that the meaning of *auca* is "warrior," unless the arrows, taken together with women's dress, signified a combina-tion of man and woman, that is, a sign for third-gender subjectivity, an iden-tity that by the early seventeenth century, when Guaman Poma wrote, might have been either eradicated or pushed underground, in which case this ritual would be but a phantasm of the precontact original. Other elements of the dance lead us to believe that *auca* did invoke the mythic Ayar Auca and his power in agricultural matters. First, Urbano reminds us that Ayar Auca's powers were associated with the "protection" of agricultural lands (50), which might also explain the arrows, as a sign of power. Second, Ayar Auca was said to have had wings, which permitted him to fly to Cuzco and select the site where Ayar Manco (Manco Capac) would found the imperial Inca city. This ability to fly suggests magical powers, associated with shamanistic dream flight, for example. Significantly, such magical powers were associated with Andesuyo, where the transgendered dance took place, because of its prox-imity to the Amazonian jungle, the Andean source of curative and magical plants. The same function in the Viracocha cycle was represented by Imay-mana, who was explicitly associated with Andesuyo.[69] Third, the song of the "*huarmi auca*" included a verse, "*chiwan waylla*," that refers to a yellow and red flower. Of course, because of the fragmented translation, we have no idea what it might have signified;[70] we must ask, however, whether it might not relate to agriculture or curative plants, refocusing our attention on the agri-cultural roots of the dance instead of on warrior women. Finally, considering the Andean correlation between female sexuality and agriculture, it seems reasonable that the *huarmi auca* dance could signify a similar belief in the An-desuyo region.[71] Whether or not the dancing, cross-dressed men were third-gender subjectivities or the ceremony is a vestige from earlier third-gender performances, the suggestive connection between myth, ritual, magic, and the feminine deserves more attention.

Again, these fragments add to the evidence that feminine characteristics were elicited in the ritual performance of agricultural rites during the colo-nial period, similar to features shared by the third-gender temple attendants recorded by Santo Tomás. Are the transgendered subjects considered de-based for participating in such activities? Should we read them as metaphors of dependency? Or, on the contrary, can we interpret these ritual attendants as liminal subjects needed in the re-creation of Andean culture? As observed above, these people were elected by the community or assumed positions held by deceased siblings. Their gender is performative in the sense that But-ler explains as the "effect of a regulatory regime of gender differences in which genders are divided and hierarchized under constraint. Social constraints, taboos, prohibitions, and threats of punishment operate in a ritualized repetition of norms, and this repetition constitutes the temporalized scene of gender construction and destabilization" ("Critically Queer," 16). Here, the repetition is literally "ritualized" in that the invocation of the feminine occurs in a ceremonial context. Ritual norms required the presence of a man who spoke in a feminine voice, perhaps as the *chacrayupay* and *mujonomiento* ceremonies considered above required the cross-dressing of a male. We are left with a "temporalized scene" of a gender subjectivity neither male nor female, but third. To understand why the society called for third-gender presence in important community ceremonies, we must consider possible mythological sanctions that Andeans felt compelled to follow in their mediations between their world, *kaypacha,* and the worlds of their deities and between the complementary genders, the *quari* and the *warmi.*

THIRD-GENDER SUBJECTIVITIES AND ANDEAN MYTHS

To explore the nexus between mythology and third-gender subjectivities, I analyze pivotal figures in myths recorded by a native Andean. I concentrate on Juan de Santacruz Pachacuti Yamqui Salcamaygua's (Santacruz Pachacuti) *Relación de antigüedades deste reyno del Perú* (1613), I also refer to Pedro Sarmiento de Gamboa's *Historia Indica* (1572), a history of the Andean region written for the colonial viceroy, Francisco de Toledo. In the conclusion of this chapter, I am particularly interested in how the gender and sexuality of mythic figures are represented in Santacruz Pachacuti's history of Tawantinsuyu. I analyze Ayar Ucho and the *huaca* Guanacauri, and the cosmological drawing's representation of Viracocha Pacha Yachachic.

An indigenous descendent of *curacas* from the area of Canas and Canchis, Santacruz Pachacuti offers us a unique perspective on Andean beliefs and practices. Only recently have scholars recognized the exceptional view of the early colonial period that Santacruz Pachacuti offers us. Regina Harrison was one of the first to vindicate the quality of the text, not for Santacruz Pachacuti's ability to conform to Renaissance Spanish rhetoric and stylistics, which had been attacked by traditional historians,[72] nor for the much-cited cosmological drawing I analyze below, but for the manipulation of linguistic codes that achieves the communication of "the essence of Andean cognition in the language and liturgy of the Spanish lords" (68). For Santacruz Pachacuti was, as Rolena Adorno has recently emphasized, a *"ladino,"* that is, a native Andean "competent (speaking, and possibly reading and writing) in the language of the colonial overlords."[73] This linguistic ability, as both Harrison and Adorno point out, positioned him to relate pre-Hispanic Andean culture to Christian history. Verónica Salles-Reese has proposed that Santacruz

Pachacuti's motivation for writing the *Relación* came from campaigns to extirpate idolatries in which he may have played a role as translator. Reading the text as a *probanza,* a legal petition commonly used by *ladinos* to establish their rights under Spanish law as well as to respond to accusations of idolatry, Salles-Reese suggests that Santacruz Pachacuti may have feared that his status as a Christian was in jeopardy. Therefore, at the insistence of the fearsome extirpator, Francisco de Ávila, he wrote the *Relación* to defend himself,[74] and he implicitly responded, as the voice of his people, to the overall attack on Andean culture in the name of Christianity.[75] Duviols and Itier's introduction to their recent edition stresses the didactic nature of the text, suggesting that it may have been destined for the recently established *Colegio de Caciques,* a Jesuit school founded for the indoctrination of the children of the Andean elite.[76] We can imagine that the structure of the narrative would have made a nice history primer, for Santacruz Pachacuti organized his story in three distinct epochs: *purun pacha,* in which the Andean people were still barbarous; the age of Tunapa, in which the apostle Saint Thomas was said to have preached the gospel, being accepted by only Manco Capac's father; and, finally, the age of the Incas, who under Manco Capac, are chosen by God to prepare the way for the Spaniards' Christian message.

A Homoerotic Encounter between a Huaca and Ayar Ucho

Santacruz Pachacuti's history of the Incas begins with a journey: the foundational family of the Incas travels from Lake Titicaca where Manco Capac had received the *tupayauri,* a magical staff given to his father by Tunapa, or the apostle Saint Thomas, from his grandfather and grandmother, Apo Tampo and Mama [*pachamama*] Achi (f6: 193). As in any epic narrative, Manco Capac and his siblings meet different challenges and suffer certain setbacks during their journey toward Cuzco. The first occurs as they approach Sañuc, a village near Cuzco, where the youngest brother sees a sitting figure:

> And arriving they say that he saw him seated like a fierce and cruel Indian, with reddened eyes, then one of the brothers arrived (the youngest one, the one that looked like a person) [the Indian] called him to his side and then as he neared closer he touched them on the head, saying: very good that you have come looking for me, finally you have found me, I was also looking for you, finally you are in my hands.[77]

The figure, here described as a fierce and cruel-looking Indian, seems to have inexplicably drawn Manco Capac's youngest brother to him. Mysteriously, the Indian speaks of the encounter as an inevitable certainty in which each searched for the other. The control of the Indian over the youngest brother keeps him there until finally Manco Capac sends another male sibling looking for him, who also stays with the Indian and the younger brother: "[A]nd they both remained there, *ojeado* by that huaca from Sañuc."[78] Thus, we learn that the Indian is actually a huaca, with whom the two siblings have become "*ojeado*," or entrapped through enchantment.[79] Manco Capac finds them "half dead," and they signal to him that "that idol and huaca had done him that evil."[80] At this point, exactly what the huaca has done to them is ambiguous, but then Manco Capac becomes angry and starts hitting the huaca on the head with the *tupayauri* given to him by the apostle at Lake Titicaca. The huaca then speaks, threatening Manco Capac that if it were not for the *tupayauri*, the huaca would have "also done him." The mysterious act perpetrated on the siblings is clarified when the huaca says: "Go away now that you have achieved great fortune, I want to enjoy your brother and sister because they have seriously sinned (carnal sin), and it is fitting that he be in the place where I am, that will be named Pituciray, Sauasiray."[81] The two male siblings who originally became entangled with the huaca are now said to be a brother and a sister, converted into two tall peaks in the region. The original manuscript carries an annotation in the margin, believed to be written by Ávila, that explains the meaning of the two peaks' names: "[T]hey are probably together, one stuck to the other," a likeness that reiterates the sexual imagery suggested in the narrative.[82]

While Duviols and Itier, in their introduction to their edition of the *Relación,* interpret this story as an "*exemplum cristiano*" that warns against incest (87), I would like to think through the evangelical veil that shrouds the myth and consider the encounter between the brothers and the huaca in native terms of same-sex, ritual sexuality.[83] Perhaps what is most interesting about this possibility is the rhetorical maneuvers employed by Santacruz Pachacuti in presenting this myth in a form recognizable to Christian moralists. As an Andean *ladino,* one whose purpose for writing might have been to teach the new generations of Andeans their history in such a way that they could be proud of their heritage in the new colonial context, Santacruz Pachacuti obscures the original meaning of a local myth. I propose that the original obscured story established the basis for a ritual relationship between mountain deity and Inca priest—one that was figured through same-sex sexuality and that mythically sanctioned third-gender ritual practices.

First, it is significant, given what we learned from Zuidema, that the first brother who is drawn to the huaca is the youngest. We recall that the younger brother in Andean kinship could be symbolically considered a third gender, an *ipa,* and he reportedly played priestly roles in ritual contexts. In Sarmiento de Gamboa's version of this myth, the only brother involved with the huaca is named Ayar Ucho, the Ayar sibling that served a religious function among the founding Incas.[84] In that version, after the huaca seduces him, Ayar Ucho is transformed into Guanacauri, an important ritual site for the Incas, where adolescent boys undergo ceremonial initiation. Second, the fact that he does not return to his family indicates that he remained alone with the huaca, unable to escape his "enchantment." That the youngest brother was physically attached to the huaca is metaphorically suggestive, as well, of a sexual liaison, especially in light of the fact that Ayar Ucho was left, "as if dead" but still enchanted, after the encounter. Third, the huaca's comment of how he was going to "enjoy" the siblings that remained behind is enigmatic. Duviols has interpreted it in terms of the devil enjoying a lost soul in hell, understanding the encounter as an incestuous one between brother and sister and that Santacruz Pachacuti implied the huaca was a demon (84).[85] This explanation, however, ignores the initial sexual imagery between the huaca and the brothers (and Sarmiento's account in which the encounter was limited to the huaca and Ayar Ucho). I interpret the sex change from two male brothers in the beginning to a male and a female sibling couple at the end as Pachacuti's attempt to Christianize the local myth, changing the original meaning by combining the Ayar story with a local Andean myth related to the two peaks.

If we read this hybrid myth in light of my explication of third gender, then the episode can be understood as the vestige of an origin myth that explains and sanctions same-sex, ritual sexuality that took place with the huacas. Could the homoerotic encounter between the huaca and Ayar brother, in which the powerful deity seduces and sexually exhausts the priest, serve as a phantasmic original for what will later become third-gender ritual sexuality? In the continuation of Santacruz Pachacuti's foundational narrative, Manco Capac travels on to Cuzco, where he establishes the Inca lineage. The narrative immediately following the encounter between Manco Capac's younger brother (Ayar Ucho in Sarmiento de Gamboa) and the huaca is marked by the spatial division of the Cuzco valley, in which the dual sectors of *hanan* and *hurin* are established. Following this symmetrical figuring of the sacred space, Manco Capac marries his sister, Mama Ocllo. Was the homoerotic encounter between the younger brother and huaca a necessary prelude to the union of the Inca foundational couple, one which provided the symmetrical reflections needed to achieve the *yanantin* that ultimately united Manco Capac and Mama Ocllo? Can we recover the same ritual patterns Platt identified in the Macha ceremonies from the foundational story of the Incas?

Sarmiento had other goals in mind when he transcribed the Inca myths; therefore, he represented the story of the huaca and Ayar Ucho more explicitly as a same-sex, sodomical encounter. Sarmiento thus implied a fundamental sexual immorality among the Incas in the heart of their culture's religion, as represented by the huaca Guanacauri. Santacruz Pachacuti, perhaps in fear of an idolatry trial, could not afford to be so bold in revealing obviously idolatrous practices in the Inca's founding family. While it would seem more compelling for him to restate a local myth in Christian discourse to reinforce the prohibition against incest, as Duviols insightfully observes, he also left traces of other meanings, as he did in other parts of his *Relación* (explored further in the last section of this chapter).

Viracocha as Androgyne

Perhaps the most widely commented aspect of Santacruz Pachacuti's *Relación* is his cosmological drawing of the Andean creator god, an image that supposedly adorned the wall of *Coricancha*, Cuzco's sun temple. Billie Jean Isbell, expanding on Zuidema's unpublished interpretation of the drawing, proposed that the sketch represents the complementary nature of gender in the Andean worldview and compares this colonial drawing with Andean children's drawing from the early 1970s to demonstrate the continuity of these conceptions. As we have seen, Duviols and Itier's recent introduction to the *Relación* privileges the European influence in Santacruz Pachacuti's writing; in a similar fashion, their analysis of the cosmological drawing centers on how it reflects Western paradigms rather than Andean ones (30–64). Harrison, on the other hand, highlights the importance of the visual code in Andean cognition ("Modes of Discourse," 74–75; *Signs, Songs, and Memory*, 57–71), and argues that Santacruz Pachacuti's drawing is just one instance of his dependence on the visual to express Andean cultural concepts. She also finds the same code in his discussion of Inca social ranking (*Signs, Songs, and Memory*, 58), the *Tocapu* sign system and *Pacarina* ordering of ethnic housing (60), and in Andean divination practices (62). Harrison contextualizes Santacruz Pachacuti's drawing in the more general discursive strategy that included resorting to visual as well as verbal representation; her reading encourages us to search for the autochthonous meanings of Santacruz Pachacuti's *Relación* in the drawing as we did in the text.

Instead of repeating a thorough analysis of this drawing, for which I direct the reader to Duviols and Itier's introduction to Santacruz Pachacuti's *Relación*, Harrison, and Isbell, I simply pull out three elements that relate to third-gender subjectivity. First, the overall structure of the drawing, agreed upon by all scholars mentioned, reflects the complementary relationship between genders in the Andes, given the symmetrical presentation of a male-identified left side and a female-identified right side. On the male side we find, in descending order from the top, etchings of the sun, the morning star, summer stars, a rainbow, a lightning bolt, *camac pacha* (male earth), a male human figure, and some eyes. On the female side, more or less parallel to the male elements, are the moon, the evening star, winter clouds, *choquechinchay* (a feline figure), *mama cocha* (female lake), a female figure, and a *mallqui* (a tree that represented Andean ancestors; see Santacruz Pachacuti, 208).

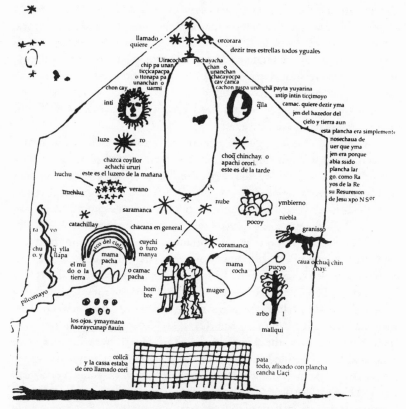

Figure 3 Cosmological drawing of the Andean creator god Viracocha Pacha Yachachic (from Juan de Santacruz Pachacuti Yamqui, *Relación de antigüedades deste reyno del Perú*, [1613])

These correspondences remind us of the symmetry discussed above, in which I hypothesized the third gender as a symbolic, liminal subjectivity mediating for the *quariwarmi* in the context of *yanantin*.

Here, in Santacruz Pachacuti's drawing (figure 3), the only element that transcends and connects the parallel gender divisions is the oval figure identified by the author as Viracocha Pacha Yachachic, the creator god of the Andes, a shape that was said to have adorned the sun temple. Harrison and Isbell have recognized the androgynous nature of this representation of the progenitor of the gendered vertical lines of descent listed above (*Signs, Songs, and Memory,* 70; "La otra mitad esencial," 38). If we think of the oval in terms of an egg-like figure, which has correspondence in Andean myths, as identified by Lehmann Nitsche and as seen in the Huarochirí myths, then the notion of an androgynous source of life seems reasonable.[86] The notion of androgyny is confirmed by recalling the feminine qualities of Viracocha highlighted in Urbano's structural analysis of the Andean mythic cycles. In addition, Silverblatt's observation that the Huari creator-god's gender was ambiguous, reportedly either "hermaphroditic" or female (70), adds more evidence of a pan-Andean tendency to represent the creator deity as androgynous. There is a relationship between an Andean notion of divine androgyny and third-gender subjectivity in ritual contexts. The metaphorical androgyny in the mythic discourse sanctions third-gender subjectivities as mediators between the male and female genders.

In addition to the ambiguous gendering of Viracocha Pacha Yachachic, Santacruz Pachacuti also included another credible mythological sanction of third-gender subjectivity: the *choquechinchay*. Harrison glosses this image as "a fierce puma constellation with brilliant eyes" (*Signs, Songs, and Memory*, 68), which is confirmed by Urton's study of southern Andean astronomy. Duviols and Itier refer to an Amazonian stellar cult in connection with this figure (35). For our purposes it is important to relate the figure in the drawing with Santacruz Pachacuti's own comments about the animal, which he presents after recounting Pachacuti Inga Yupangui's expansion of the Inca empire (f19–f21: 219–24). Upon returning to Cuzco and finding his father old and ill, the Inca celebrates several rituals, including *capac raymi* and rites associated with the birth of his son (f21: 224). After expelling all the "wild animals" from Cuzco, "the chieftains (from Carabaya) bring a *chuqui chinchay* an animal that is painted in all the colors. They say that it was the *apo* of the jaguars, *in whose protection were the hermaphrodites or Indians of two genders*."[87] Here we discover that there was an *apo*, or mountain deity, for the "hermaphrodites or Indians of two genders." Given that *hermaphrodite* was a commonly mistaken term used by colonial chroniclers to signify a berdache or third gender, it is likely that the *choquechinchay* was the protector of the third-gender subjectivities I have discussed in this chapter. While we do not know precisely why the *apo* was called to Cuzco at this time, it is suggestive that its presence played a ritual role in Andean society during liminal moments, the near death of an Inca and the birth of a new generation. The connection to the jungle star cult and its clear association with the moon, and therefore the feminine sphere of Santacruz Pachacuti's drawing, is further substantiation of the relationship between the feminine, Andesuyo, and the supernatural mentioned above.

As John McDowell has recently stressed, more study is needed in exploring the connection between the Andean highlands and the Amazon lowland jungles,[88] where "vibrant peripheries such as the Sibundoy Valley, areas that never came under the influence of Incaic empire-building, hold their own clues to the enigmatic quality of 'Andeanness'" (112). In McDowell's ethnographic work on the northern Amazonian, Quechua-speaking jungle culture of the Sibundoy, we find a myth with strong transgender content. In the myth, the hostile sun deity's daughter, the moon, transforms herself into human form and promises to marry a human miner. She gives the man a wad of cotton after rubbing it on her body, which he then stores away in his gear (103). The man's younger brother discovers the cotton and rubs it all over his body, including his crotch area, causing him to transgender into a woman (104). The older brother takes him/her to the river and allows animals to lick his/her vagina, but he/she ends up being devoured by the animals. Only his/her head remains, which the older brother sends down the river in a drum, to be found by washerwomen who, upon opening the drum, find an infant in place of the head. The infant is said to be Wangetsmuna, who is figured as a Viracocha-like civilizing hero in Sibundoy mythic tradition (104). In fact, McDowell identifies Wangetsmuna as "probably cognate with Viracocha of the central and southern Andes" (112). Again we are confronted with a younger brother who becomes gendered female, reminiscent of Ayar Ucho, Manco Capac's younger brother, who was enchanted and implicitly sodomized by the huaca, and of the *ipa* in Andean kinship relations. That the civilizing demigod of the Sibundoy is produced from such a magical, and sexualized, encounter with the moon suggests a parallel between Santacruz Pachacuti's androgynous Viracocha and the tacit, transgendered androgyny of Wangetsmuna. These myths, involving younger brothers and deities, together with the supernatural figure, *choquechinchay,* indicate the complexity of the third-gender subjectivity and its role in Andean ritual practices. Through both visual and written codes, Santacruz Pachacuti recorded mythological sanctions for the performance of third-gender subjectivity in ritual contexts.

CONCLUSIONS

The preceding pages reconsider a marginalized subjectivity in colonial historiography while meeting a significant challenge: to discuss possible readings of these tropes and their corresponding claims of representation of indigenous referents without falling into well-worn patterns of trying to make intelligible to a Western audience something that does not correspond to Western notions of subjectivity. In previous scholarship on this topic, these subjects have been pathologized as degenerates, posited as analogous contemporaries of the European and Middle Eastern sodomites, and, more recently, as forerunners of modern homosexual identity. I asked myself, Is there not another way of rendering intelligible cross-gender subjectivity and same-sex sexuality? I have refocused the study of subjectivity, concluding that we can only render colonial subjects intelligible to our students and colleagues by focusing on the discursive practices that interpellated them in the first place, the tropes that claim to represent them in colonial historiography. The result is an alternative interpretation written from the margins of heteronormative discourse and from an Andean cultural paradigm. From this perspective, the ideologically charged tropes of sexuality become accessible knowledge of cultural difference.

Through analysis of multiple fragments taken from colonial discourse, pre-Hispanic material culture, and more recent ethnography of the Andean region, I have reconsidered the cultural meaning of third-gender subjectivity, traditionally referred to as berdache, or stigmatized by colonial scribes as sodomites. By parting from an Andean theory of gender symmetry that includes the conceptualization of same-sex sexuality as symbolically necessary in the context of ritual community building, I have proposed that we should not appraise the Andean third-gender performances of subjectivity found in the historiography as debased, sexual subordinates subjugated by a gender politics that demeaned the feminine elements of the culture. Instead, I have shown how the feminine is repeatedly invoked through the various performances of third-gender characteristics. The iteration of transgendered behavior, such as transvesting, "speaking like a woman," and ritual same-sex sexuality is often related to agriculture and other community rituals and is sanctioned by Andean mythology. Through the repetitive interpellation of the ritual, these subjects become agents in the performance of sacred sexuality. Understanding third-gender subjectivity in performative rather than traditional constructionist terms allows us to appreciate the fluidity of gender even in gender cultures that seem to be as hermetically dualistic as the Andean. For in the liminal moments of ritual, the gender binaries, so crucial for the complementary symmetry of symbolic and social relations, are broken to allow for mediation performed by a third gender.

Focusing only on political hierarchies, basing analysis on Western cultural assumptions about gender and sexuality, and reading across hemispheres are analytical approaches that obscure the cultural specificity that informs gender relations in particular regions or cultures. Nor does a strictly constructionist model of gender analysis account for the gender fluidity and diversity represented in a region's historiography. In the case of the Andes, such methodologies ultimately erase the agency of women and third-gender subjects, who, as I have demonstrated above, enjoyed both mythological and community sanctions in their public roles. The complex process of gender negotiation in the daily and ritual reproduction of Andean culture was not completely replaced by emerging ideologies associated with the Inca's early state formation. As I have aimed to demonstrate in this chapter, the performance of third-gender subjectivity in the pre-Hispanic and colonial periods was associated with localized rituals involving liminal moments in Andean culture. Phantasms of these earlier performances of third-gender subjectivity continue to appear in ceremonies today.

This reconstruction of the ritual significance of third-gender subjectivity in the Andes calls for a revision of what has traditionally been considered a dimorphic gender system in the region. The very presence of what have been considered unintelligible subjectivities encourages us to question the essentialist postulations of strict gender binaries such as male and female. By recognizing the existence of third gender in culture-producing rituals, we move a step toward recognizing the importance of gender diversity in the Andes. More field research is needed in order to comprehend contemporary, indigenous understandings of the ceremonies that continue to reproduce Andean culture. Finally, these projects require careful readings of the colonial sources and critical methodologies that deconstruct the biases and misunderstandings of the colonial chroniclers and historians. Armed with a methodology that approaches tropes of colonial discourse as accessible knowledge of transculturated subjectivities, scholars can gain new understandings of the gender culture in colonial contact zones, and thereby better consider subsequent reiterations of those figures in national literatures. In turn, future generations might develop a new appreciation for gender diversity and recognize the roles all people play in the reproduction of culture and society, even those whose sacredness has become abject through the construction of hegemonic discourses such as the colonial and neocolonial representations of indigenous Andean gender and sexuality.

NOTES

I acknowledge the generous critical advice and comments offered by Regina Harrison, William Leap, and Lynda Klich. They read previous versions of this essay and were supportive in its development. Pete Sigal was very encouraging and helpful throughout the editing process. Special thanks go to Nick Murray for his precise copyediting and other critical suggestions. Research for this chapter was originally funded by an NSEP Graduate International Fellowship and a U.S. Department of Education Foreign Language/Area Studies Fellowship.

1. See Arboleda, "Representaciones artísticas de actividades homoeróticas"; Bleys, *Geography of Perversion;* Goldberg, "Sodomy in the New World"; Gutiérrez, *When Jesus Came, the Corn Mothers Went Away,* "Must We Deracinate Indians to Find Gay Roots?" and "A Gendered History of the Conquest of America"; Horswell, "Third Gender"; Trexler, *Sex and Conquest;* Ugarteche, *Historia, sexo, y cultura en el Perú.*

2. It is important to understand the physical and cultural spaces and peoples represented in this chapter as "the Andes," "Andeans," and "Andean culture." Tawantinsuyu, the Inca empire encountered by the Spanish in 1532, was a multiethnic, multilingual region that stretched along the Andes mountains from today's southern Colombia to northern Argentina; it included territories that spread from the highlands eastward to the Amazonian jungle basin and westward to the Pacific ocean. The Incas were but one of the ethnic groups in this region, a group that began an imperial expansion in the middle of the fifteenth century, quickly establishing reciprocal governing relationships between their southern, highland capital and place of origin, Cuzco, and other ethnic centers throughout the Andes. This rise to power was accomplished in a short, eighty-year period. Therefore, many non-Inca cultures retained much of their identity and language. As I discuss Tawantinsuyu and the subsequent Spanish invasion and colonization, I attempt to differentiate the distinct cultural areas. For problematization of the historical use of the term "Andean," see Kaliman, "Sobre los sentidos del concepto de lo Andino" and "La palabra que produce regiones."

3. References to Butler's concepts are hereafter cited in the text by work and page number.

4. I follow Peter Hulme's definition of colonial discourse as one that is "an ensemble of linguistically based practices unified by their common deployment in the management of colonial relationships, an ensemble that could combine the most formulaic and bureaucratic of official documents . . . with the most non-functional and unprepossessing of romantic novels" (*Colonial Encounters*, 2).

5. I develop the reading of these transculturated texts in my Ph.D. dissertation, "Third Gender, Tropes of Sexuality, and Transculturation in Colonial Andean Historiography" (hereafter cited by page number). In tracing the textual representation of gender and sexuality in premodern Iberian culture, and later in Andean colonial culture, I problematize notions of a "natural," inherent, or essential gender and sexuality in the peninsula and Andean region by interrogating their discursive constructedness. However, as Diana Fuss has pointed out, we need not be caught between false theoretical binaries; even for those who maintain that there is no prediscursive gender or sexuality, that all manifestations of identity are constructs of a given discourse, a reading begins at some point in time, which implies starting from an essence (Fuss, *Essentially Speaking*, 3–4). While a constructionist reading strategy often resorts to a historicism that is itself an essentialized version of the social process, and while there are essentialist aspects of psychological and deconstruction theories as well, as Fuss indicates, the critic must accept, in terms dating to Locke, "nominal essence"; that is, identities are "merely a linguistic convenience, a classificatory fiction we need to categorize and label" (4). Similar to Spivak's "strategic essentialism," this conception of identity enables an identity politics based on unstable identity categories, for example, man or woman.

6. In the West, for example, sexual dimorphism cannot be taken as a naturalized condition, for as recent scholarship reveals, the body has at times been considered as a single-sexed entity. See Laqueur, *Making Sex*.

7. Mary Louise Pratt defines the "contact zone" in *Imperial Eyes* as "social spaces where disparate cultures meet, clash, and grapple with each other, often in highly asymmetrical relations of domination and subordination" (4).

8. For an explanation of "sodomy trope," see Goldberg's groundbreaking article, "Sodomy in the New World," and the introduction to Horswell, "Third Gender," 6–10. For histories of Iberian gender culture in the early modern period, see Carrasco, *Inquisición y represión*; Perry, *Gender and Disorder*; Trexler, *Sex and Conquest*; and Horswell, "Third Gender," chap. 2.

9. Herdt's work is subsequently cited in the text by page number.

10. Trying to avoid Western paradigms of gender and sexuality, Roscoe and other anthropologists and historians have worked hard to develop ethnographies that describe third genders from the perspective of the native people's culture. Roscoe's model, as first presented in "Gender Diversity in Native North America," includes several components. The first dimension to analyze is the role of third gender in society, specifically "productive specialization," "supernatural sanction," and "gender variation" (65). Next, we must ask if the third genders were "accepted and integrated members of their communities" (66). Finally, by analyzing how the berdache fit into the society's larger gender culture, we can determine if the Andean berdache is indeed a third gender. A unified analysis of the gender diversity in a society, as suggested by Roscoe, would take into consideration the sociocultural processes that construct gender in a society and would address the cultural meanings of social relationships, the power relationships among genders, and how historical discourses have affected the subject positions in question (70). Roscoe's works are hereafter cited parenthetically by title and page number.

11. A new collection of essays edited by Sue-Ellen Jacobs, Wesley Thomas, and Sabine Lang, *Two-Spirit People: Native American Gender Identity, Sexuality, and Spirituality*, is a unique collaborative effort between anthropologists and contemporary "two-spirit-identified" people. ("Two-spirit people" is the preferred term of the Native American gay, lesbian, and third-gender community [6], who seek to disavow the colonial term *berdache* used by most social scientists.)

The essays, focused entirely on North American native ethnic groups, bring into dialogue Native American "two-spirit people" and anthropologists in order to clarify points of contention and misunderstandings.

12. In my research and writing I have opted to use the term *third gender* except when the specific indigenous word for the subjectivity in question is known. I employ the term *berdache* only when discussing other researchers' use of the term and do not adopt the term *two-spirit*, whose cultural specificity relates directly to the contemporary North American Native American community and issues of self-identification.

13. Walter Williams's *The Spirit and the Flesh: Sexual Diversity in American Indian Culture* was the first book-length study devoted to revising Western knowledge of the berdache. Combining archival research with field investigations, Williams reconstructed a more integral understanding of the berdache's roles in native societies, calling particular attention to their often sacred status in many ethnic groups. Roscoe followed Williams's pan-American survey with a detailed ethnohistory of the Zuni berdache, *The Zuni Man-Woman*. On the basis of Roscoe's research, as summarized in his article, "How to Become a Berdache" (hereafter cited by page number), I offer a summary of the characteristics often shared by the North American berdache. This consensus does not necessarily predict that we will find the same gender constructs in the Andes; indeed, I refrain from making explicit comparisons in my analysis of the Andean context in order to respect the cultural specificity of different gender cultures. However, it is instructive to have a sense of other American cultures' third genders in order to have at least one other point of reference in addition to the European tradition that pervades the historiography.

First, male berdaches are known to have productive specialization in the areas of crafts and domestic work, including the care of children, and they are often marked as overachievers in their occupations (334). Second, berdaches often enjoyed supernatural sanction and fulfilled religious functions in their communities. Due to their reputations in both of these specializations, berdaches were integrated members of society (335). Gender variation in relation to the culture's norms for male and female genders varies; berdaches often cross-dress or dress completely differently than either males or females (334). Their sexuality also varies, from exclusively same-sex (male biological sex) relationships to bisexual and heterosexual partnerings. Their sexual activities range from casual encounters to long-term relationships (335). Roscoe notes that, increasingly, scholars are abandoning "deterministic hypotheses concerning the 'cause' of 'berdache' behavior" (336). The trend is to recover the berdaches' agency in taking on their social roles, rather than accepting the practices of biased discourses that "predetermine and overdetermine berdaches as objects of action, never the subjects" (336). I return to this point below. Finally, as I discuss more fully throughout this chapter, some berdaches are increasingly categorized as third genders. Rather than conceptualize them as crossing genders or in terms of sexual object choice (homosexual), third-gender theory posits them as "a separate gender within a multiple-gender gender system" (338). For an alternative reading of Roscoe's scholarship and the subject of gender and power among the Pueblo Indians, see Gutiérrez, "Must We Deracinate Indians to Find Gay Roots?" and "A Gendered History of the Conquest of America."

14. Irene Silverblatt's *Moon, Sun, and Witches* (hereafter cited parenthetically by page number in the text) has provided us with one of the most complete histories of gender systems and their evolutions in the pre-Hispanic and colonial Andes. For further studies on Andean gender relations, see Allen, *The Hold Life Has;* Harrison, *Signs, Songs, and Memory;* Isbell, "La otra mitad esencial," and *To Defend Ourselves;* and Platt, "Mirrors and Maize."

15. The scope of the meaning of the Quechuan concept, *ayllu,* varies, as Salomon and Urioste have pointed out in their glossary definition from *The Huarochirí Manuscript:* "social group, often localized, self-defined as ancestor-focused kindred" (254). For a fully developed view of an *ayllu's* structure, see Allen (95–124).

16. This explanation of the Andean cultural concept of *tinku* is based on Tristan Platt's study ("Mirrors and Maize," hereafter cited by page number in the text) of the Quechua-

speaking Macha, who live in the region north of Potosí. For an explanation of the concept in Aymara culture, which is similar, see Bouysse-Cassagne and Harris, "Pacha: En torno al pensamiento Aymara."

17. See Murra's classic study of this concept, *Formaciones económicas y políticas del mundo andino.*

18. See Allen, *The Hold Life Has,* 183–85; hereafter cited parenthetically by page number.

19. The González Holguín Quechua-Spanish dictionary (1608) further corroborates the notion of "pairing" in the Quechua term *tinquichi:* "Tinquini: Hermanar dos o muchas cosas o parerlas" (to bring together two or many things or to pair them; 1: 343). All translations are my own unless otherwise indicated.

20. In Spanish: "Los indios hechiceros hacían tinquichi: ajuntan al hombre con la mujer para que se enamoren y haga gastar al hombre" (Guaman Poma, *El primer nueva corónica,* f276: 203; hereafter cited by folio and page number in the text).

21. At this point, a reader unfamiliar with the Andes might ask how important could these reflections of symmetry really be to a culture? For the highlanders, they seem to be central to their entire worldview. A brief look at the textile tradition, and at stone carving as well, reveals an incredible attention to symmetrical design, especially to geometrical doublings. The remarkable samples of textiles that have survived the ravages of time, for example, from the time of the confluence of the Nazca and Huari cultures, show the importance of reflected images. The weaving technique named "sprang" is characterized by the mirror effect, in which the image in the upper half of the piece is the exact reflection of that in the lower half. The two sides come together in a central dividing line, just as the cosmic divisions are separated by *kaypacha,* and the ecological zones by *chawpirana.* This information is drawn from a lecture entitled "Textilería Andina," given by Isabel Iriarte at the Colegio Andino, Centro Bartolomé de Las Casas, Cuzco, Perú, 23 July 1996. For other studies of Andean textiles and their cultural significance, see Cereceda, "The Semiology of Andean Textiles"; and Paul, *Paracas Ritual Attire.* Cereceda's study of the dual division of the *telega* bags and their center dividing space is suggestive of the kinds of symbolic symmetry I am discussing here (155–56).

22. In Spanish: "abrazarse dos mujeres desnudas"; cited and translated by Platt (252).

23. In Spanish: "servirse un hombre de otro, o el demonio, o el pecado del hombre"; cited and translated by Platt (252).

24. See Horswell, "Third Gender." Here, I briefly note the ideological difference between the two entries. The first was written by a Dominican sympathizer of the indigenous in the early years of conquest; the second, compiled forty-eight years later, was written by a Jesuit missionary implicated in the process of efficient evangelization and colonization. The first carries no moral judgment in its definition, while the second glosses the Quechua with a moralizing rhetoric, equating same-sex praxis with demonical idolatry and sin. González Holguín's first gloss, "servirse un hombre de otro," seems to echo the Spanish conception of same-sex sexuality in which the relationship is a prostitution of the passive. Of course, another possible reading of these entries would be that the same-sex praxis of women posed less of a threat to patriarchal masculinity than did the male same-sex activity implied by González Holguín's entry, resulting in Santo Tomás's nonjudgmental entry.

25. For recent research on the place of women in spheres of power in the Moche culture and region, see Donnan and Castillo, "Excavaciones de tumbas"; and Gero, "Field Knots and Ceramic Beaus." For a comprehensive review of the feminist-inspired study of gender in archeology, see Conkey and Gero's "Programme to Practice."

26. Bawden, *The Moche,* 8; hereafter cited by page number in the text.

27. For a brief review of the literature on this subject, see Manuel Arboleda's article, "Representaciones artísticas de actividades homoeróticas" (hereafter cited by page number in the text). Trexler reviews this topic as well, analyzing Larco Hoyle's *Checan* (111–14).

28. For further critique of Larco Hoyle's descriptions, see Horswell, "Third Gender," 113–15.

29. Golte, *Iconos y narraciones*, 40; hereafter cited in the text.

30. Donnan, *Moche Art and Iconography*, 72–75; hereafter cited by page number in the text.

31. In Spanish: "[Q]uizás la presencia de estas características en un solo individuo represente una tradición antigua de representar 'berdache,' o sea, individuos masculinos que asumen y desempeñen el papel del género opuesto" (102).

32. Trexler, *Sex and Conquest*, 109–10; hereafter cited by page number in the text.

33. Hocquenghem, *Iconografía Mochica*, 137.

34. Isbell, *To Defend Ourselves*, 209; hereafter cited by page number in the text.

35. My discussion of feminine political agency in the Huarochirí manuscript also makes the connection between female sexuality and agriculture. See Horswell, "Third Gender," chap. 2.

36. I treat the gendered nature of cosmological equilibrium below in my discussion of native chronicler Santacruz Pachacuti. Isbell discusses this balance in Santacruz Pachacuti's cosmological drawing (207–14), a reworking of her earlier article "La otra mitad esencial."

37. Paul, *Paracas Ritual Attire*, 17; hereafter cited by page number in the text.

38. In the words of Luis Alberto Sánchez, Cieza "escribe la historia a puro episodio, sin examinar razones, sin 'moralizar,' según el giro grato a los cronistas conventuales" (75). Sabine MacCormack has observed that Cieza's "was the first account to combine observation with sustained reflection and analysis" (*Religion in the Andes*, 80). MacCormack's work is subsequently cited by page number in the text; Cieza's is cited by short title (to distinguish Spanish or English edition) and page number.

39. Foucault, *The Order of Things*, 29.

40. For a more in-depth reading of Cieza's portrayal of gender and sexuality, in particular his depiction of sodomy, see Horswell, "Third Gender," chap. 3.

41. See Mannheim, *Language of the Inca*, 140.

42. See also Trexler, *Sex and Conquest*; Arboleda, "Representaciones artísticas de actividades homoeróticas"; and Harrison, "'True' Confessions."

43. In Spanish (from the 1995 Spanish edition): "[P]orque es justo, que los que somos Christianos tengamos alguna curiosidad: para que sabiendo y enteniendo las malas costumbres destos, apartarlos de ellas, y hazerles entender el camino de verdad, para que se salven" (199). The translation is mine, since the English-language edition from which I cite below did not include this preamble.

44. Fossa has gone so far as to suggest that the ideology informing Cieza's chronicle can be stripped away in order to obtain a more indigenous reading of his observations, a strategy she implements in her reading of the Inca ritual, Capac Hucha ("Leyendo hoy a Cieza de León," 34).

45. "Verdad es, que generalmente entre los serranos et Yungas ha el demonio introduzido este vicio debaxo de specie de sanctidad. Y es, que cada templo o adoratorio principal tiene vn hombre o dos, o más: según es el ydolo. Los cuales andan vestidos como mugeres dende [*sic*] el teimpo que eran niños, y hablauan como tales: y en su manera, trage, y todo lo demás remedauan a las mugeres. Con estos casi como por via de sanctidad y religión tienen las fiestas y días principales su ayuntamiento carnal y torpe: especialmente los señores y principales. Esto sé porque he castigado a dos: el vno de los indios de la sierra, que estaua para este efecto en un templo que ellos llaman Guaca de la prouincia de los Conchucos, término de la ciudad de Guánuco: el otro era en la prouincia de Chincha indios de su magestad. A los quales hablándoles yo de esta maldad que cometían, y agrauándoles la fealdad del pecado me respondieron: que ellos no tenían culpa, porque desde el tiempo de su niñez los auían puesto allí sus Caciques, para vsar con ellos este maldito y nefando vicio, y para ser sacerdotes y guarda de los templos de sus Indios. De manera que lo que les saqué de aquí es, que estaua el demonio tan señoreado en esta tierra: que no se contentando con los hazer caer en pecado tan innorme: les hazía entender, que tal vicio era especie de sanctidad y religión, para tenerlos más subjetos" (*La crónica*, 199–200).

46. Bertonio recruited indigenous informants from the Juli area and trained them in Christian doctrine and in writing in Aymara (*Vocabulario*, xxxi). From these writings, the linguist

would select words to be defined in his dictionary. Xavier Albó, in his edition of the dictionary, has expressed the value of Bertonio's dictionary as a source of ethnographic information: "His acuity and fidelity as an observer, researcher, and systemizer provides us an important archive of facts of Aymara life and culture from his times" ["Su agudeza y fidelidad como observador, indagador, y sistematizador nos permite tener hasta el día de hoy un archivo importante de datos sobre la vida y cultura Aymara de su tiempo"] (54). Bertonio's *Vocabulario* is hereafter cited parenthetically by page number.

47. In Spanish: "Uno que vive, viste, habla, y trabaja como mo muger, y es paciente en el pecado nefando, al modo que antiguamente solía aver muchos en esta tierra" (154).

48. "Destos se tiene, que aborrescían el peccado nefando: puesto que dizen que algunos de los rústicos que andaban guardando ganado los vsauan secretamente: y los que ponían en los templos por induzimiento del demonio: como ya tengo contado" (*La crónica*, 278). This comment leads us to understand that there was both a profane and sacred use of sodomy in the Lake Titicaca region. Evidently, shepherds were known to indulge in same-sex erotics.

49. For recent studies of the idolatry campaigns carried out in the colonial Andes, see Griffiths, *The Cross and the Serpent*; and Mills, *Idolatry and Its Enemies*. Duviols's *La destrucción de las religiones andinas* is still an authoritative account of the campaigns as well.

50. *Huacas* were sacred sites in Andean religious practice, often the places of ritual ceremonies. Frank Salomon defines *huaca* in his introduction to *The Huarochirí Manuscript* as "any material thing that manifested the superhuman: a mountain peak, a spring, a union of streams, a rock outcrop, an ancient ruin, a twinned cob of maize, a tree split by lightning. Even people could be huacas" (17).

51. For more on the ecclesiastical literature's treatment of sodomy in the Andes, see Harrison's "'True' Confessions."

52. See Harrison, *Signs, Songs, and Memory*, and Horswell "Third Gender," chap. 2.

53. "Todas estas diligencias se hacían por amor de la república y aumento de la grandeza de la magestad del Inga" (f205: 154).

54. For an exploration of young male participants' roles and attitudes in ritual, same-sex fellatio in the Highlands of New Guinea, see Gilbert Herdt's *Guardians of the Flutes*. Roscoe discusses Mohave children's paths to berdache status, noting that "Mohaves credited a combination of predestination, occupational preferences, social influences, and, above all, dreams" ("How to Become a Berdache," 365). Williams reports that dreams and visions were common methods of self-identification among berdaches of many North American native ethnicities, including the Papagos, Yumas, Yaqui, Yokuts, Lakota, and Omaha (*The Spirit and the Flesh*, 25–30).

55. "Muchos destos se ofrecían desde mochachos y duraban, no sólo en continencia hasta la vejez, pero en virginidad. . . . Muchos destos o los más eran eunuchos, que ellos dicen corasca que, o ellos mismos se castraban, en reverencia de sus dioses, o los castraban otros cuando eran mochachos, para que sirviesen en esta manera de vivir" (Valera, *De las costumbres antiguas*, 83; hereafter cited by page number).

56. "Cuando salían por las calles y las plazas, llevaban tras sí toda la gente, que los tenían por sanctos" (83).

57. In Spanish: "Oraban publicamente por el inga y por el pueblo" (83).

58. I am indebted to Regina Harrison for suggesting this possibility to me.

59. Godenzzi and Vengoa, *Runasimimanta Yuyaychakusun*, 116.

60. Zuidema, *Inca Civilization*, 29; hereafter cited by page number.

61. Silverblatt analyzes this story in greater detail, highlighting how the sacrificed girl's tomb became an important *huaca* in her region. The younger brothers who became her priests seemed to channel her voice from beyond (99), thus "speaking like a woman." This raises the question as to whether the transgendered priests described in this chapter were always associated with female-identified *huacas*.

62. González Holguín, *Vocabulario*, 281.

63. "Y al son de ello [una flauta] hacen fiesta, andan al ruedo asidos las manos unos con otros, se huelgan y hacen fiesta y *bailan huarmi auca todos los hombres vestidos como mujer con sus flechas* dice así el que tañe tambor: uarmi auca chiauan uaylla uruchapa panascatana anti auca chiuan uaylla (f323: 242; my emphasis).

64. Bertonio's entry follows: "*Memillaatha o memillachatha:* disfrazar a uno en habito de muchacha, commo si fuesen en danzas o mascaras" (to masquerade in the dress of a girl, as if he were in a dance or using masks; *Vocabulario*, 221).

65. See Szeminski's translation in Guaman Poma, *El primer nueva corónica*, 3: 198.

66. Trexler builds his case of native Andean women's scorn for the third-gender subjectivity on one comment in Montesinos's *Memorias antiguas*, whose goal it was to show how the Incas entered into moral decline because of the implicitly effeminate influence of lowland invaders (151).

67. Urbano, *Wiracocha y Ayar*, hereafter cited by page number. As Urbano points out, there are multiple fragments of other mythic traditions in Andean historiography, but due to the intense scrutiny of the Toledo viceroyalty in the Cuzco area we have more complete myths from the southern Andean region (20).

68. In Spanish: "señor y protector de los campos agrículas" (59).

69. Urbano clarifies the significance of the relationship between the magical-agricultural function and the Andesuyo region (32–33).

70. In his translation of Guaman Poma's work, Szeminski glosses the Quechua as "*flor colorada y amarilla*" but cannot translate the other words in the song (198).

71. I have discussed more fully this connection in chapter 2 of "Third Gender" by analyzing the Huarochirí manuscript, relating these observations to Regina Harrison's translation and analysis of Ecuadorian women's Quichua language songs, in which female agency is expressed through agricultural metaphors.

72. Harrison, "Modes of Discourse," 67; hereafter cited by page number.

73. Adorno, "Images," 235.

74. Salles-Reese, "Yo Don Joan," 112; hereafter cited by page number.

75. The manuscript was found, along with the Huarochirí manuscript and other important documents related to Spanish observation of native traditions, in Ávila's papers (see the introduction to the *Relación* by Duviols and Itier, 15).

76. See p. 94 of the introduction by Duviols and Itier, editors of the 1993 edition of Santacruz Pachacuti, *Relación*. All subsequent citations are to this edition by page number.

77. In Spanish: "Y llegado dizen que le bio sentado como a un yndio más fiero y cruel, los ojos colorados, luego como llegó uno de los ermanos <que fue el menor, el dicho que parecía persona> le llamó junto a sí, y luego como lo llegó los tentó de la cabeza diziendo: muy bien abéis benido en mi busca, al fin me hallasteis, que yo también os andava en busca buestro, al fin estáis ya en mi mano" (f7: 195).

78. "[Y] se quedó el uno y el otro, ojeado de quel uaca de Sañuc" (f7: 195).

79. I take this interpretation of *ojeado* from Ana Sanchez's comment in the edition of the *Relación* that she edited with Henrique Urbano. Her explanation is based on the Andean folk belief in the *mal de ojo*. See p. 185, n. 28.

80. In Spanish: "aquel ydolo y guaca lo avían hecho aquel mal" (f7: 195).

81. "Andad que abéis alcansado gran fortuna, que a este su ermano y ermana lo quiero gozar porque pecaron gravemente <pecado carnal>, y así combiene que esté en el lugar donde estubiere yo, el cual se llamará Pituciray, Sauasiray" (f7: 196). The ambiguity as to the number of siblings and their gender can be observed in the Spanish version's use of a singular direct object pronoun, *lo*, while the narrator speaks of "brother and sister."

82. In Spanish: "[Q]ue quiere dezir estarán juntos apegados uno sobre otro" (f7v: 196; the *v* indicates a marginal note added by a reader—probably Father Ávila).

83. I am indebted to Henrique Urbano for calling my attention to this passage.

84. Sarmiento de Gamboa, *Historia Indica*, 216; hereafter cited by page number.

66   MICHAEL J. HORSWELL

85. Duviols notes Santacruz Pachacuti's refashioning of Sarmiento de Gamboa's version of the Ayar myth, arguing that he substituted the two peaks for Guanacauri because the mountains represented a local myth related to incestuous erotics and therefore would have been meaningful to local natives (86).

86. For a summary of Lehmann Nitsche's analysis, see the introduction to Duviols and Itier's edition of the *Relación,* especially pages 103–6. Duviols and Itier disregard the theory of Viracocha as "cosmic egg," arguing that the oval in the drawing comes from Christian architecture's church facades. However, such a refutation does not address the presence of the egg as progenitor in the other Andean myths that Lehmann Nitsche identified. I believe that one interpretation does not exclude the other, for Santacruz Pachacuti's text and drawings are hybrid compositions, influenced by both Christian and native Andean traditions.

87. In Spanish: "Los curacas y mitmais <de Carabaya> trae a *chuqui chinchay,* animal muy pintado de todos los colores. Dizen que era apo de los otorongos, *en cuya guarda da a los ermofraditas yndios de dos naturas*" (f21–f22: 224–25; my emphasis).

88. McDowell, "Exemplary Ancestors"; hereafter cited by page number.

WORKS CITED
Adorno, Rolena. "Images of *Indios Ladinos* in early Colonial Perú." In *Transatlantic Encounters: Europeans and Andeans in the Sixteenth Century,* ed. Kenneth J. Andrien and Rolena Adorno, 232–70. Berkeley: University of California Press, 1991.

Allen, Catherine. *The Hold Life Has: Coca and Cultural Identity in an Andean Community.* Washington, DC: Smithsonian Institution Press, 1988.

Arboleda, Manuel. "Representaciones artísticas de actividades homoeróticas en la cerámica Moche." *Boletín de Lima* 16–17–18 (edición especial) (1981): 98–107.

Arriaga, Pablo José de. *La extirpación de la idolatría del Perú.* [1621]. In *Crónicas peruanas de interés indígena,* ed. Francisco Esteve Barba. Biblioteca de Autores Españoles, vol. 209. Madrid: Atlas, 1968.

Bawden, Garth. *The Moche.* Cambridge, MA: Blackwell Publishers, 1996.

Bertonio, P. Ludovico. *Vocabulario de la lengua aymara.* [1612]. Cochabamba: Centro de Estudios de la Realidad Económica y Social, 1984.

Bleys, Rudi C. *The Geography of Perversion.* New York: New York University Press, 1995.

Bouysse-Cassagne, Thérése, and Olivia Harris. "Pacha: En torno al pensamiento Aymara." In *Tres reflexiones sobre el pensamiento andino.* La Paz: Hisbol, 1987.

Butler, Judith. *Bodies That Matter: On the Discursive Limits of "Sex."* New York: Routledge, 1993.

———. "Critically Queer." In *Playing with Fire: Queer Politics, Queer Theories,* ed. Shane Phelan. New York: Routledge, 1997.

———. *Gender Trouble: Feminism and the Subversion of Identity.* New York: Routledge, 1990.

Carrasco, Rafael. *Inquisición y represión sexual en Valencia: 1565–1785.* Barcelona: Laertes S.A., 1985.

Cereceda, Verónica. "The Semiology of Andean Textiles: The Talegas of Isluga." In *Anthropological History of Andean Polities,* ed. John V. Murra, Nathan Wachtel, and Jacques Revel. Cambridge: Cambridge University Press, 1986.

Cieza de León, Pedro de. *La crónica del Perú. Primera parte.* [1553]. Lima: Fondo Editorial de la Pontificia Universidad Católica del Perú, 1995.

———. *The Incas of Pedro de Cieza de León.* Translation of *La crónica del Perú. Primera parte.* Ed. Harriet de Onis, trans. Victor Wolfgang von Hagen. Norman: University of Oklahoma Press, 1959.

Conkey, Margaret W., and Joan M. Gero. "Programme to Practice: Gender and Feminism in Archeology." *Annual Review of Anthropology* 26 (1997): 411–37.

Donnan, Christopher B. *Moche Art and Iconography.* Los Angeles: UCLA Latin American Center Publications, 1976.

————. *Moche Art of Peru: Pre-Columbian Symbolic Communication.* Los Angeles: UCLA Latin American Center Publications, 1978.

Donnan, Christopher B., and Luis Jaime Castillo Butters. "Excavaciones de tumbas de sacerdotisas Moche en San José de Moro, Jequetepeque." In *Moche: Propuestas y perspectivas,* ed. Santiago Uceda and Elías Mujica. Lima: Travaux de l'Institut Francais d'Estudes Andines, 1994.

Duviols, Pierre. *La destrucción de las religiones andinas (conquista y colonia).* Trans. Albor Maruenda. Mexico: Universidad Nacional Autónoma de México, 1977. [*La lutte contre les religions autochtones dans le Pérou colonial (L'extirpation de l'idolatrie entre 1532 et 1660),* Lima: Institut Francais d'estudes Andines, 1971].

Fossa Falco, Lydia. "Leyendo hoy a Cieza de León: de la Capacocha a la Capac Hucha." *Boletín de Lima* 73 (enero 1991): 33–41.

Foucault, Michel. *The Order of Things.* New York: Vintage Books, 1973.

Fuss, Diana. *Essentially Speaking: Feminism, Nature, and Difference.* New York: Routledge, 1989.

Gero, Joan M. "Field Knots and Ceramic Beaus: Recovering Gender in the Peruvian Early Intermediate Period." Presented at Pre-Colombian Studies Symposium, Dumbarton Oaks, Washington, DC, 12 October 1996.

Godenzzi, Juan Carlos, and Janet Vengoa Zúñiga. *Runasimimanta Yuyaychakusun: Manual de lingüística Quechua para bilingües.* Cuzco, Peru: Centro de Estudios Regionales Andinos "Bartolomé de Las Casas," 1994.

Goldberg, Johnathan. "Sodomy in the New World: Anthropologies Old and New." *Social Text* 9 (1991): 45–56.

Golte, Jürgen. *Iconos y narraciones: La reconstrucción de una secuencia de imágenes Moche.* Lima: Instituto de Estudios Peruanos, 1994.

González Holguín, Diego. *Vocabulario de la lengua general de todo el Perú, llamada lengua Quichua, o del Inca.* [1608]. Ed. Ruth Moya. Quito: Corporación Editora Nacional, 1993.

Griffiths, Nicholas. *The Cross and the Serpent: Religious Repression and Resurgence in Colonial Peru.* Norman: University of Oklahoma Press, 1996.

Guaman Poma de Ayala, Felipe. *El primer nueva corónica y buen gobierno.* [1615]. Ed. Franklin Pease, G.Y. Translations by Jan Szeminski. 3 vols. Mexico City: Fondo de Cultura Económica, 1993.

Guerra, Francisco. *The Precolumbian Mind.* New York: Seminar Press, 1971.

Gutiérrez, Ramón. "A Gendered History of the Conquest of America: A View from New Mexico." In *Gendered Rhetorics: Postures of Dominance and Submission in History,* ed. Richard C. Trexler. Binghamton, NY: Medieval and Renaissance Texts and Studies, 1994.

————. "Must We Deracinate Indians to Find Gay Roots?" *Out/Look* 1, no. 4 (1989): 61–67.

————. *When Jesus Came, the Corn Mothers Went Away: Marriage, Sexuality, and Power in New Mexico, 1500–1846.* Stanford, CA: Stanford University Press, 1991.

Harrison, Regina. "Confesando el pecado en los Andes: Del siglo XVI hacia nuestros días." *Revista crítica de literatura latinoamericana* 19, no. 37 (1993): 169–85.

————. "The Language and Rhetoric of Conversion in the Viceroyalty of Peru." *Poetics Today* 16, no. 1 (1995): 1–27.

————. "Modes of Discourse: The *Relación de antigüedades deste reyno del Perú,* by Juan de Santacruz Pachacuti Yamqui Salcamaygua." In *From Oral to Written Expression: Native Andean Chronicles of the early Colonial Period,* ed. Rolena Adorno, 65–99. Syracuse, NY: Syracuse University, 1982.

————. *Signs, Songs, and Memory in the Andes: Translating Quechua Language and Culture.* Austin: University of Texas Press, 1989.

————. "'True' Confessions: Quechua and the Spanish Cultural Encounters in the Viceroyalty of Peru." University of Maryland Latin American Studies Center Series, no. 5. College Park: University of Maryland Press, 1992.

Herdt, Gilbert. *Guardians of the Flute: Idioms of Masculinity.* Chicago: University of Chicago Press, 1994.

———. *Third Sex, Third Gender: Beyond Sexual Dimorphism in Culture and History.* New York: Zone Books, 1994.

Hocquenghem, Anne Marie. *Iconografía Mochica.* Lima: Fondo Editorial de la Pontificia Universidad Católica del Perú, 1987.

Horswell, Michael J. "Third Gender, Tropes of Sexuality, and Transculturation in Colonial Andean Historiography." Ph.D. diss. University of Maryland at College Park, 1997.

Hulme, Peter. *Colonial Encounters: Europe and the native Caribbean, 1492–1797.* London: Methuen, 1986.

Iriarte, Isabel. "Textilería Andina." Presented at the Colegio Andino, Centro Bartolomé de Las Casas, Cuzco, Perú, 23 July 1996.

Isbell, Billie Jean. "La otra mitad esencial: Un estudio de complementaridad sexual andina." *Estudios Andinos* 5 (1976): 37–56.

———. *To Defend Ourselves: Ecology and Ritual in an Andean Village.* Austin: University of Texas Press, 1978.

Jacobs, Sue-Ellen, Wesley Thomas, and Sabine Lang. *Two-Spirit People: Native American Gender Identity, Sexuality, and Spirituality.* Urbana: University of Illinois Press, 1997.

Kaliman, Ricardo. "La palabra que produce regiones. El concepto de región desde la teoria literaria." Tucumán: Universidad Nacional de Tucumán, Instituto de Historia y Pensamiento Argentinos, 1994.

———. "Sobre los sentidos del concepto de lo Andino." Unpublished essay, 1995.

Kauffman-Doig, Federico. *Sexual Behavior in Ancient Peru.* Lima: Kompaktos, 1979.

Laqueur, Thomas. *Making Sex: Body and Gender from the Greeks to Freud.* Cambridge, MA: Harvard University Press, 1990.

Lavrin, Asunción, ed. *Sexuality and Marriage in Colonial Latin America.* Lincoln: University of Nebraska Press, 1989.

MacCormack, Sabine G. *Religion in the Andes.* Princeton, NJ: Princeton University Press, 1991.

Mannheim, Bruce. *The Language of the Inca since the European Invasion.* Austin: University of Texas Press, 1991.

McDowell, John H. "Exemplary Ancestors and Pernicious Spirits." In *Andean Cosmologies through Time,* ed. Robert V. H. Dover, Katherine E. Seibold, and John H. McDowell. Bloomington: Indiana University Press, 1992.

Millones, Luis. "Reflexiones en torno al romance en la sociedad indígena: Seis relatos de amor." *Revista de crítica literaria latinoamericana* 8, no. 14 (1981): 7–29.

Mills, Kenneth R. *Idolatry and Its Enemies: Colonial Andean Religion and Extirpation 1640–1750.* Princeton, NJ: Princeton University Press, 1997.

Montesinos, Fernando. "Memorias antiguas historiales y políticas del Perú." [1644]. *Colección de libros españoles raros y curiosos,* vol. 16. Madrid: Miguel Ginesta, 1882.

Murra, John V. *Formaciones económicas y políticas del mundo andino.* Lima: Instituto de Estudios Peruanos, 1975.

Murray, Stephen O. *Male Homosexuality in Central and South America.* San Francisco: Instituto Obregón, 1987.

Paul, Anne. *Paracas Ritual Attire: Symbols of Authority in Ancient Peru.* Norman: University of Oklahoma Press, 1990.

Perry, Mary Elizabeth. *Gender and Disorder in Early Modern Spain.* Princeton, NJ: Princeton University Press, 1990.

Platt, Tristan. "Mirrors and Maize: The Concept of Yanantin among the Macha of Bolivia." In *Anthropological History of Andean Polities,* ed. John V. Murra, Nathan Wachtel, and Jacques Revel, 228–59. Cambridge: Cambridge University Press, 1986.

Pratt, Mary Louise. *Imperial Eyes: Travel Writing and Transculturation.* London: Routledge, 1992.

Roscoe, Will. *Changing Ones: Third and Fourth Genders in Native North America.* New York: St. Martin's Press, 1998.

———. "Gender Diversity in Native North America: Notes toward a Unified Analysis." In *A Queer World,* ed. Martin Duberman. New York: New York University Press, 1997.

———. "How to Become a Berdache: Toward a Unified Analysis of Gender Diversity." In *Third Sex, Third Gender: Beyond Sexual Dimorphism in Culture and History,* ed. Gilbert Herdt, 329–72. New York: Zone Books, 1994.

———. *The Zuni Man-Woman.* Albuquerque: University of New Mexico Press, 1991.

Salles-Reese, Verónica. "Yo Don Joan de Santacruz Pachacuti Yamqui Salcamaygua . . . digo." *Revista Iberoamericana* 61, nos. 170–71 (1995): 107–18.

Salomon, Frank, and George L. Urioste, eds. and trans. *The Huarochirí Manuscript.* [1608]. Austin: University of Texas Press, 1991.

Sánchez, Luis Alberto. *La literatura peruana, Tomo II.* Buenos Aires: Editorial Guarania, 1950.

Santacruz Pachacuti Yamqui, Juan de. *Relación de antigüedades deste reyno del Perú.* [1613]. Ed. Pierre Duviols and César Itier. Cuzco: Centro de Estudios Regionales Andinos "Bartolome de Las Casas," 1993.

———. *Relación de antigüedades deste reyno del Pirú.* [1613]. In *Varios: Antiguidades del Perú,* ed. Henrique Urbano and Ana Sánchez, 175–269. Madrid: Historia 16, 1992.

Sarmiento de Gamboa, Pedro. *Historia Indica.* [1572]. Biblioteca de Autores Españoles, vol. 135. Madrid: Atlas, 1965.

Silverblatt, Irene. *Moon, Sun, and Witches: Gender Ideologies and Class in Inca and Colonial Peru.* Princeton, NJ: Princeton University Press, 1987.

Trexler, Richard C. *Sex and Conquest: Gendered Violence, Political Order, and the European Conquest of the Americas.* Ithaca, NY: Cornell University Press, 1995.

Ugarteche, Oscar. *Historia, sexo, y cultura en el Perú.* Lima: Abraxas Editorial, 1993.

Urbano, Henrique. *Wiracocha y Ayar: Héroes y funciones en las sociedades andinas.* Cuzco: Centro de Estudios Regionales "Bartolomé de Las Casas," 1981.

Valera, Blás. *De las costumbres antiguas de los naturales del Perú.* [1590]. In *Varios: Antiguidades del Perú,* ed. Henrique Urbano and Ana Sánchez. Madrid: Historia 16, 1992.

Williams, Walter L. *The Spirit and the Flesh: Sexual Diversity in American Indian Culture.* Boston: Beacon Press, 1986.

Zuidema, R. Tom. *Inca Civilization in Cuzco.* Trans. Jean-Jacques Decoster. Austin: University of Texas Press, 1990.

CHAPTER TWO

Gender Subordination and Political Hierarchy in Pre-Hispanic America

RICHARD C. TREXLER

It is a widespread characteristic of patriarchal conceptions of political order that power in polities is said to belong to males or those perceived as male, while dependency is said to be the fate of the female. Not for nothing did the half-native Garcilaso de la Vega, historian of the collapse of the Inca empire at the hands of macho Spaniards, insist that there never was a more manly people than his beloved Inca![1] Indeed, in traditional societies, the very notion of independence is commonly glossed as something masculine and that of dependence as feminine or as childish, so that those lowest in the political echelons or excluded from them are viewed as "girls," to use a term employed in today's armies, prisons, and offices, even though they may be biologically male.[2] In short, whatever their lineage arrangements or the symmetry of their cosmologies, most societies, for all their variety, in what touches political power and order are at one in assigning femininity to what is further down, masculinity to what is up.[3] Obviously, like the husband who is conceptualized as a "girl" at work or when unemployed, but as a male as head of a household, a person may be simultaneously gendered in both directions depending on the social context. To be sure, there is much contingency in matters of gender, which it is the task of the historian to ferret out. But the general rule enunciated above—that the exercise of power is perceived as totally male in patriarchal societies—should not be ignored or forgotten. That way lies the land of Cocaigne, where the suffusive ubiquity of power itself may be doubted, and, for those with their own agendas, what is down may be made up.

To be sure, in every political entity, as well as in personal relations, there is a process at work by which persons and corporations are judged to be in concord or at odds with either their biological sex or, in the case of corporations, with a male or female gender said to be "natural" to them. Now, one problem in studying this gendering process is that, as a general rule, patriarchal societies limit formal political, and often ritual, participation to adult men; that is, they exclude all females and young men. Yet—what is less often recognized—that male political institution itself soon takes on a gendered character: The adult political males build or define hierarchy within their male polis in part by assigning a feminine gender in that hierarchy to males who by reason of status or age are lower down on the political scale. A political hierarchy is thus imagined and characterized at one level as the corporation of males, who defend all the women and children outside, but at another as a register that has males at the top and male "females" and "children," or those addressed and insultable as such, at the bottom. In patriarchal ideology, "women" appear within, though women are outside, the political hierarchy, just as "women" may appear in, though women may be excluded from, for example, a dance. How then is such an obvious political inconsistency or ambiguity—gender is, after all, ambiguous by definition—represented in human societies?

After studying the gendering of politics in late medieval and early modern Europe,[4] I became interested in the same process when after 1980 I turned my attention to American studies and especially to the pre-Hispanic period in the area we today call Latin America. Given my previous study of collective insults in late medieval Italy, I was hardly surprised to find that participants in the wars of conquest between the Spaniards and the indigenous Americans, as well as subsequent commentators, genderized those conflicts. It soon became clear to me that military and diplomatic activities were the most obvious areas in which relations between people were expressed in gendered language, and I deal first with that realm of political relations in this chapter.

It was when I turned to descriptions of political and social relations in innerpolitical native contexts that I encountered something new to me. At the time of contact, the majority of American tribes in what has come to be called Latin America included a particular social figure, the berdache, who may be defined as a transvested biological male who until death represented himself as a female in all possible ways, usually including his sexually receptive or "passive" self-"presentation" to other, penetrating, males. One of this figure's prime functions in that place and time was, I would ultimately argue, to serve as a visual embodiment of the gender hierarchy and to express to the whole community just what I have stated above: the relation between force and masculinity on the one hand, dependence and femininity on the other. This chapter continues my discourse on the subject of the berdache.

The berdache, it seems, was one American means of representing all those males who were not "men," that is, those males who were in fact dependent on other men. The trivial admonition that if you weren't on top, you would be on the bottom was embodied in a particular social creature, the berdache.

This figure, as he was encountered during the Spanish conquests of what we today call Latin America, became the subject of my 1995 book, *Sex and Conquest: Gendered Violence, Political Order, and the European Conquest of the Americas,* and that work in turn has become the object of some heated dissent, especially by Michael Horswell, both in his dissertation "Third Gender, Tropes of Sexuality and Transculturation in Colonial Andean Historiography" (1997) and now in his chapter in this volume, and by Will Roscoe, in his *Changing Ones: Third and Fourth Genders in Native North America* (1998). Both of these works have helped me to better focus some of my findings, for which I am thankful. But what follows will also show the price these and other researchers pay when they allow their own personal search for identity to determine their reading of the past.[5]

In the following pages I want to bring the figure of the "Latin American" berdache, that is, the figure encountered by the Iberians at the time of their conquests, to the foreground once again.[6] This chapter is not about women, nor does it discuss the Spaniards' sexual treatment of the Americans,[7] nor is my work concerned with mentalities, that is, with native mythology or philosophy, which were, after all, attempts to explain established behaviors. This chapter is about Native American power, which may be suggested in thought but is manifested in the indigenous behavior of men made out to look like these societies' images of women so as to represent, in gendered form, the principle of dependence in society.[8] Specifically, it describes the political significance of the berdache, understanding the word *politics* in the broadest sense.[9] Needless to say, political power is not the only force that peoples represent in gendered fashion. So, once we have described this outright political figure, I will try to place the image of the berdache alongside some other gendered representations in Middle America.

Of all areas of social and political life, certainly the military and diplomatic spheres are those where the influence of gendering is most quickly and keenly recognized. For perhaps universally in the heat of battle and in the first flush of victory, engaged warriors defame their opposite numbers by calling them women. Yet, interestingly, as time passes after a war, these gender assignments lose their military aggressiveness and yield to diplomatic considerations: victors and losers are forced by circumstances to become different grades of "brothers" if they are to live in comity with each other.[10] This general dynamic certainly matches the behavior of the Spaniards and the Americans in confronting and later coming to terms with each other. But more important to our present theme, it concurs with what we know of military and diplomatic relations between the American peoples themselves. In sum, in the military sphere gender assignments are often not at all definitive, but can change to accommodate shifting political conditions. This is true not only of individuals but of gendered corporations as well. It is well known, for example, that in another part of the Americas at a later point, corporate relationships between whole peoples were described in gendered fashion, with the subordinate tribe of the Delaware being "the woman," and the superior tribes of the Iroquois being made up of "the men."[11]

Moving now from verbal to bodily gendering, we can quickly pass in review some of the actions taken in warfare and diplomacy. They ranged from practices carried out on corpses to castration and sodomitic rape through depilation and the like. These practices usually had a gender insult at their base, and even when none is mentioned, the "womanly" character of a person or tribe who would let such things happen to him was clear to one and all. Nor were the Americans unique in these regards.[12]

But the most relevant practice of this type for our purposes is that victors forcibly transvested losers as women to emphasize their subordinate status, a habit the Spaniards were well acquainted with from Europe. Thus, in the pre-Hispanic tradition of the Aztecs, written down after the conquest, we find the ruler of one Valley political unit forcing the ambassador of another to dress as a woman for the return home to Tenochtitlan.[13] Let us not surmise, however, that warriors only perpetrated this insult against military enemies. Within the same ethnic unit, we find forced transvestism visited upon subordinates by superiors. Thus, in the Andes, Inca Huascar is said to have forced his general to dress up as a woman because he had lost a battle.[14] Other examples of this behavioral humiliation by gendering are common enough, and Cecelia Klein has found convincing evidence in the Aztec record showing this culture's soldiers being spurred on to heroism with threats to the effect that, otherwise, they would be denounced as women,[15] a threat which, as we have seen, did at times include forced transvestism. The derision of women implicit in this practice will hardly surprise anyone familiar with the treasury of misogyny in the oral traditions of these, and other, American peoples.

Let us be clear: In these military-diplomatic examples, we are talking predominantly about forced transvestism that could have been only temporary in nature. Of course a humiliated soldier returning home accused of cowardice would never again be thought of as fully male, and just as probably, some prisoners who had been "made women," perhaps through rape or depilation, remained so. Yet the evidence does not allow the presumption that berdaches, who were permanent transvestites, were usually products of the battlefield.[16] I believe only that the creation and maintenance of political authority within the polities derived from the same principle of violent transformations of gender that we have now seen outside, on the battlefield. Just as contestants on the battlefield gendered losers female, so were polities

capable of forcing their own domestic "cowards" (the native word for berdache sometimes was identical to that for coward) into womanhood in the
context of civil life, to which we now turn.

    In this world where gendering was so ubiquitous in inter- and intratribal
relations, we have now come finally to the berdaches, who were a fixture
across the Americas as well as among various Middle Eastern and east Asian
peoples. How do we know about the American berdaches? In the time and
geographical region that are our sole concern—the Latin American world
before and during the contact period with the Spaniards—Spanish writers,
both ecclesiastical and lay, are our most important sources, followed by several mestizo writers. There are obvious advantages in this fact, especially because churchmen wrote about these cultures to the end of more successfully
converting the native, and thus filled their accounts with often ethnographic
information. But there are also disadvantages because, as with sources in general, those used in this study are interested; that is, they write about these
cultures—which were largely alien to them—from a particular point of view.

    Thus, historians have the duty to read sources carefully, and to evaluate
their promise and problems. They will begin with a study of European sexual discourse at the time of the conquests, so as to recognize the conventional
shibboleths used by European sources, and the first two chapters of my *Sex
and Conquest* do precisely that.[17] They will of course dismiss generalizations
to the effect that Americans were "all sodomites." When dealing with other
sources on the Americas where ideology is at play, the historian will also
seek out primary source authorities with polarized opinions, such as those
separating Fernández de Oviedo and Las Casas, cited below. These authorities, for instance, give fairly detailed information on such homosexual behavior and on cross-dressing, often distinguishing between the two acts, as
sources inexperienced in the Americas do not, all in the attempt to refute each
other's notions as to the extent of homosexual behavior. Yet, as the most
reliable sources, the student will prefer those offhand observations of sexual
behavior whose point of emphasis lies elsewhere and whose nature is not
directly ideological. This is regularly the case with references to sodomy in
the New World record. Scholars unfamiliar with the primary sources may
imagine that the Europeans regularly combine the "crime" of sodomy with
cannibalism and human sacrifice into a package whose purpose was merely to
justify conquest, but the overwhelming number of references to sodomy in
this record actually occur alone, with no link to those other, more serious
"crimes."[18]

    Perforce, in the absence of police records, the information at the histo-
rian's disposal is largely anecdotal, because there were no scientific studies of
sexuality in these ages.[19] But nonetheless, from such anecdotes comes a trove
of knowledge of undoubted value precisely because it is not trying to make a

large point and is so commonly devoid of any reference to larger questions. Given the offhandedness of so many of these records, and the fact that they commonly were set down by people with no interest in such questions, one marvels at the naïveté of the notion that the Spaniards referred to the berdache so often merely because "the conquerors were collecting evidence to justify their conquest."[20] This trove of information I have collected will not of course answer all or even most questions about the American berdache of these contact centuries; the sources are too fragmentary for that. But the historian will bear in mind what it is that he or she sets out to demonstrate, and be sure that the sources used are adequate to prove that point. They will prove to be fully adequate on that score.

We should be clear that for all their problems, there is no alternative to the use of these European records, because no purely American record from the time of the Spanish conquests exists regarding the berdaches and their role in society. One may hope that some day such indigenous sources on the berdache in native languages will come to our aid. But certainly, no one will wait on them, or be so naive as to believe that a native American source would be any less interested. Nor can we uncritically project backward into Hispanic colonial times the more available information on berdaches gathered by nineteenth- and twentieth-century ethnographers of North America, much less retroject into the contact past the concerns of today's sexual identity groups. I return to this point at the end of this chapter. It is reckless to disregard the historical nature of these contact period human beings. Once the European materials are understood, bemoaning their problems is mere provincial bathos, and a waste of time.[21]

A second historiographical problem must also be addressed, and that is the relative scarcity of source materials concerning the berdaches among any particular people. Needless to say, if more were known at the ethnic level from the historical period that interests me—the period of contact and colonization—the position of the preconquest berdache among any given people might form the subject matter of who knows how many dissertations. But the material referenced in my recent book contains everything I could find available on them for the period in question. Certainly someone—like Michael Horswell elsewhere in this volume—mainly interested in the mentality or cosmology of a given people can use the behavioral material he or she encounters in this chapter and in my monograph to develop a broader understanding of gender within that given ethnic group; such an effort is to be encouraged. But my concern has been with the berdache as a living individual, and that led me perforce to a large range of (almost wholly) Spanish sources from across the Latin American world as it is defined today. To be sure, there were substantial differences among the berdaches of that world, and I have insisted upon them in earlier work when I found them, as I do here. But the bulk of these sources also reveals strong similarities, which I want to emphasize in this chapter. These similarities are so fundamental and straightforward as to allow the general argument I shall present.

We begin by noting that sixteenth-century Iberian and mestizo chroniclers quickly labeled the subject of this chapter and the objects of their curiosity "berdaches," a term that was current in the Old World. Roscoe and others claim to the contrary that the term was applied to our figure only in the eighteenth century. However, the evidence is clear that this originally Persian word meaning a servant or slave boy—the word is still used in vernacular Italian with the same intonation of dependence—was a rooted part of the historical literature of Mesoamerica at the end of the sixteenth century.[22]

Turning now to the vital statistics of these persons, we ask if these berdaches, who may have numbered three or four to a village, but whose number in cities proves impossible to estimate, played any significant role in group politics narrowly defined: Horswell has laid out a vast claim in this regard, going so far as to state that "castrated or transvested, [third-gender persons] participated in the power structure of Tawantinsuyu" or the Inca state.[23] What are we to make of such a claim? Transvestites at least do in fact occasionally appear as actors in military and diplomatic contexts, and describing them will plunge us quickly into the berdaches' intragroup social significance. A more cautious reading of the evidence will not sustain broad claims.

The all but universal rule for the berdaches described in this chapter is that they did not take part in actual warfare.[24] Like the Floridian Tumucua, they carried provisions and gathered up the wounded. But they did not carry arms, or, to be still more precise, they did not bear the arms proper to male warriors.[25] The exception that proves the rule in Mesoamerica is in a report of Nuño de Guzmán, writing in 1530 and describing a "Chichimec" he encountered at Cuizco west of Tenochtitlan. The Spaniards thought he was a woman because of his clothing, and were dumbfounded to find this "woman," presumably armed in the same way as the other combatants, the last to surrender. They soon enough discovered that he was a man in woman's clothing, and killed him.[26] The exceptional nature of this report is the more clear cut because those relatively few men I found assuming the role of berdache only at an advanced age did so, if we are to credit later records, to avoid fighting in any more wars.[27]

Not surprisingly, Latin American sources in this period never document these men who did not fight as ever having provided counsel to those responsible for the tribe's or village's military and diplomatic policy. Berdaches were neither counsellors nor politicos, to judge by the sources for this time or place. Even outside the Latin American area, it is not until 1673 that we encounter any sign of berdaches being relied upon for military or diplomatic advice.[28] Significantly, that source suggests that the Illinois consulted their berdaches on military matters because of their spiritual powers.

We turn now to the question of the berdache's possible role in native religion, to find that almost from the beginning of the conquests in Latin America, the berdaches played a significant religious role in intratribal social life. Yet we must be clear what that role was, and when it is that we encounter changes in this regard presumably brought about by the Spanish occupation. Let it be said first of all that the occult powers ascribed to the Illinois berdaches in 1673, mentioned above, are nowhere to be found in the contact period in Latin America. One of the first European sources on America— Peter Martyr—mentions one group, the *piaches* of the South American Tierra Firme, who did indeed function as *curanderos* by recourse to spirits, and who also prognosticated for their people (and soon for the Spaniards *piaches*).[29] But, alas, in these early sources they apparently neither transvested nor engaged in homosexual acts. During the sixteenth century, there is no indication that Latin American berdaches claimed any occult powers.

At a later date, however, the berdaches did begin to have occult powers attributed to them. In the very year 1673 when the Illinois berdaches were said to have charisma, far to the south and within our Latin American sphere, the writer Nuñez de Pineda published his account of the Araucanians, including a description of two types of shamans (*machis*).[30] One such, called *hueyes* or *weye*, were berdaches, that is, transvestites engaging in passive homosexual acts. These were identifiable by their ugliness, said Nuñez de Pineda, but tolerated by the Araucanians because they were said to have a pact with the devil, which made them effective *curanderos*. This singularly important information was, of course, clearly influenced by Christianity: The "devil" is a Christian deity, not an American one. In any case, what is to be emphasized is that nowhere else, in the century and a half before the Araucanian description, could I find berdaches who, from occult resources, cured the sick and spoke to the politicos about the future.[31] In large parts of Latin America, the end of the third quarter of the seventeenth century seems to mark a divide between the world of the berdache as he was at contact and a new world in which—in certain tribes, at least—he had occult powers and some limited political weight.[32]

What then was the berdaches' religious role on contact with the Spaniards? Rather than being prophetic politicos, the berdaches seem to have held a role best described as sacrificial. The stage for this discussion may be set by an insightful, but to date unreplicated statement of Las Casas, who claims that natives in the Tierra Firme thought the gods were pleased if young boys were prettified as girls before they were sacrificed.[33] Sacrifice appears close to the surface in much that touches on the berdache in religion.

As we shall see in the Andes, mid-sixteenth-century berdaches were cere-monially and sacrificially raped by big men during temple services, while the nineteenth-century Pueblo Americans still practiced something similar on their berdaches during corn festivals. In such instances, the berdaches appear to have been sacrifices to the deities, and, in my view, this practice is at one with the sexual sacrifice accorded the Peruvian god Pachacama, which seems to have consisted in bent-over subjects at prayer presenting their hindquarters for anal penetration to the god, that is, to his priests.[34] In New Spain, as we shall also see, the information linking berdaches to sacrifice appears in Mexico before the Spaniards ever set foot in Peru. Further, the repeated Spanish claim that the "devil" encouraged the natives to engage in homosex-ual behavior in the temples—a claim probably also put forward by savvy natives as well—when rightly understood, does argue for "sodomy" being at least partially sacrificial in character, as does the claim that sodomitic activity in the temples was routine.[35] The question then becomes, was the position of the sacrificee an honorable one?

It is Michael Horswell's merit to have pointed out that in the Andes, ac-cording to the Jesuit Blás Valera, to whom this anonymous source is ascribed, eunuch priests prayed for the Inca and the community, and that when they went through the streets they were followed by the people, "who considered them saints."[36] Alas, this author wants these honored priests, whom Valera does not say were transvested, to be the more exotic, unmutilated berdaches, assuring readers that "Valera is careful to use terms [like "eunuch"] that the European reader could understand." Yet even if these men were eunuchs and not berdaches—and Valera leaves no doubt on that score—Horswell can make them serve his purpose. In a flash and uniquely, eunuchs join berdaches in the ranks of Horswell's "third gender" (!) because both, he says, assume "the effeminized position," a position whose honor Horswell is determined to defend throughout his work.[37]

All Horswell's effort with this source proves vain. First, Valera specifically says that these castrated priests were virgins (who would not have assumed the effeminized position). And second, once Valera is rightly read, it is clear he was not stating that these figures were honored for being either berdaches or eunuchs. In fact, the author only meant to say that the Andean priests as priests were considered saints. That is, this Jesuit was making the usual missionary observation that, so much superior in this to lax Christians, these non-Christian people considered their priests, "prideful pharisees" though the Jesuit knew them to be, saints.[38]

Such veneration is scarcely surprising for any sacrificial figure. It was after all common for the Aztecs before the conquest to worship those they would sacrifice, and in the later history of the berdache, we encounter many an abused berdache simultaneously honored. As I showed in my book's dustcover reproduction of George Catlin's striking painting of the Sauk or Fox "Dance to the Berdash," there was no incoherence between violating the berdache and venerating him, indeed, the one might be a condition of the other. Horswell's fancy to the contrary, Valera's text shows not at all that even these eunuchs, and definitely no berdache as berdache, were participants "in the power structure of Tawantinsuyu."[39]

Thus, within our time frame and area, the berdache played no significant role in the formal political life of these nations and assumed a largely passive one in the latters' religious life. Clearly, few young boys would choose this type of life, and none are said to have done so. We have come now to the question of how one became a berdache, and the picture that will emerge from our sources is one in which young boys were forced into the life of a berdache either by older men or by circumstances beyond their control. The following pages document that claim.[40] An important early source concerned with the religious role of berdaches provides us with the beginning of an answer to this question of origins: becoming a berdache was predominantly a social process. Said otherwise, in this process berdaches were not usually atomized individuals, but social creatures. Writing in mid-sixteenth-century Peru, the linguist-missionary Fray Domingo de Santo Tomás introduces us to the coercion that was commonly present in the making of a berdache in conquest Latin America. On interrogating two berdaches in a temple practicing the sexual aspect of their craft, Santo Tomás found them of course quick to resist any responsibility for their status or their passive homosexual behavior: "They answered me that it was not their fault, because from childhood they had been put there by the caciques to serve them in this cursed and abominable vice [of sodomy], and to act as priests and to guard the temples of their idols."[41] Presumably the boys said in 1529 by a missionary in Tenochtitlan to have been "abused" by priests in the temples of Tenochtitlan would have pleaded the same guiltlessness.[42] They were doubtless right to do so.

The forced disposition of children for purposes of tribute, or as hostages, or as temple servants, is not unknown in these or in many other cultures. At the very beginning of the Spanish conquest, Campeche natives offered the conqueror Grijalva a boy as a gift. The early historian Oviedo narrates how Muiscan (northern Colombian) caciques returned from their temple with at least one small boy each, whom they raised to puberty before sacrificing to the sun. And Guatemaltecans told the late-sixteenth-century historian Fray Juan de Torquemada that the ancient Olmecs had required conquered villages to surrender on demand two boys each,[43] perhaps for sexual purposes. In the light of this type of evidence, the fact that Peruvian caciques consigned the two berdaches interviewed by Fray Domingo to perpetual rape hardly comes as a surprise.

This evidence has been inadequately credited in the literature. Horswell, for example, will not have Santo Tomás's witness, thorough kenner and supporter of the Andeans though the latter was. In the first place, this author intimates, the fact that young people so quickly adopted their sex's division of labor shows that at just as early an age, they were "responsible" for the passive sexual roles they adopted! This unscholarly view is not unique in the literature. Compare Horswell's statement for instance to Roscoe's argument that the rape of a Mohave *girl* would have had no negative psychological effect because rape was no different from many other things a tribal member was constrained to do or undergo.[44] Horswell continues: The source itself is not reliable. Because Santo Tomás was a friar and the boys were natives, "his two punished [*sic!* (actually *castigado* here means "reprimanded")] and *perhaps* repentant subjects *naturally* would blame their 'errors' on others" (my emphasis). Thus Horswell seeks to dismiss a firsthand, knowledgeable, primary source, one sympathetic to the Andeans, just as he wants the Inca Huascar to have gifted rather than transvested his losing general, and just as he leaves unmentioned the humiliating obeisance that Pachacamac's subjects, presumably old and young alike, paid the god through their presentations. Of course Horswell ignores the imposing evidence of constraint exercised against such youngsters beyond the Andes, for he studies the Andes alone, and in them, so he wants the reader to believe, "the passive sodomical [*sic*] role and to cross-dress were not considered inferior activities."[45]

There were in my view no laws against sodomy in these lands,[46] and some of those with power sequestered or seduced boys as well as girls to their own ends then, much as they so evidently do now in developing as well as in developed countries.[47] An occasional Iberian source of the time describes young American boys who of their own free will market their wares to all comers, but we must dismiss this perverse notion of *children's* free will then— "agency," Roscoe calls it—as most of us would now.[48] In full awareness that many cultures justify such practices and call them by another name, the scholar must not hesitate to label as force or constraint the transvestism and sodomization of the young here, any more than we want there to call female clitoridectomies a mere expression of African custom. Nor is this just a historiographic difference of opinion: Our sources repeatedly point out the coercive sociality that was at the origin of becoming a berdache. Thus, according to his first letter from the American mainland, Hernan Cortés warned the caciques of Zempoala that they must not just break their images, but "that also, they had to be pure of sodomy. Because they keep [*tenian*] *muchachos* in women's clothes who go about profiting in that infamous office."[49]

Thus, boys sounding like entrepreneurs turn out to be kept by caciques, part of their retinue and, as I argue elsewhere, a model protostructure of the state in formation. Berdaches were not isolated individuals of the Western ideological stamp. They were created and raised within a social nexus: Repeatedly, the berdaches of the Spanish conquest centuries, who earn their keep through prostitution, turn out to belong to lords, who "kept them" in their possession.[50]

The actual process by which a young boy attained this status of berdache seems to have occurred in either a societal or a familial context. The societal procedure may in turn be further subdivided. Either an older man dressed the boy up as a woman and then violated him—since in the native view "women" not men were meant to be penetrated or to fellate—or the older male first raped the boy, and then dressed him up as a woman as punishment for not acting male. The late-sixteenth-century Peruvian historian Murúa provides the most straightforward formulation of the former scenario with his description of Cuzceñans who first appointed males to be women, then dressed them as such, then penetrated them.[51] But the evidence for the latter scenario comes from the much earlier royal historian Oviedo, who resided for years in the Tierra Firme and thus deserves all the greater attention. He says that sodomy was common among many native peoples, then immediately contextualizes this remark as follows: "And the Indians who are *señores y principales* and who sin in this way keep young men [*tienen mozos*] publicly with whom they consort in this infamous sin. And once they fall into this guilt [of sodomy], these passive *mozos* then are dressed in *naguas*, like women."[52]

Unsurprisingly, Roscoe will not have such a translation, straightforward though it may seem, and he quickly reassures his readers, without explaining how he does so, that "there is no mention of rape or force, however, and the wording clearly indicates that the acts were voluntary."[53] In fact, Oviedo and Murúa only disagree on whether the boy got his woman's skirt before or after being sodomized. As do all the sources that comment on the matter, both agree that the initiation to the estate of berdache was coercive, carried out, that is, within the company of older men. Indeed, as I have already indicated, in 1529, years before even Oviedo set pen to paper, the famous Franciscan lay missionary Peter of Ghent called these actions against Tenochtitlan boys at times under six years of age by their proper name, "abuso."

Let us be clear. To speak of children having agency, and of exercising free will, now or then, is itself a type of abuse. Yet Roscoe and Horswell repeatedly insist that, to use the former's words, "the large majority of those who became berdaches did so entirely of their own volition."[54] Indeed, Roscoe goes further, at more than one point excluding forced or coerced boys from the very ranks of "true berdaches."[55] The reader may rightly be perplexed to find a self-proclaimed social constructionist like Roscoe vehemently protesting all the free choices made by his berdaches, but the deeper irony is that both he and Horswell, who imagine themselves latter-day *defensores indorum* against the sexual repression they (rightly) impute to "the Europeans," actually adopt the thoroughly Pauline or European view that, because man has free will, each person is responsible for his own immortal soul, or body, in the process merrily abandoning the context which must be the basis for such constructionism.

But the Latin American sources, Oviedo and Murúa, Domingo de Santo Tomás, Peter of Ghent, and many others, all describe young boys below the "age of reason" being coerced into homosexual activity by *a Herr*, even though no source of the time describes an autonomous *Knecht* who "willingly" became a berdache—whatever that might mean for a youngster.[56] Later I explore why these authors adopt this stance. But it must be said that those who would argue the free will of these boys in "Latin America" at the time of the conquests must come up with some evidence to support their belief. *All* the Latin American documentation in the conquest centuries points decisively in the opposite direction.

But the evidence presented so far only scratches the surface of the berdaches' originological history of subordination. Regularly, sources like Oviedo and Murúa speak of the "office" filled by such children, and on careful examination, a picture emerges of them being *appointed* to the role of women. What could be more illustrative of appointment to gender than Cieza de León's Andean report that "[the devil] made it understood that service to him could properly take the form of some boys [*mozos*] of childhood age [*niños*] being kept in the temples, so that at times, and when sacrifices and solemn festivals were executed, the lords and other principals would copulate with them in the notorious sin of sodomy."[57]

Once we have grasped this quite structural indigenous approach to gender, which the Andeans shared with many of their cousins across the Americas,[58] we can begin to comprehend how a social-political entity might make these appointments not only after a boy was born, but when the fetus was still in the womb, where there can be no talk of youngsters choosing to become berdaches. A description and analysis of such appointments will not only confirm the presence of constraint in the making of berdaches, but begin to highlight the significant social roles that the berdaches did play in their respective societies. For if the berdaches were not military, diplomatic, political, or charismatic figures in the time and place under consideration, they definitely did play significant social roles, which emerge in what follows.

The conquest evidence for the practice of appointing a male *fetus* to be a berdache once born features the community as the decision-making agent. While traveling among the Yuma in the lower Colorado River valley in 1541, Hernándo de Alarcón encountered a village which maintained four berdaches. After one died, the next-born male was appointed to be converted into a woman for life, joining his three existent fellows.[59] As Alarcón makes clear, these berdaches were a public sexual resource, providing hospitality to visitors to be sure, but also procuring peace and tranquility within the group. The four berdaches, he says, could "be used by all marriageable youths of the land."[60] Obviously, this communal institution aimed to discourage young unmarried males from having relations with girls and women of the tribe, which would have complicated social relations. We may characterize this berdache function as demographic in nature, and reemphasize that in such cases, obviously no talk of free will may be entertained. Needless to say, Roscoe passes over in silence the significance of Alarcón's document,[61] while Walter Williams obviously "doubts the validity" of sources to this effect.[62]

Turning now to the familial context from which berdaches might emerge, we immediately reencounter this phenomenon of appointment, but now in a postnatal context where parents are determined to control the gender of their offspring. Surely the most characteristic source of this particular demographic phenomenon in Latin America is Bishop Fernández de Piedrahita in his mid-seventeenth-century report on the Laches of Colombia. Our author says that fathers among this people took into account the sex distribution of their children, and if they found there to be too many males (to be specific, five) and no females, they were permitted to change one of those boys, once he reached one year of age, into a girl (to use Piedrahita's words), because fathers obviously desired to be served.[63] Similar motivations for such a switch are found elsewhere in the ethnographic literature, and indeed, outside Mesoamerica can be found applied to girls where there were no boys in a family.[64] But to the point: in the early Mesoamerican record, cases like the one involving one-year-old Laches leave no room for talk of choice.

What is so impressive about this practice of appointing unborn or infant males to the role of berdaches is its tenacity, for in fact, the same procedure was still being followed in the Hispanic sphere in modern times. Thus in the 1820s the Franciscan friar Boscana in his masterful ethnography of the natives of the San Gabriel Valley in the Mexican province of California describes how "while yet in infancy [*chiquitos*] were selected, and instructed as they increased in years, in all the duties of the women."[65] Displaying the same historical romanticism from which Horswell and Roscoe ultimately descend, Alfred Kroeber, no matter how much he admired Boscana, could not accept the straightforward lesson of the learned and experienced friar. Twice in his authoritative *Handbook of the Indians of California*, the anthropologist returned to his master Boscana's troubling lines, to assure his readers that Boscana to the contrary, the berdaches were "not delegated to their status, but entered it, *from childhood on, by choice* or in response to an irresistible call of their nature" (my emphasis). He insists again: "That they were deliberately 'selected' in infancy as stated [by Boscana], seems inconceivable." Alas, the only evidence Kroeber presents for his conviction is "the lack of repression customary in Indian society," a perfect example of circular reasoning.[66] Kroe-

ber concludes therefore that femininity could come to the surface unim-
peded, where it was welcomed. Again, we see free will thoughtlessly imputed
to children, a train of thought Kroeber would never have used in referring
to Anglo children. Such is the "cant of the [anthropological] conquerors," to
echo Roscoe, that the best of scholars may bring to the study of native Americans.

Yet another case in Hispanic America where female gender was assigned
to infants or children is encountered in the ethnographic record of early-
twentieth-century Zuni—near enough to the Yumas who had indulged in
the practice three and a half centuries earlier. According to the anthropologist Elsie Clews Parsons, "If a household was short on women workers, a boy
would be more readily allowed to become a *lámana*"—without any compul-
sion, her sources predictably assured the Anglo anthropologist. How old
might such a boy be? Without a trace of curiosity, Parsons says that the
youngest of that tribe's four berdaches, one Lasbeke, was only six years old,
not at all an age at which an Anglo mother would have spoken of her own
child's "free will."[67] And in fact, Arnold Pilling recently determined that in
that very time frame, at the end of the nineteenth century, "the emergence of
a cross-dresser in a Zuni household was nearly always a response to the lack
of a sister or female matrilateral cousin in the household."[68] Roscoe himself
cites Edward Gifford to the effect that as late as 1940, the same people might
bring up a boy as a girl if there was no girl in the family.[69] Thus, well into the
twentieth century, at least this American people was still assigning female
gender to male children for social and economic reasons.

In all these "appointments to office," either the community or a household
was the active party, with the child obviously constrained by force and circumstances to do their bidding. With this background in mind, then, we can
readily understand the forces at work behind Fray Bernardino de Sahagún's
mid-sixteenth-century dramatic description of parents deciding what was
to be the gender of their "small boy." What "should [they] make of him," he
has the parents ask themselves, and one possibility ran as follows: "Is he
perchance a woman? Shall I place, perchance, a spindle, a batten, in his
hands?"[70] To answer that question, the parents may well have weighed this
small boy's limited past behavior, but what is more decisive here as elsewhere
is that the executive power to assign gender was vested in those parents,
rather than being the boy's own choice. Indeed, this passage of Sahagún's
hints in the sixteenth century at a means of parental decision making found
repeatedly in later times: the test. In different variations, parents presented
children with some emblem of masculinity, like a bow and arrow, alongside
another that stood for femininity, like a spindle or beads. Then in reaching for one or the other, the child—and the context regularly makes clear
this was commonly a child—would betray his "true" gender, and the parents

would then raise the young person in that gender.[71] I need hardly point out that such a ritual procedure is a fine example of parental or communal control—for these authorities prescribed the meanings of such symbols—rather than of free choice by the child.[72] This would be true even if Sahagún had said that the parents proceeded with the rite only after the child betrayed "womanly" behavior—which neither he nor any other of the sources of this time and place does—for in any case, such an action still comes down to an assertion of parental authority. What the orthodox defenders of (occidental) free will among the native Americans fail to keep in mind is the extremely widespread native American perception that at certain times they themselves control and assign the (malleable) gender—what they called sex—of their children. The artisanal role of the parents in shaping the gender of their children is not open to dispute.

I have argued that the phenomenon of appointing young children to the office of berdache unavoidably involved coercion. Some last, but no less significant pieces of evidence in this regard concern the Mesoamerican institution of same-sex marriage, as it is portrayed for us first in the mid-sixteenth century by Bartolomé de Las Casas. This scholar/bishop describes how highland Maya fathers provided their (unmarried) youth with niños or young boys, whom they would treat as wives, presumably until the youth married and cohabited.[73] Clearly, such an arrangement helped preserve the honor of the future bride and groom, as well as order within the community at large.[74] But it also coerced youngsters into the life-long position of berdaches, either through the force of circumstances—if the boys had no one to defend them—or through outright gifting of such niños by their parents to the families of such young men. Thus Las Casas not only documented the self-evident fact that, here as elsewhere,[75] younger boys in the nature of things were (and are) at the sexual mercy of older boys, but he saw that in Guatemala, at least, this disadvantage had been institutionalized.

The experienced Franciscan ethnographer Gerónimo Boscana documented a similar case in the San Gabriel Valley in the early nineteeth century, that is, a half-century after the conquest of that area of Mexico by the Spaniards. Recall Boscana's infants mentioned above whom adults selected to be berdaches and then instructed over the years in the duties of women. They then assumed one of two assignments, according to our source. Some became public prostitutes (rameras), while others were claimed by chiefs (capitanes), who married them, not just for sex, Boscana says, but to prepare their meals and other domestic tasks, for "the berdaches were always stronger" than women.[76]

Looking back over the foregoing material, we see in the contact period in the area we today call Latin America a social figure who is fundamentally sacrificial in nature, a condition seen not least in the fact that circumstances or big men usually forced boys into accepting this estate. Further, the data so far show a figure who has a set of social roles to which he is willy-nilly appointed, but which have still not been systematically enumerated. Let me do so at this point, summarizing these social roles or tasks as prostitutional, economic, and demographic in quality.

By a prostitutional role in political society, I mean to describe the berdache's sexual functioning as an exchange object in the political realm, and it is because of this political angle that I place this role first. I have described groups of berdaches who remain in the sexual and other service of their lords. They might reside in male brothels, or they might live with an ally of the lord, but in any case their sexual and other services could be rented out by a cacique or a *curaca*.[77] To be sure, this situation can only be clearly documented in a handful of Latin American situations, and no transregional claim is made in this regard. Nevertheless, there can be little doubt that in many tribes of these expansive realms, berdaches were under the control of political figures who used them as instrumentalities of their power. In fact, I have shown by evidence describing Peru that these transvested, yet corporeally powerful "women" in fact formed the retinue of such powerful men.[78] If a retinue of powerful men—even without "masculine" arms—was an early form of the primordial state, as I have suggested it was, then the berdaches, dressed as women but as men fully capable of defending their lord, represented one type of state formation and expression in the Americas. Comparable to the youth of many societies who are dressed up in ornamental uniforms and then brutally lord it over the dependents of the Señor, these berdaches exercised a certain political authority, at sufferance, even if it was not institutionalized.

I have already described what I call the demographic role of the berdaches, who, as we have seen, were sometimes the product of gender-distribution practices aimed at guaranteeing either the legitimacy of family members or the "unbalanced" family's attainment of a normative sexual distribution of male and female children. So we may turn now to the economic role of many berdaches. What were these "women's" tasks? Two Spanish historians of the sixteenth century, describing the Tierra Firme and Nicaragua, listed them as sweeping and washing, grinding corn, spinning and cooking, thus reinforcing a gender hierarchy that was surely more flexible.[79] But there were other tasks assigned different berdaches, and the anthropological literature raises the possibility that because of their strength, berdaches were often put in charge of village production units otherwise made up of females. I have been unable to confirm the idea through the conquest literature, but it may well be sound. Thus in the mid-nineteenth century William Hammond encountered a dozen Pueblo women working together on their metates, and because of their identical appearance, he was amazed when his host pointed to one of them as actually a berdache, with whom Hammond could "do what [he] pleased."[80]

However, another type of evidence is at hand that does tend to confirm this view, and it is domestic rather than communal in nature. As early as Piedrahita in the mid-seventeenth century, Latin American sources refer to the "robustness" of the berdaches, and the Franciscan Boscana in early-nineteenth-century California followed up with almost identical language. Piedrahita pointed out that because of this robustness, men preferred the Laches berdaches as wives, and Boscana's observations of San Juan Capistrano natives in 1822 confirmed that for California. "Being more robust than the women," the friar noted, berdaches, *who had been selected as infants,* "were better able to perform the arduous duties of the wife, and for this reason they were often selected *by the chiefs* and others."[81] Once again, the sociopolitical importance of some of these berdaches is obvious.

The previous pages, and the book that lies behind them, offer the first study of the institution of the berdache in Latin America before the nineteenth century. In that work I repeatedly insisted that this early history may be different from the profile of the berdaches elsewhere in the eighteenth through twentieth centuries. Yet several of the commentators on this work have failed to keep these distinctions of time and place clearly in mind— one thinks immediately of Roscoe's intentional misstatement of the time and place of my argument, which I quoted at the beginning of this chapter. Roscoe and others have gone on from there to wildly denounce this work. Whence this heat?

Some part of such behavior is, to be sure, mere professional jealousy of a perceived outsider who dared address a topic that had been ignored by early colonial scholars. I am repeatedly identified in the reviews as a "European historian" who, in one reviewer's words and typical sentiment, "has undertaken to become a Latin Americanist," even though I have been writing and publishing colonial American history for a score of years.[82] More interesting are the critiques of those who put themselves forward on the one hand as modern-day defenders of past "homosexuals," and on the other as *defensores indorum,* or modern-day historical romanticists. I have touched on this latter problem of romanticism as regards Native Americans earlier in the chapter, so here I limit my remarks to the former—gay defenders of past homosexual behavior. One such scholar, Randolph Trumbach, in a discussion following a public lecture I delivered, announced that my approach to the preconquest berdache "hurts us," meaning today's gays.[83] But most germane of all are those writers who, like Walter Williams, Horswell, and particulary Roscoe, look back, determined to find a nonrepressive and thus non-Anglo historical past when "homosexuals" were allowed their freedom.[84]

The quasi-monopoly that gays have on studies of historical homosexual behavior in general and berdaches in particular is understandable enough. The former have been marvelously productive—one thinks of the work of Michael Rocke and John Boswell—but, as Boswell's work itself shows, one's own lifestyle can complicate the pursuit of historical truth.[85] For example, modern gay studies spend much time on the notion of homosexuals as a third or fourth sex. Of course humans represent a variety of genders. Let a thousand genders bloom! But a review of the literature on third genders shows that that notion often is little more than an identity politics within a discourse meant to circulate mainly among other gays. This is not the place to critique the notion, only to state that, whatever the situation may be later and elsewhere, I have seen no source of the period and in the places I have studied which supports the notion of a third or fourth sex or gender among these berdaches.

If the notion of a third gender is primarily a discourse with the like-minded about the writer's own identity, it is not surprising that that search for positive identity is too often transformed into a false understanding of the past. In his recent book, Roscoe provides nothing short of a road map on how such antihistory is done. I point out in my work that there was no "homosexuality," there were no "homosexuals," in this period. Homosexuality as a lifestyle is at most an eighteenth- or nineteenth-century notional innovation, and for that reason, as I explained, I avoided those terms and referred at most to "homosexual behavior," while also allowing the sources their customary use of the word "sodomy," meaning (usually same-sex) anal or fellative intercourse.[86] But Roscoe has an agenda, and it is not that of the professional historian—or anthropologist. History, says this author, "provides the models and language for lesbian and gay natives to open dialogues about homophobia and (re)claim a place in their communities."[87] Now, the professional may be charmed to find this white man putting himself forward as a defender of Native Americans. But for those who think history must provide first and last the elements for arriving at past truths, as does this historian, Roscoe's assertion is a recipe for mere propaganda. First, Roscoe wants to convince his (gay) readers that an essential identity exists between the berdaches of yesteryear and the (native American) gays of today.[88] And so, ignoring the reasoning I and others have given for avoiding the terms *homosexual* and *homosexuality* in dealing with earlier centuries, and indeed bizarrely misunderstanding what early modern Europeans meant by "sodomy,"[89] this author continually employs the former usages. His agenda explains why. Using the terms *homosexual* and so forth solves both Roscoe's own identity problem and that of other contemporaries, including, of course, his Native American gays. Since in today's parlance the modern lifestyle word *homosexual* refers both to the gay who penetrates and the one who receives, by using that term to describe berdaches, Roscoe leaves the impression that this historical figure

might both receive and penetrate. Indeed, Roscoe positively states at one
point that the berdache was "sexually active"![90] Yet Roscoe knows perfectly
well that the berdache was a male who, in whatever cavity, *only* received, and
did not advance, the penis.

This is the second point of Roscoe's agenda, which reflects the author's inability to meld his own sense of contemporary gay self-assertion with the
reality of his historical berdaches' passivity. The astonishing thing about
Roscoe's work, in fact, is that he regularly represses, if he does not omit alto-
gether, the fundamental fact that berdaches were as good as always sexually
passive. Failing to distinguish between the berdache who is active in other
areas of life but—to use the the technical term—"sexually passive," Roscoe
rails against those whose descriptions of berdaches make them seem, well,
passive, indeed even "slaves."[91] Still more astounding: In his latest work,
Roscoe spends more than a chapter in proving that berdaches were mili-
tarily valorous, "great warriors." Now, I myself referred earlier to a case in
which the Spaniards encountered a berdache warrior. But whereas I labeled
this the exception that proves the rule, pointing out that the berdaches in
warfare were used all but exclusively as provisioners, porters, cooks—in short,
in the roles of women—Roscoe labors to leave the impression that his later
berdaches were often involved in actual warfare as warriors,[92] apparently
finding it hard to imagine a person who is courageous yet does not want
to engage in warfare. Yet there is no doubt whatever that across the hemisphere—and here I do for once exceed my self-imposed boundaries—Roscoe's claim of berdache militarism is nonsense. From then till now, with the
rarest of exceptions, berdaches across the hemisphere almost never lifted
manly arms, because that was not their assignment.

From these previous elements proceeds a third part of Roscoe's—and of
Horswell's—agenda, which is to deflate the evidence that coercion and force
were common elements in the making of the berdache by the pre-Columbian
peoples in today's Latin America. The reasoning is evident, as I have previously suggested: If it can be shown that at the time of contact with the Spaniards, natives had mostly entered the berdache status through political or
familial constraint, that might be taken to mean that today's homosexual
also became so through constraint, rather than having become "what he is."
What follows is predictable. My repeated insistence that I could only speak
for the situation in Latin America in the early centuries of conquest, and
specifically not speak for the later history of the American berdache, was beside the point. For these critics, the Latin American berdache must also have
entered his status voluntarily. Contradictions do not stand in the way. If
Roscoe once affirms that "most tribal cultures, especially those in which visions are credited with bestowing skills and inclinations, do *not* view gender
identitites as being chosen" (my emphasis), he soon enough doubles back,

vaunting the fact that these "individual[s] [do] choose or desire an alternative gender identity."[93]

So central has (the Western, Pauline) notion of free will become for Roscoe that at one point he is driven to use a nonsource to make his point. He cites the 1985 memoir of the eighty-five-year-old Carolyn Reynolds, who recalls how the aged Crow berdache Maracota Jim "was probably glad to get away from his native tribe . . . [because] at home, he was forced to dress like a woman."[94] Troubled by this text (Reynold's "understanding of the Crow third-gender role was [obviously] faulty"), Roscoe cites what he calls a keepsake that had been inserted into this book by its publisher to the effect that Reynolds, after completing her memoirs, did after all conclude that "Crow mothers would not force cross-dressing on their children; this would be contrary to the 'free and easy life.'" Instead, Maracota Jim—Roscoe's erstwhile "third-gender warrior," Osh Tisch—"was garbed like a woman, and Crow friends tell me, he dressed like a woman because he wanted to." Roscoe's invincible naïveté here becomes pulp fiction. Of course the Crow would deny constraint, as native Americans long ago were taught to deny such matters to the white man. But Roscoe does not hesitate to convert this guilty, romantic, white publisher's word into ethnography!

I hope that this critique of other scholars has served its purpose, which is to illustrate the perils of making one's own lifestyle the point of departure and the predominant reason for research into the past. It really will not do in the absence of evidence to have one gay arguing for the "effeminate position" as having been honored in the past, while another lays claim to the berdache's "third-gender warrior" position, knowing that warring was foreign to the berdaches. I would indeed welcome more straight scholars in this field—to establish its bona fides—but I nonetheless believe deeply that the eros that gays bring to the study of historical sex and gender can and often does contribute to first-class historical scholarship. Not for nothing did I thank the gay and lesbian rights movement for inspiration in introducing my book, even if its dedication was "For the Children," who have so commonly been the victims of these and other adult societies.

There are so many questions to which a dispassionate study of the berdaches can still contribute. Certainly foremost among these is a better understanding of early American women. Of course the comparison between the male berdache and the so-called female berdache is one such area, and it has been getting increased attention recently. But what I have in mind is a subject that lies in the interstices between the berdaches and the broad mass of early American women, viewed and treated as dependents. It cannot be too forcefully stated that such boys in the time and place I have studied were made and kept "girls" as an expression of processes of humiliation that helped inform and define social structure: The treatment of the (male) berdaches documented in my work is in fact also about some native treatment of, and attitudes toward, women, attitudes that, by the way, struck the Spaniards (!) as starkly misogynous.[95] The information on treatment of the berdaches is the more valuable for the history of women in this age because women themselves so rarely appear in the historical record of the conquest and early colonial period.

Two further areas of needed research beckon strongly. As has often been pointed out, an analytically fundamental distinction needs to be made between berdaches, who their lives long played the roles of women to the tens, and several other native American types who transvested, to be sure, but only for limited periods of time.[96] Yet as far as I know, no real study of this matter has been done: We have a long way to go before a broader picture of cross-gender representations is possible in these societies. Then there is the matter of the often striking difference between how peoples imagined or ritually represented the gendered organization of their universes and the way they manifested power.[97] This disparity continues to bedevil historical studies—how could it not?—but, especially in a world like that of the Aztecs, where philosophical and cosmological rather than historical documents are most of what we have for the contact period, the de facto centrality of behavior over thought as an etiological principal needs always to be asserted, and that disparity more seriously investigated.

Penultimately, let me address a matter of anthropological debate. At the time native Americans came into contact with the Spaniards in today's Latin America, what was the relative importance of the berdache's sexual behavior in comparison to his/her other behaviors and functions? Recently, a debate whirled about studies of the berdaches of Oman and Mombasa by Wikan and Shepherd, the one arguing that questions of gender and sexuality were the primary motivations in homosexual "marriages," the other asserting that the moving force was not sexual but economic: Commonly, poor passives joined with actives of greater affluence and often more elevated social station for economic reasons. Questions of sexuality and gender were secondary.[98]

Alas, our Spanish sources so despised merchandising that they say little enough about the economic role of the berdaches, so we are hamstrung indeed for this period, and cannot contribute much to the debate. However, I do think that my approach to the berdaches calls for a broadening of the Wikan-Shepherd argument. In my view, the Latin American institution of the berdache during the contact period was significantly a phenomenon of representation, and specifically the representation of political and social dependence. The berdache's public representation of his/her sexual and economic activities is, in my view, marked enough in these early sources that the question might more properly be phrased, Are not the gender and economic frames of Wikan and Shepherd rather themselves epiphenomenal expressions of a dominant need to portray political and social power? The meaning of the American berdaches at the time of the conquest is certainly rooted both in sexual and economic activity—the former the better documented— but all such activities of these "appointed" berdaches proclaimed a hierarchy of power and dependence. It may well be asked how personages who appear to conceal the fact that they are male can be representational. I would reply that what berdaches in fact represented was the political reality that all men, though they may have called themselves brothers, were not. Rather, the berdaches were the patriarchy's girls.

Finally, let me once again position the research in this chapter within the more general study of the berdache. I have insisted throughout that my subject here has been the berdache in those areas conquered by the Spaniards during the conquest periods; I have made but a rare claim regarding the North American berdache, and certainly not regarding those of more recent times. Yet on the surface, an impressive degree of similarity, still to be analyzed, seems to link the Mesoamerican berdache of the fifteenth and sixteenth centuries to those of North America during the eighteenth and nineteenth centuries. How then can we ultimately come to an evaluation of the perceived similarities among berdaches who lived among hunter gatherers, sedentary agrarians, and even city dwellers?

My hypothesis for explaining that perceived similarity is already a matter of record: A male figure whose female gender expresses the ideological basis of a certain type of early state formation, the berdache may appear so similar across the American ecumene because in general, and despite the apparent differences, the level of state formation of the various peoples of the Americas was comparable enough to tolerate this largely uniform figure. Yet clearly, this hypothesis is inadequate. What is needed now are discrete *historical* studies of the berdache among the North American peoples comparable to my own on Mesoamerica, to create the basis on which a more substantial comparative hypothesis could first be formulated. The limited sources are not the only obstacle to carrying out such a study, however. What is no less necessary is the determination to look at the past dispassionately, free of the narcissism that the present—that ultimate guarantor of historiographic eros and curiosity—can bring to its study.

NOTES

1. De la Vega, *Comentarios reales de los Incas*, vol. 133, 226 (bk. 6, chap. 25). See also Trexler, *Sex and Conquest*, 150. I would like to thank my friend Jean Quataert for reading a draft of this chapter.

2. Only recently (July 1996) the press reported that Joe Arpaio, the sheriff of Arapaho County (Phoenix, Arizona), famous for his gendered treatment of prisoners, had forced the latter to wear pink clothing. Typical uses of the term *girl* to address prisoners occur in the film *The Shawshank Redemption* (dir. Frank Darabont). See further Scacco, *Male Rape*, and, recently,

Donaldson, "The Deal behind Bars," an insider's description of sexual strategies and tactics, kindly brought to my attention by Jim Senter. A broad survey of such gendering behavior, across the animal kingdom, is in the papers of the symposium I sponsored on this subject: see Trexler, *Gendered Rhetorics.*

3. Brandes provides an excellent example in his *Metaphors of Masculinity* (chap. 8, esp. 144), where he observes that during the olive harvest in "Monteros," women are invariably down, picking olives from the ground, men always up, reaching into the trees. I distinguished between dualistic symbolic systems in highland Peru and the de facto power monopoly of men in my *Sex and Conquest,* 218, n. 29; cf., however, Silverblatt, *Moon, Sun, and Witches;* Isbell, "De inmaduro a duro," 253–301.

4. See specifically Trexler, "Ritual in Florence," "Correre la Terra," and "Den Rücken beugen."

5. Horswell's dissertation was done at the University of Maryland at College Park. In what follows, I cite from this work, rather than from the chapter in the present volume, which summarizes part of the dissertation. St. Martin's Press published Roscoe's work. The author had finished a draft of his work when he received my work. Unfortunately, he chose not to incorporate information from my text into the body of his own work, merely adding a critique of my work and that of two other authors as the last chapter of his book.

6. The parameters I set are important. For instance, Roscoe writes that "Trexler argues that *throughout the Americas* berdaches were 'young men forced to dress as women,'" whereas I actually said that "*in different parts of Mexico and the Andes* we encounter young men forced to dress as women" (my emphasis). Thus, for reasons I examine later, Roscoe purposely misstates the parameters I set. I have in fact now addressed the general problem of the berdache "throughout the Americas" in "Making the American Berdache: Choice or Constraint?" In the present chapter, however, I refer to Roscoe only as his work touches on the berdache during the periods and in the spaces of the Iberian conquests, which are the focus of my book and of this chapter.

7. On this subject, see Barbosa Sánchez, *Sexo y conquista;* Herren, *La conquista erótica de las Indias.*

8. Roscoe thinks that "power in native societies is first and foremost spiritual and supernatural" (*Changing Ones,* 190). Theology not being my strong suit, I must leave that notion of power to someone else.

9. Much of the large literature on the berdache is cited in the bibliography of my *Sex and Conquest.* Literature since I finished that work includes a survey by Roscoe, "Was We'wha a Homosexual?" The recent collection of Jacobs, Thomas, and Lang, *Two-Spirit People,* has little of historical significance. Exceptions are the articles by Pilling, cited further below, and Lang, whose dissertation, *Männer als Frauen—Frauen als Männer,* 310–57, provides the best overview of the literature on the much rarer, so-called female berdaches. Like much of the literature on the berdaches, these works pay no real attention to historical change.

10. Juan Ginés de Sepúlveda provides one good example of this postbellum reassessment in his *Crónica Indiana,* 442 (bk. 7, chap. 26); others are in my *Sex and Conquest,* 72–74.

11. The seventeenth-century Delaware's structural subordination to the Iroquois in gendered form was, I argue, manifested by the former dressing as women when they received the latter. Though the principle of diplomatic gendering that I presently describe is comparable, I have not found such a corporate institution of cross-gendering at the state level in Mesoamerica. I provide an extended look at these similarities and differences in *Sex and Conquest,* 74–79; and see especially the excellent article by Speck, "The Delaware Indians as Women."

12. The readiest overview of such practices is in antiquity, through the relevant articles in *Paulys Realencyclopädie der classischen Altertumswissenschaften, neue Bearbeitung;* see also my *Sex and Conquest,* 12–37.

13. Alvarado Tezozomoc, *Crónica Mexicana* [and the] *Códice Ramirez,* 263 f., 54, 57.

14. Cabello Balboa (fl. 1576–86), *Historia del Perú,* 155 (chap. 19). For no apparent scholarly reason, Horswell essentially dismisses this account, as he will others that he thinks dishonor

Andean, not to say contemporary American women, berdaches, and "homosexuals." Here as elsewhere, he fails to mention my evidence that the identical practices—in this case insult transvestism—are found in the Valley of Mexico, not to mention in North America as well. Instead, he suggests that here the Inca may actually have been bestowing a gift of cloth upon his (losing) general! ("Third Gender," 32–33).

15. Klein, "Fighting with Femininity," 113.

16. Callender and Kochems, in "North American Berdache" (451), also caution against such an assumption; see further Trexler, *Sex and Conquest*, 217, n. 22. Alas, Horswell misreads me, to then proclaim that it is "nonsensical" of me to say—as I did not—that berdaches are "products of conquest politics in the Andean context" ("Third Gender," 25). My point that war provided a template for the erection of civil institutions was lost on him.

17. See my categorization of the primary sources according to their value and demerits in *Sex and Conquest*, 3–5.

18. See Mason's "Sex and Conquest," with my rejoinder (93 [1998], 655–66). This was followed by Mason's response and my closing observation (94 [1999], 315–16).

19. The exception are the records of the city of Florence, Italy, masterfully studied by Rocke, *Forbidden Friendships*.

20. Roscoe, *Changing Ones*, 194.

21. My experience is that some Americanists cite European sources profusely—what else is there?—until they encounter statements they do not like; then they declaim against European sources, which don't understand, and so on. Thus Roscoe refers to the "cant of conquest" even while citing it affirmatively (*Changing Ones*, 189). This practice is the more blatant among deconstructionists like Mason, for whom there is no there there.

22. Roscoe (*Changing Ones*, 173) has the word used for the first time in the New World by the Frenchman Deliette in 1704, even though my book shows the word employed by the writer Diego Muñoz Camargo ca. 1576. See the text in *Sex and Conquest*, 259, n. 86. The word was promptly reemployed by J. de Torquemada. This Franciscan first referred to the famous boy whom the Emperor Hadrian "le servia de bardaje," and then made a god (*Monarquia indiana*, 2: 393), and then a few pages later, in a long description of the berdaches of the New World, came back to the same boy, and the same Hadrian who "tenia un moçuelo de estos por muger (como en otra parte diximos)"; *Monarquia indiana*, 2: 427. My thanks to Delia Cosentino for her information on the contemporary Italian use of *bardasso(a)*.

23. Horswell, "Third Gender," 156.

24. Obviously, the explanation that they were cowards cannot be actually credited; the allegation must rather be understood as a formal quality of their condition. For Roscoe's view to the contrary, see further below.

25. Thus Marquette, in describing the Illinois in 1673, says that that tribe's berdaches did fight, but with clubs, not bows and arrows, which were the arms of men (Gold Thwaites, *Jesuit Relations*, 128 ff).

26. Presumably this warrior was a permanent, not a temporary, transvestite; see the account in *Colección de documentos ineditos*, 13: 367 f.

27. The existence of such "senior berdaches" is implied by Las Casas. I have gathered the evidence in my *Sex and Conquest*, 96–101.

28. Writing about the Illinois and Nadouessi in 1673, Marquette at first provides a classic description of berdaches: They assume the role when young, and they do all those debased things one would think only women are capable of, and so on. They do fight, as we saw above, but not with men's weapons. Interestingly, they sing in the festivals honoring the tribal god Columet, but cannot dance. Then he adds the novelty: the berdaches *are* summoned to councils, where "nothing can be decided without their advice." Marquette concludes, "They are considered Manitous, that is, spirits or persons of consequence"; Gold Thwaites, *Jesuit Relations*, 128.

29. Peter Martyr d'Anghiera, *Opera*, 255–62 (dec. 8, chaps. 8–9).

30. Nuñez de Pineda y Bascuñan, *Cautiverio feliz*, 107, 164, 157–59.

31. There are many reasons for the changes in the berdaches' roles in modern times. Perhaps the most practical has been the change in the sexual division of labor brought on by the European-imposed absence of men from native villages due to mining and other factors. The impact of Western sexual and gender notions certainly played a key role as well. That is a problem for other historians and anthropologists to tackle.

32. One is reminded of the new roles of Andean women as priests once their men had been neutralized by colonialism; Silverblatt, *Moon, Sun, and Witches,* 198–207.

33. This cross-dressing was not for reasons of sodomy, he insisted, "sino solamente por hacerles sacrificio agradable"; see Las Casas, *Apologética historia Sumaria,* 2: 232 (chap. 180). The context: Las Casas speculated that wanting to be part of any and all sins, the devil had "introducido y enseñado otro peor género de sacrificio, como fue . . . que ofrecían los moles y afeminados, porque se hallaron (según dijeron algunos españoles) algunos mozos vestidos como mujeres" (ibid.). In my "Making the American Berdache," I summarize the claims across the American ecumene that the beauty of a boy sometimes caused him to be converted to a girl because, combined with his strength, such a beauty could easily be married to a rich man.

34. On the Pueblo, see Hammond, "Disease of the Scythians," and *Sexual Impotence in the Male and Female,* 157–73. On the relation between prayer and sexual postures in the Pachacama rites, as well as in other devotions, see further Trexler, "Den Rücken beugen," and *Sex and Conquest,* 102–9.

35. See further the Guatemaltecan Maya divinity Tohil soliciting (sexual?) embrace; Trexler, "Den Rücken beugen," 242 f.

36. Horswell, "Third Gender," 156. Horswell notes that I did not cite this passage. In fact, I did not pursue it because the author was, as we shall see, talking about (eunuch) priests and not about berdaches.

37. Horswell, "Third Gender," 156.

38. Cf., for example, Peter of Ghent in 1529 observing that the pueblo "considered as saints" the priests of Tenochtitlan (see note 42 below).

39. The sources being fruitless, Horswell first equates the berdache with woman, and then, to sustain his argument about berdache "power," notes that two tombs of rich Moche women have been unearthed. By Horswell's reasoning, the many women's tombs in, say, Renaissance Florence surely prove that sex was a part of that city's power structure!

40. For the apparently less sizable number of those who entered the estate when full-grown adults ("senior berdaches"), see my *Sex and Conquest,* 96–101.

41. Cieza de León, *Crónica del Perú,* 1: 200 (pt. 1, chap. 64). This is the first of several sources across the Americas, detailed in my "Making the American Berdache," that state that boys were made girls so as to satisfy the sexual needs of older males.

42. "Algunos de estos sacerdotes no tenían mujeres, sino en lugar de ellas muchachos de que abusaban"; the full text of Peter of Ghent's 1529 report on sodomy in Tenochtitlan temples perpetrated by some priests on young boys [*muchachos*], is in García Icazbalceta, *Bibliografía Mexicana,* 398. The sodomitic substance of this report was then independently confirmed, first by the conquistador Bernal Díaz del Castillo: "Aquellos papas eran hijos de principales y no tenían mujeres, más tenían el maldito oficio de sodomías" (*Historia verdadera,* 1: 162 [chap. 162]), and by Tomás López Medel, the royal *oidor* in Mexico City who, according to some accounts, declined to succeed archbishop Zumárraga in 1546: "Tenían los mexicanos y guatemaltecas grande copia de sacerdotes en aquellos templos y allí era su perpetual mansion y morada, a donde se ejercitaban en tan abominables lujurias y pecados que es cosa abominable y torpe decir. Y tenían éstos ya adquiridos tantos derechos o, por mejor decir, introducidas tan nefandas y espurcísimas costumbres en este caso con el pueblo que, por no ofender las orejás castas, se han de pasar con silencio" (*De los tres elementos,* 233 [part. 3, chap. 20]). See also López's entry in the *Enciclopedia universal ilustrada,* vol. 3, 167. In 1593, Thomas de Bozius declared the same from Europe in his *De signis ecclesiae dei* (1: 519 [bk. 7, signum 29]). No primary source denies the existence of temple sodomy in Tenochtitlan, so the burden of proof rests with those who would dispute these

sources. For Cieza de León's observation that sodomy might be considered wrong in Peruvian villages in whose temples it was licit, see Trexler, *Sex and Conquest*, 106. In his letter cited above, Peter of Ghent was also disturbed that fathers sacrificed or mutilated their own sons—out of fear not love—and that the priests serving the "idols," considered saints by the populace, "se alimentaban solamente de niños cuya sangre bebian." See above and in the following text for earlier indications of young males similarly sacrificed, a theme that informs much early Spanish reporting on Tenochtitlan.

43. On the offer, see Peter Martyr, *Opera*, 150 (dec. 4, chap. 4). Oviedo implies that the boy was used homosexually during that year. In the meantime, the boy, as an orant, represented his master to the gods at temple (*Historia general y natural de las Indias*, 127 f. [bk. 26, chap. 30]), and cf. above Blás Valera's "eunuchs" praying for the community. Torquemada: "Asimismo les demandaban cada día, que se les diesen, de cada pueblo, dos niños; no supieron declarlos Indios, que dieron essa relación, si querían estos para sacrificar, o para comer, o para servicio" (*Monarchia indiana*, 1: 332 [bk. 3, chap. 40]).

44. The argument runs as follows: "It is risky to say that the youths truly considered themselves 'forced' into their sacred roles. . . . Furthermore . . . the practice of young children taking on responsibility, both mundane and sacred, was (and still is) the norm in Andean society. . . . The ethics of reciprocity in Andean communities is what motivated service, an ethics that the youth learned from an early age" (Horswell, "Third Gender," 154 f.). To the contrary, I consider it risky *not* to say that the youths "truly considered themselves 'forced.'" See also Roscoe, *Changing Ones*, 95. In both these utterances, the reader recognizes the language not of the scholar of juvenile development, but, *inter alia*, of NAMBLA, the North American Man/Boy Love Association.

45. Horswell, "Third Gender," 154. Horswell presents no evidence to that effect, and indeed, as I have indicated, the misogynistic strain in Peruvian culture in no way lags behind that in other traditional cultures.

46. Claims that such laws did exist are postconquest constructions with obvious ideological purposes; see Trexler, *Sex and Conquest*, 156–61, 257. In the Nahuatl realm, one can trace the claim of anti-sodomy laws not to Tenochtitlan (!) but to ca. 1538 Texcoco (see *Sex and Conquest*, 257, nn. 61 and 63). A further link in that Texcocan string of claims is in Alva Ixtlilxochitl, *Historia de la nación chichimeca* (2: 101). It appears evident to me that the Franciscans imputed antisodomitic enlightenment to Texcoco because that town was the home of the acclaimed philosopher-king Nezahualcoyotl, whose family would quickly convert under the influence of Peter of Ghent, who often lived in Texcoco.

47. The discourse in this chapter can scarcely surprise anyone aware of the massive reality of (male as well as female) child abuse in our own contemporary world. My conclusions about pre-Hispanic child abuse in the person of the berdaches are by now much like those of scores of studies of sexual abuse of children, including some of a historical character, emerging almost daily in the periodical and monographic literature.

48. This author imagines me horrified that berdaches, exerting "agency," may have wanted to be penetrated (*Changing Ones*, 196). This and a score of other insults in his pages do nothing for his argument. My point is that both the context of their being "brothelized" and the age of the youngsters, prohibit talk of free will, much less of agency.

49. Díaz del Castillo, *Historia verdadera*, 1: 162 (chap. 52).

50. See the repeated cases of this in *Sex and Conquest*, 94–95 and passim. Obviously, the fact that these boys were constrained to become berdaches did not preclude some developing into self-confident adults capable of handling the wrong done them as children. Unfortunately, in our period no such accounts survive.

51. Murúa, *Historia de los Incas*, 122 f. (bk. 2, chap. 4). On appointment to the status of berdache, see below. Juan Ossio is preparing an important new edition of Murúa replete with many original drawings. Will Roscoe in his attempt to discredit Murúa's account while reviewing my book embarrassingly characterizes the friar, well-known to all Peruvian historians of the

period, as an "obscure" source; see Roscoe, "Mapping the Perverse." Cf. above for the Andeanist Horswell's no less embarrassing determination that Cabello Balboa, another Peruvian historian whose message did not please, was also "obscure." Apparently for them, obscurity equals falsity.

52. "Entre los indios en muchas partes es muy común el pecado nefando contra natura, y publicamente los indios que son señores y principales que en esto pecan tienen mozos con quien usan este maldito pecado; y los tales mozos pacientes, asi como caen en esta culpa, luego se ponen naguas, como mujeres" (*Sumario de la natural historia de las Indias,* chap. 81, 508). With no justification, Roscoe says the text suggests that the boys rather did this voluntarily. Oviedo, however, clearly has cacique power coming first and last: the principal's sodomitic will, then the construction of a brothel, then the same principal's penetration of these boys. But Roscoe's mistake was predictable, since he also misunderstood who Oviedo was talking about: He says that Oviedo was describing Cueva-speaking people, but Oviedo was clearly referring to "los Indios en muchas partes" (Roscoe, "Mapping the Perverse," 861).

53. Roscoe, *Changing Ones,* 193.

54. Ibid., 200.

55. Ibid., 9, 194.

56. Generally speaking, males were thought able to resist coercion after they were fourteen or fifteen years old; details are in Trexler, *Sex and Conquest,* 201–3, nn. 28, 29, 41.

57. Cieza de León, *Crónica del Perú,* 1: 99 (pt. 1, chap. 64).

58. A point I examine in detail in my "Making the American Berdache."

59. "E che la prima di esse [donne] che partoriva mascio, era deputato a dover far quell'esercizio muliebre" (Ramusio, *Navigazioni e viaggi,* 6: 652; the oldest text is in Italian).

60. "Questi tali non possono aver commercio carnale con donna alcuna, ma sí ben con essi tutti i giovani della terra che sono da maritarsi" (Ramusio, *Navigazioni e viaggi,* 6: 652). In my "Making the American Berdache," I document seventeenth-century berdaches in the present-day United States who were "made" for precisely the same reason.

61. Instead, he imagines that the authorities were replacing a dancer! Obviously, Roscoe says only that the "antierotic lens of counter-reformation Catholicism" produced Alarcón's "distorted account of this process," without stating what that process was (*Changing Ones,* 143–44). I need hardly point out that the Counter-Reformation had not begun in 1541, that Alarcón was a soldier not a priest, who as such betrays no antieroticism in his account.

62. See Williams, *The Spirit and the Flesh,* xii, and for where Williams stands in the historiography of the berdache, see Trexler, *Sex and Conquest,* 6. A rarity in this regard, Bleibtreu-Ehrenberg recognized that young boys were reclassified as girls "bereits *vor* der Geburt eines Kindes" (*Der Weibmann,* 104).

63. "Ambición que tienen de estar bien servidos. Tienen por ley que si la mujer paría cinco varones continuados, sin parir hija, pudiesen hacer hembra a uno de los hijos a las doce lunas de edad" (Fernández Piedrahita, *Historia general del nuevo reino de Granada,* 1: 25).

64. In "Making the American Berdache," I study this phenomenon across the hemisphere and beyond, to Greenland. For general ethnography, the verification in southern climes of such gender switching at or near birth will prove to be the most significant discovery I have made regarding the berdache, since it ties together the hemisphere in this regard.

65. Boscana, *Chinigchinich,* 54. Cf. Reichlen and Reichlen, "Le manuscrit Boscana," 233–73, esp. 252–53, containing the variant Harrington translation. Boscana's work was originally entitled *Relación historica de la creencia, usos, costumbres, y extravagancias de los Indios de esta Misión de S. Juan Capistrano, llamada la Nación Acâgehemem.*

66. Kroeber, *Handbook of the Indians of California,* respectively, 497, 647.

67. Parsons, "The Zuñi La'mana," 521, 525–26.

68. Pilling, "Cross-Dressing and Shamanism among Selected Western North American Tribes," 72.

69. Roscoe, *Changing Ones,* 199.

70. Sahagún, *Florentine Codex,* bk. 9, 14. This "small boy" was clearly a child: When he

accompanied the older merchants, he bore nothing on his back except the group's drinking vessels.

71. See, for example, S. Jacobs, "Berdache: A Brief Review of the Literature," 276. A study of these tests is needed.

72. In "Making the American Berdache," I emphasize that the famed visions of the Plains Indians, which are often understood as free-will exercises leading some adolescent boys to become berdaches, have rather authoritatively been understood as exercises in which the communities controlled the substance and meaning of what was viewed.

73. Las Casas, *Apologética historia Sumaria,* 2: 522 (chap. 239).

74. A cautionary note: Elsewhere in the ethnographic literature (including that of Europe) there is evidence of young *girls* of low status being provided to nubile young men of some social standing for sexual purposes, obviously to comparable ends of avoiding the violation of "honest" nubile young women.

75. I encountered similar problems, and practices, in late medieval and early modern Florence, Italy; *Public Life in Renaissance Florence,* 382.

76. In Reichlen and Reichlen, "Le manuscrit Boscana," 252–53.

77. The evidence is provided in Trexler, *Sex and Conquest,* 90–94.

78. "No ay principal que no trayga quatro o cinco pajes muy galanes Estos tiene por mancebos"; Ruíz de Arce, *Servicios en Indias,* 32.

79. Fernández de Oviedo, *Sumario de la natural historia de las Indias,* 508 (chap. 81); Herrera, *Historia general de los hechos de los castellanos,* 8: 339 (dec. 4, bk. 6, chap. 1).

80. "I observed that he used the masculine pronoun *el* in referring to the individual," said Hammond in "Disease of the Scythians," 343 f.

81. My emphasis. "Ejercitaban los oficios de mujeres con robustecidad de hombres" (Fernández Piedrahita, *Historia general del nuevo reino de Granada,* 1: 25); "Being more robust than the women, [berdaches, who had been selected as infants] were better able to perform the arduous duties of the wife, and for this reason they were often selected by the chiefs and others" (Boscana, *Chinigchinich,* 54). George Catlin said the same of the Mandan berdaches later in the century: "[The berdaches] performed the duties of women with the robustness of men" (*Letters and Notes,* 2: 15).

82. The characterization is by E. Couturier, from a review in *The Americas,* 55 (1998): 144.

83. This transpired at the Columbia University Seminar on Gay and Lesbian Studies in spring 1996; I have verified Trumbach's statement with others at the gathering. The basic argument of this point of view, silly as it sounds, is that any historical study of homosexual activity that determines that the passive was not doing what he wished to do implies that the modern gay in pursuing his lifestyle is not freely doing what he does; see further at the conclusion of this chapter. The upshot of all this is that such authors presumably carefully excise anything in the past that, in their view, might "hurt" today's gays.

84. My criticism of Williams's work is in *Sex and Conquest,* 6.

85. I refer of course to Boswell's unfounded conviction that there was a "gay" culture in the Middle Ages, that is, partners whose relationship was equal rather than pederastic in character (see *Christianity, Social Tolerance, and Homosexuality*).

86. Unfortunately, Roscoe proves himself ill-equipped to discuss this language: He defines "sodomites" as "males who were receptive in sex with other males"—whereas, as I clarified in my *Sex and Conquest* (169), "sodomite" usually refers in the sources to the active party; see *Changing Ones,* 181. Our critic then proceeds to define sodomy as "an act that in European societies was usually understood as a rape of a younger man by an older man" (*Changing Ones,* 182, 186). News indeed. This is the expertise Roscoe brings to reading the historical sources, all of which routinely describe homosexual behavior as "sodomy."

87. Roscoe, *Changing Ones,* 198.

88. Ibid., 10, 183–187.

89. See above, note 86.

90. Roscoe, *Changing Ones*, 9.

91. I am said to describe slavery in describing berdaches (Roscoe, *Changing Ones*, 191). The institution of slavery plays no part in my book's discussion of the berdache. Roscoe's passionate use of the term shows how far his book strays from scholarly discourse.

92. Cf. Roscoe, *Changing Ones*, 31 f., 148, 197 f.

93. Roscoe, *Changing Ones*, 130, 196. In this latter context Roscoe claims that "whether or not berdache status was coercively imposed, the rules of European discourse required that berdaches be described as if it were and that the possibility of an individual choosing or desiring an alternative gender identity never be represented." He added that "Europeans never sympathized with berdaches as victims." But as I pointed out above and in my book, European sources did occasionally refer to just such entrepreneurs who had (allegedly) chosen their way. And, as I explained in detail in my book, there is a clear pattern in late medieval Spanish law that exempts passives beneath ca. fifteen years of age precisely because they were victims who could not freely choose. The persecution of berdaches by both their own peoples and the Iberian conquerors is of course a matter of fact, but self-persecution as a modern historiographical strategy surely diminishes this type of work.

94. Roscoe, *Changing Ones*, 37.

95. Such observations were made of Mexico and of the Tierra Firme; Trexler, *Sex and Conquest*, 122, 162. Needless to say, these (male and foreign) assertions must be treated with care. But they also should not be ignored as part of a historical romanticism privileging the better position of women in the good old days.

96. Such transvestisms, in festivals or as the result of battlefield "cowardice," may have remained temporary because they did not proceed to rape.

97. In a different time and place, I studied this problem: *Public Life in Renaissance Florence.*

98. The Wikan-Shepherd debate is in *Man*, n.s., 12 (1977): 304–19; n.s. 13 (1978): 663–71.

WORKS CITED

Barbosa Sánchez, Araceli. *Sexo y conquista.* Mexico City: Universidad Nacional Autónoma de México, 1994.

Bleibtreu-Ehrenberg, Gisela. *Der Weibmann: kultischer Geschlechtswechsel im Schamanismus: Eine Studie zur Transvestition und Transsexualität bei Naturvölkern.* Frankfurt am Main: Fischer Taschenbuch Verlag, 1984.

Boscana, Gerónimo. *Chinigchinich: A Revised and Annotated Version of Alfred Robinson's Translation of Father Gerónimo Boscana's Historical Account of the Belief, Usages, Customs, and Extravagancies of the Indians of This Mission of San Juan Capistrano Called the Acagchemem Tribe.* Banning, CA: Maliki Museum Press, 1978.

Boswell, John. *Christianity, Social Tolerance, and Homosexuality: Gay People in Western Europe from the Beginning of the Christian Era to the Fourteenth Century.* Chicago: University of Chicago Press, 1980.

Bozius, Thomas de. *De signis ecclesiae dei.* Cologne, 1593.

Brandes, Stanley. *Metaphors of Masculinity: Sex and Status in Andalusian Folklore.* Philadelphia: University of Pennsylvania Press, 1980.

Cabello de Balboa, Miguel. *Historia del Perú bajo la dominación de los Incas.* Lima: Sanmartí, 1920.

Callender, Charles, and Lee Kochems. "The North American Berdache." *Current Anthropology* 24, no. 4 (1983): 443–70.

Catlin, George. *Letters and Notes on the Manners, Customs, and Conditions of North American Indians.* 2 vols. New York: Dover, 1973.

Cieza de León, Pedro de. *La crónica del Perú.* Lima: Pontificia Universidad Católica del Perú, 1984.

Colección de documentos ineditos relativos al descubrimiento, conquista y organización de las antiguas posessiones españoles en America y Oceania. Vol. 13. Madrid: Academia de la Historia, 1870.

De la Vega, el Inca, Garcilaso. *Comentarios reales de los Incas.* 3 vols. Biblioteca de autores españoles, vols. 133–35. Madrid: Atlas, 1963–65.

Díaz del Castillo, Bernal. *Historia verdadera de la conquista de la Nueva España.* Mexico City: Editorial Porrúa, 1968.

Donaldson, S. "The Deal behind Bars." *Harper's Magazine,* August 1996, 17, 20.

Fernández de Oviedo, Gonzalo. *Historia general y natural de las Indias.* Biblioteca de autores españoles, vol. 119. Madrid: Atlas, 1959.

———. *Sumario de la natural historia de las Indias.* Biblioteca de autores españoles, vol. 22. Madrid: Atlas, 1946.

Fernández de Piedrahita, Lucas. *Historia general del nuevo reino de Granada.* Bogotá: Editorial ABC, 1942.

García Icazbalceta, Joaquín. *Bibliografía Mexicana del siglo XVI.* Mexico City: Andrade y Morales, 1886.

Gold Thwaites, Reuben, ed. *The Jesuit Relations and Allied Documents: Travels and Explorations of the Jesuit Missionaries in New France, 1610–1791.* Vol. 59. New York: Pageant, 1959.

Hammond, William A. "The Disease of the Scythians (Morbus feminarum) and Certain Analogous Conditions." *American Journal of Neurology and Psychiatry* 1 (1882): 339–55.

———. *Sexual Impotence in the Male and Female.* Detroit: George S. Davis, 1887.

Herren, Ricardo. *La conquista erótica de las Indias.* Barcelona: Planeta, 1991.

Herrera, Antonio de. *Historia general de los hechos de los castellanos en las islas y tierrafirme del mar Océano.* 17 vols. Madrid: Real Academia, 1934–57.

Horswell, Michael. "Third Gender, Tropes of Sexuality and Transculturation in Colonial Andean Historiography." Ph.D. diss. University of Maryland at College Park, 1997.

Isbell, Billie Jean. "De inmaduro a duro: Lo simbólico femenino y los esquemas andinos de género." In *Más allá del silencio: Las fronteras de género en los Andes,* ed. Denise Arnold. La Paz: CIASE, 1997.

Ixtlilxochitl, Fernando de Alva. *Historia de la nación chichimeca.* In *Obras Historicas.* Vol. 2. Mexico City: Universidad Nacional Autónoma de México, 1977.

Jacobs, Sue-Ellen. "Berdache: A Brief Review of the Literature." In *Ethnographic Studies of Homosexuality,* ed. Wayne R. Dynes and Stephen Donaldson. New York: Garland, 1992.

Jacobs, Sue-Ellen, Wesley Thomas, and Sabine Lang, eds. *Two-Spirit People: Native American Gender Identity, Sexuality, and Spirituality.* Urbana: University of Illinois Press, 1997.

Klein, Cecelia. "Fighting with Femininity: Gender and War in Aztec Mexico." In *Gendered Rhetorics: Postures of Dominance and Submission in History,* ed. Richard C. Trexler. Binghamton, NY: Medieval and Renaissance Texts and Studies, 1994.

Kroeber, Alfred. *Handbook of the Indians of California.* Berkeley: University of California Press, 1953.

Lang, Sabine. *Männer als Frauen—Frauen als Männer: Geschlechtsrollewechsel bei den Indianern Nordamerikas.* Hamburg: Wayasbah, 1990.

Las Casas, Bartolomé de. *Apologética historia Sumaria.* Mexico City: Universidad Nacional Autónoma de México, 1967.

López Medel, Tomás. *De los tres elementos: Tratado sobre la naturaleza y el hombre del Nuevo Mundo.* Madrid: Alianza Editorial, 1990.

Mason, Peter. "Sex and Conquest: A Redundant Copula?" *Anthropos* 92 (1997): 577–82.

Murúa, Martín de. *Historia de los Incas, Reyes del Perú.* Lima: Sanmartí, 1922.

Nuñez de Pineda y Bascuñan, Francisco. *Cautiverio feliz y razón de las guerras dilatadas de Chile.* Santiago, 1863.

Parsons, Elsie Clews. "The Zuñi La'mana." *American Anthropologist* 18 (1916): 521–28.

Peter Martyr d'Anghiera. *Opera: Legatio Babylonica. De orbe novo decades octo. Opus epistolarum.* Graz, Austria: Akademische Druck- und Verlagsanstadt, 1966.

Pilling, Arnold. "Cross-Dressing and Shamanism among Selected Western North American Tribes." In *Two-Spirit People: Native American Gender Identity, Sexuality, and Spirituality*, ed. Sue-Ellen Jacobs, Wesley Thomas, and Sabine Lang. Urbana: University of Illinois Press, 1997.

Ramusio, Giovanni Battista. *Navigazioni e viaggi.* 6 vols. Turin: Einaudi, 1978–85.

Reichlen, H., and P. Reichlen. "Le manuscrit Boscana de la Bibliothèque nationale de Paris: Relation sur les indiens Acâgchemem de la mission de San Juan Capistrano, Californie." *Journal de la société des Américanistes* 59 (1970): 233–73.

Rocke, Michael. *Forbidden Friendships: Homosexuality and Male Culture in Renaissance Florence.* New York: Oxford University Press, 1996.

Roscoe, Will. *Changing Ones: Third and Fourth Genders in Native North America.* New York: St. Martin's Press, 1998.

———. "Mapping the Perverse." *American Anthropologist* 98 (1996): 861.

———. "Was We'wha a Homosexual? Native American Survivance and the Two-Spirit Tradition." *GLQ: A Journal of Lesbian/Gay Studies* 2/3 (1995): 193–235.

Ruíz de Arce, J. *Servicios en Indias.* Madrid: Tip. de Archivos, 1933.

Sahagún, Bernardino de. *The Florentine Codex: General History of the Things of New Spain.* Book 9. *The Merchants.* Ed. Charles E. Dibble and Arthur J. O. Anderson. Santa Fe: School of American Research and University of Utah Press, 1980.

Scacco, Anthony, ed. *Male Rape: A Casebook of Sexual Aggression.* New York: AMS Press, 1982.

Sepúlveda, Juan Ginés de. *Crónica Indiana.* Valladolid: Seminario Americanista, 1976.

Silverblatt, Irene. *Moon, Sun, and Witches: Gender Ideologies and Class in Inca and Colonial Peru.* Princeton, NJ: Princeton University Press, 1987.

Speck, F. "The Delaware Indians as Women: Were the Original Pennsylvanians Politically Emasculated?" *Pennsylvania Magazine of History and Biography* 70 (1946): 377–89.

Tezozomoc, H., and Fernando Alvarado. *Crónica Mexicana* [and the] *Códice Ramirez.* Mexico City: Editorial Porrúa, 1975.

Torquemada, Juan de. *Monarquia indiana.* 3 vols. Mexico City: Editorial Porrúa, 1975.

Trexler, Richard C. "Correre la Terra: Collective Insults in the Late Middle Ages." In *Dependence in Context in Renaissance Florence.* Binghamton, NY: Medieval and Renaissance Texts and Studies, 1994.

———. "Den Rücken beugen: Gebetsgebärden und Geschlechsgebärden in frühmodernen Europa und Amerika." In *Verletzte Ehre: Formen, Funktionen und Bedeutungen in Gesellschaften des Mittelalters und der fruhen Neuzeit*, ed. Klaus Schreiner and Gerd Schwerhoff. Cologne: Böhlau, 1995.

———, ed. *Gendered Rhetorics: Postures of Dominance and Submission in History.* Binghamton, NY: Medieval and Renaissance Texts and Studies, 1994.

———. "Making the American Berdache: Choice or Constraint?" *Journal of Social History* 35 (2002): 613–36.

———. *Public Life in Renaissance Florence.* New York: Academic Press, 1980.

———. "Ritual in Florence: Adolescence and Salvation in the Renaissance." In *Dependence in Context in Renaissance Florence.* Binghamton, NY: Medieval and Renaissance Texts and Studies, 1994.

———. *Sex and Conquest: Gendered Violence, Political Power, and the European Conquest of the Americas.* Ithaca, NY: Cornell University Press, 1995.

Williams, Walter. *The Spirit and the Flesh: Sexual Diversity in American Indian Culture.* Boston: Beacon, 1986.

CHAPTER THREE

Gendered Power, the Hybrid Self, and Homosexual Desire in Late Colonial Yucatan

PETE SIGAL

The effects that the Spanish conquest had on Native American constructions of homosexuality have not been studied in a systematic manner.
Part of the reason for this lack of scholarship is the relative dearth of documents which directly discuss the topic. Additionally, many scholars who have
studied the history of sexuality have posited that no homosexual identity
existed before the birth of the modern era in the middle of the nineteenth
century (and then only in Western societies).[1] This chapter has two purposes:
First, it shows how relatively new historical methodologies allow scholars to
understand ways that sexual desires have been negotiated and changed with
the imposition of different sexual paradigms. Second, it shows how late colonial (seventeenth- and eighteenth-century) Maya ideas of homosexual desire
were influenced by a variety of forces related to Maya, Nahua, and Hispanic
traditions, and to hybrid or syncretic practices. The reader will see that late
colonial Maya ideas of homosexuality had been changed by the imposition
of a Spanish hegemonic culture.[2] While Spanish hegemony never was
completely established, the Catholic discourse on sin influenced and altered
Maya sexual desires and behaviors.[3]

HOMOSEXUALITIES IN SIXTEENTH-CENTURY SPAIN AND MESOAMERICA

In order to understand the forces that altered concepts related to homosexuality in colonial Yucatan, one needs to analyze the ways in which the various
societies in Spain and Mesoamerica viewed homosexuality at the time of the
conquest.

The Spaniards saw sodomy as sinful.[4] This concept of sin was extended to both partners in sodomy, thus suggesting a negative identification with the action of sodomy itself (as opposed to the vilification of people who were seen as possessing an intrinsic internal identity based on sexual desires—although see below regarding the case of the *puto*).[5] To understand Spanish attitudes toward homosexual acts, one must uncover three levels at which these acts were condemned: the religious sphere, the state, and popular culture. To the early modern Christian clergy,[6] sodomy was seen as sinful in a framework within which all sexual activity was described as sin. Of course the clergy ranked the levels of sin, and vaginal intercourse in marriage was viewed as the least sinful. All other sexual acts were condemned to one degree or another, and the clergy did not hesitate to try to enforce their views. Clerical opposition to sodomy stemmed from a particular reading of the Bible, related to the story of Sodom and Gomorra. The clergy used this story in order to attempt to get people to avoid such activity.[7] Yet, in New Spain at least, the Church was not successful in preventing such sexual activity.[8] In this framework, both partners in sodomy were condemned, since the activity itself was seen as sinful.

The Spanish state condemned sodomy on a different level: that of the law. Spanish law, similar to Italian law of the same period, condemned the active partner in sodomy to criminal penalties, but the passive partner received no penalty.[9] Advocates of the "Mediterranean model" assert that Hispanic notions of sodomy condemn the passive partner but allow the active partner great latitude. As he is the penetrator, he is seen as playing the appropriate masculine role. However, early modern Spanish law appears to contradict this. Richard Trexler argues that the rationale behind Spanish law was the concept of punishing the perpetrator of an act of illicit domination. The passive partner was seen as somebody who had no choice in the act, who essentially was raped.[10]

Spanish popular culture, on the contrary, condemned the passive partner. Spaniards racialized sodomy by asserting that it was a dominant practice among the Moors. In the wars between the Spaniards and the Moors, Spanish soldiers were seen as the active partners to the passive Moors. In Spanish popular culture, therefore, the passive was condemned and in many ways seen as equal to a Moor, a racially inferior being. Spaniards further condemned the passive partner as a *puto,* an effeminate male who was perceived as being anally penetrated. *Puto* was a common insult used against people, and being a *puto* was perceived as a horrendous fate.[11] Note, however, the difference between a *puto* identity and that of a modern homosexual. The *puto* was defined primarily by his effeminacy and his passivity, and only secondarily by the gender of his sexual object choice. Nor was he seen as an equal partner to the active.

Spanish culture combined these three discourses into an overall condemnation of all types of sodomy. However, there also was some normative acceptance of the existence of sodomy in Spanish society.[12] Different types of sodomy (male/male; male/female; male/animal; and, occasionally, female/female) often were distinguished from each other, but the discourses as a whole condemned all kinds.

Sodomites formed communities in sixteenth- to eighteenth-century Spain. Rafael Carrasco has worked through the Inquisition sources in Valencia, and he has found that sodomites were able to find each other in urban areas throughout the region. They came from various sectors of society, but through their participation in a sodomitical subculture, the people became marginalized. Carrasco, in fact, finds evidence that the Inquisitors and popular society both linked sodomy directly with prostitution.[13] Sodomitical desires, according to Carrasco, reproduced many aspects of heterosexual desire, while also establishing a strong division between actives and passives.[14] Carrasco's conclusions are important for understanding the relationship between broader cultural norms and the creation of homosexual desires.

The documentation related to homosexual activity in Mesoamerican societies at the time of the conquest is rather limited. Trexler shows that the Nahuas of central Mexico condemned passivity in men. The Florentine Codex was clear in its position on sodomy: it condemned the passive partner.

> PASSIVE PARTNER IN SODOMY, CATAMITE: Corruption, perverted, excrement, feces, infamous, corrupt, vicious, mocker, scoffer, provoker, repugnant, loathsome. He fills people's noses with the smell of excrement. Effeminate. He passes himself off as a woman. He deserves to be cast in the fire. He burns. He is cast in the flames. He talks like a woman. He passes himself off as a woman.[15]

This condemnation came from a document where the Nahua informants were talking to a Franciscan friar, but this particular friar was interested in ethnographic accuracy.[16] Moreover, other documents suggest perceived feminization and weakness in the passive partner.[17] The Nahuas also preserved a role for passives to meet the sexual desires of noble men.[18] Nahuatl-speaking peoples had significant influence on the Maya, and they no doubt had much influence on Maya ideas related to homosexual behavior.[19]

The Maya of Yucatan at the time of the conquest had similar views to the Nahuas. In several documents written in the colonial period, but about preconquest times,[20] the Maya writers stressed that they found sodomy and pederasty to be important factors in the reasons that rulers were overthrown, people were killed, and communities were conquered.[21] They generally degraded their enemies by calling them passive sodomites.[22] An early colonial Maya noble alleged that there was a furnace in Mayapán that had been used to kill sodomites.[23] But the Maya, like the Nahuas, reserved a role for ritualized sodomy (that may explain the fact that Bernal Díaz del Castillo found idols showing sodomy between men), which showed the power and desire of the active partner to control and penetrate the passive.[24]

For the Maya and the Nahuas, passivity in men generally was condemned. But both also found a place for ritualized sodomy, which emphasized both desire and power, as an element of the social structure. This was different from the Spaniards, primarily because of different notions of culture, politics, ritual, and religion.

IDEOLOGIES OF CONTROL, CONQUEST, AND CONTAMINATION

Most of the evidence that I present in the next two sections relates to the symbolic construction of homosexual desire. In the cases discussed here, homosexual activity, in all likelihood, did not actually occur. The Maya-language texts which I have used in the bulk of my work are extremely esoteric, consciously philosophical documents. They intend to analyze the relationships that people have with the gods and that the nobles have with the commoners. They use sexual, including homosexual, desire to make specific arguments about the ways in which people are supposed to imagine, fantasize about, and fear their relationships with their superiors. My analysis of these texts is a discussion of the symbolic structures of Maya life.

While the Maya at the time of the conquest held views of homosexual behavior that differed from those of the Spaniards, these views changed through the colonial period. The ritualized kinship connection of Maya nobility with the gods, an important connection which gave the Maya nobles legitimacy, was to be altered by the Spaniards. With the advent of Christianity, the Maya nobles could not be considered direct descendants of the Christian God, Jesus, the Virgin Mary, or even the saints. Still, much Maya religious tradition survived through the colonial years, in the form both of rites hidden from the Spaniards and of syncretic elements that developed in Yucatecan Christian rituals.[25] These connections allowed for some sense of the survival of tradition, and Maya notions of homosexual behaviors and desires followed this same pattern of the perceived maintenance of some tradition in a different context.

The Maya of eighteenth-century Yucatan had developed coping strategies to deal with two centuries of Spanish rule over the bulk of the more populated areas in the peninsula. The few Spaniards who chose to settle in Yucatan certainly attempted to dominate the region in order to get the maximum amount of labor from the indigenous population.[26] Yet, even by the middle of the nineteenth century, there were few creoles and mestizos who lived among the Maya in the outlying communities.[27] Most Hispanic peoples lived in the three cities established by the original Spanish settlers in

Yucatan: Campeche, Mérida, and Valladolid. Yet the Spaniards were able to have significant influence from these cities. They participated in the economies of the outlying areas through the *encomienda* and *hacienda* systems.[28] Perhaps more important, a significant number of people of Maya descent headed toward the three cities in an attempt to gain employment and escape the difficulties of rural colonial life. These people, many of whom did not sever their ties with the indigenous communities, effectively worked as cultural transmitters, allowing indigenous community members, even in the far reaches of southern Yucatan, to understand various aspects of Hispanic traditions.[29] The clergy and others who lived among the indigenous peoples also acted as cultural liaisons.[30] These phenomena resulted in meaningful changes in Maya life.

As these changes took place, the clergy wrote about the ways in which they had transformed the religious lives of the Maya and other Latin American indigenous peoples. This is what other scholars have called the spiritual conquest of Latin America.[31] Yet, in more recent research, anthropologists and historians have said that such a spiritual conquest never took place.[32] I argue here, however, that the Spaniards significantly altered Maya values by asserting a cultural system that had different notions of history, religion, and self-identity.[33] Traditional Maya notions of the ways in which the gods worked as gods/ancestors who were progenitors of the nobles changed dramatically. Maya history and self-identity could not be linked as closely to ritual life and the gods.

These changes were complex, and they related closely to Maya concepts of sexual behavior. For the Maya, appropriate sexual behavior was intimately linked with notions of religion. The Dresden Codex pictured the sexual behavior of the Maya gods.[34] Sexual acts among gods and between gods and humans were pictured as creating humanity. Most strongly shown was the relationship between these sexualized gods and the lineages of the nobles. These gods were seen as the progenitors of the nobles, who thus were provided with legitimacy.[35] Maya sexual behavior at the time of the conquest also was linked closely with notions of warfare and sacrifice (auto, animal, and human). All of these sacrifices, like sexual activity, were viewed as acts of penetration central to the maintenance of religious and social life.[36] With appropriate sexual behavior linked so closely both with concepts of sacrifice and with the relationship of the nobles to the gods, the alterations of these elements of ritual and religious life, which were mandated by Christianization, changed the nature of appropriate and inappropriate sexual desires. These sexual desires were linked with the gods and with Maya notions of conquest and power. As the colonial period progressed, the desires became more closely linked with ideas of conquest and contamination in the European sense of the terms.

Maya historians wrote of pederastic political rituals in which elder noble politicians asserted their power as sexual actives over their younger colleagues. These ceremonies were not ostensibly about sex, and the people did not engage in sexual activity during the rituals. Moreover, the language itself is evocative of masculine bravado and joking. Despite the fact that the ceremonies were not about sex, the sexual subtext is clear.[37] These rituals were ceremonies which discussed the relationship between pedagogy and the sexual politics of nobility. The Maya historical texts, the *Books of Chilam Balam*, called these rituals *suiua than,* "Zuyua speech" or the "Zuyua word."[38] This translated as "unintelligible speech," textually represented as a test in which the nobles made unintelligible speech intelligible.[39] The tests were about knowledge: Those who had knowledge of society could rule over that society. This knowledge was represented as both libidinal and kinship-oriented.

Zuyua speech, which has been called a "language of Zuyua," has intrigued scholars of the *Books of Chilam Balam.* These scholars have stated that Zuyua specifically was intended to confuse people and hide meaning.[40] It is true, as the reader will see, that Zuyua speech was made up of a series of riddles, but my research has shown that these riddles were intended to enlighten rather than confuse. The enlightenment came when those to whom the riddles were directed solved the problems presented. Zuyua was representative of a set of standards designed to determine nobility and truth. The rituals showed the power of the *halach uinic,* "the true person," over the rest of the nobility.[41] The power relationship presented by the riddles showed the *halach uinic* as a trainer and teacher of noble youth.

My interpretation shows that these rituals involved adolescent boys aspiring to become nobles.[42] The many discontinuities in Maya life before the conquest and throughout the colonial years made it difficult to establish the proper kinship ties for a noble. The nobles wanted to have a way of separating the true nobles from the others. This theoretically was accomplished by a test given to adolescent noble aspirants. Those who passed the test may have gone on to take political office, or they simply may have lived their lives as nobles, but at least their nobility was "proven." The kinship ties to the *halach uinic* who, by his very name, had proven the truth of his nobility, showed a connection to a very "real" noble lineage. The adolescent boys were called *batabs* ("governors") in an effort to imply both their unity with and their dependence on the *halach uinic.* This relationship was both pederastic and pedagogical: The leader taught the adolescent boys how to rule, and, in doing so, he required the services of these adolescents.

Initially the guardian, the *halach uinic,* was seated, showing his ascension into political power. This person "guarded" the semen and the blood, two interrelated elements.[43] Semen and blood stratified his relationship with the adolescent nobles, for this was the symbolic knowledge they sought to gain.

The sexual connotations represented political desires: In order to gain the political power of the *halach uinic*, the youth had to gain knowledge of his semen and blood. Whether this ritual was attained through actual sexual activity or simply through the use of semen and blood as symbols of power is something that we may never know.[44] The symbolic relationship was a homoerotic and pederastic one, with the leader imparting his knowledge to the younger male nobles through semen. The blood, either representing menstruation (and thus suggesting the semen/blood connection as one which maintained the *halach uinic* as the guardian of men and women) or penis piercing,[45] located the desires of the adolescent nobles.

The "phallic signifying economy"[46] represented here stratified the political system based on gender and age. The adolescents desired the blood of the various rituals, the blood of the lineage. The ceremonies, designed to test knowledge of blood and semen, both gendered and phallic,[47] showed that these adolescents were required to understand lineage, directly related to political power. The rituals of blood were seen as replacements for secure lineage alignments. The stratification of the lineage, apparent in both warfare and politics,[48] allowed for a homoerotic desire to emanate from both of these fields.

The often quite humorous questions and answers led the aspiring nobles to the possibility of political power. This text constructed asymmetrical relationships, however humorously, in an effort to gain (perhaps fictive) political office. The heart, blood, and semen were central symbols in this construction. While other documents described narratives of universality in which all people were created, this ritual discussed a narrative to which all aspired: to be declared the "true person." The text, although representing universal aspirations, was a highly particularized story which represented the lives of few people. The people shown were all male and all nobles. They desired to represent the "truth" through the phallus, constructed as political power.

The pedagogical relationship implied between the established noble and the aspiring nobles is familiar to those who have studied Melanesia and the ancient Greeks. For the Greeks, this relationship was sexualized, although it had to be controlled.[49] For some Melanesian groups, this relationship represented the ritual exchange of semen in order to promote masculinity and growth.[50] In both cases these relationships were played out through actual pederastic homosexual acts.

For the Maya the pedagogical relationship was somewhat less explicit than either that of Melanesia or of ancient Greece. Zuyua speech made a humorous attempt to require those aspiring to be nobles to have knowledge of rituals of politics, religion, and creation, relating these to notions of sexual desire, symbolically represented as semen and blood. While the text never said how the adolescents gained the knowledge of semen and blood that the leader possessed, these elements represented sexual acts, creation, childbirth, warfare, penis piercing, and human sacrifice. The *halach uinic* may or may not have literally pierced the youthful penises (or have had them pierce his: the active/passive dichotomy is unclear in this act). His semen may or may not have literally penetrated their bodies. He tested them on their knowledge of semen and blood. He showed them that he had this knowledge because it represented his knowledge of all aspects of society.

The stories themselves actually showed the bi-eroticism of political and sexual desire, as they primarily discussed sexual acts between men and women while they represented the male body in an erotic manner, attaining the pederastic relationship. Some clearly showed an erotic connection between the older noble and the adolescents. For example, the elder noble stated,

> Son, bring me your trousers[51] so I may smell their odor here and get rid of their odor, the odor of my trousers, the odor of my cloth . . . and the great odor of the center of the sky and the center of the clouds. . . . If you are the *halach uinic*, let it be done.

The younger one answered, and the narrator/historian described as follows:

> "Father, I will bring it," are his words. Here is the odor of the trousers for which he asks, the great odor of the center of the sky: it is incense burning in the fire. This is the green garden plant for which he asks. This is ground cacao seeds.[52]

The joking language allowed the older man to contemplate his desire to sniff the pants of the younger. The young male body was associated with creating pleasure for an older, superior man. This pleasure was associated with great ritual power as the youth's body was equated with the smell of the center of the sky. As the older noble searched for something in the pants of the younger, he enjoyed the adolescent's odors. The search, likely for the anus, situated the homoerotic tenor of the ritual. It also sexualized political power through the phallic connotations. It was the desire for the phallus that allowed access to political power. But, of course, we know little about the desires of the youth, as this text was structured through the desires of the leader, who was looking for the anus.

The discourse showed that nobles were allowed to engage in intergenerational erotic games that stressed the power of the elder noble over the younger. Among the Maya, unlike among the Greeks,[53] we find no textual discussions about the nature of inter-generational sexual relationships. The pedagogical relationship was eroticized through the provision of service by the younger male for the elder. While the younger obtained some power in the act of creating pleasure for his partner,[54] the elder male had power over the younger in a sexual, political, and educational sense. The event thus maintained the hierarchical social order.

The younger noble, of course, played a joke on the elder, legitimizing both of their positions. The position of the younger noble represented a position of desire for and access to political office. The older noble represented the old leadership, a group which maintained its dominance of rituals, but which was both pompous and ridiculous.[55] The elder noble was powerful, and he maintained that power through his discourse and actions. However, he would not always have been powerful, and it served his strategic interests to allow others to laugh at him.

In another example, the leader maintained his stance as a protector of his people by the instructions he gave to the youth:

> "Son, go bring me an old man, but don't confine his testicles, his water balls. Hom Tochac [Submerged Impotent] is his name."[56]
> "That is how it shall be, father."
> Here is what he asks for: armadillo.[57]

The younger noble was required to take care of the impotent man's testicles. The male body, constructed as somewhat broken down, needed care to re-energize the impotent and to prevent further damage of the goods. The elder noble "taught" the younger how to care for the bodies of other men and, in doing so, expressed concern over the loss of the phallus. While the unconscious representation may have suggested a concern related to a castration complex, it more clearly showed the relationship between sexual desire among men and the power relationships developed in such desire.[58] Both the older noble and the younger had certain political responsibilities. The phallic symbolism represented a concern for the future of society, which was unveiled in a concern for the place of the male body in the reproductive act. Here the authors had some anxiety about the fact that the male body may have become incapable of engaging in intercourse and reproduction. The potential impotence of the man required the care of the youth in order for the male body to be rejuvenated. While the text did not specify the actual acts performed, the youth may have been required to engage in a variety of activities to get the elderly man potent. It was the youthful body that was placed at the center of the discourse. The homoerotic desire represented (in the idea that the older man would desire these youth so greatly) was an element constructing particular power relationships such that the youth were required to sexually service older nobles. Of course, one must recall that the discourse is only sexual banter, and that the sexual acts may never have been performed.

As the riddles of "Zuyua speech" became more clear, they asserted the patrilineage, allowing the actors access to speech and power only if they were male. However, access to the social and political hierarchy in colonial Maya society required nobility determined through both patrilineage and matrilineage. The riddles, rather than asserting a male social dominance, provided a reference point to male dominance in the political sphere.

The *Books of Chilam Balam* from Chumayel and Tusik included a variety of related texts that implied the ritual importance of homoerotic and bierotic desire marking the body. This sexual contact, both in the documents and in the ethnographic context, did not disavow age or gender-structured homosexual desire. The various desires presented in the texts represented the "truth" that the "true leader" sought to impart to the noble youth. This "truth," symbolized as blood and semen, was linked explicitly to the libido. The Maya structured the political power of pederasty by placing a variety of bodies at the hands of the leader of society. These bodies, at least fictionally, represented and maintained a social and political hierarchy.

As I have previously noted, Maya tradition related homosexual desires to conquest. The conqueror was perceived symbolically as the active partner, while the conquered was perceived as the passive.[59] In the Yucatecan historical texts covering the preconquest period, the Maya writers asserted that those who lost wars were cowardly passives who "surrendered their spirit" as they turned and "spread" their backsides to the conquerors.[60] Because of the actions of the cowardly passives, Maya society was destroyed by the Spaniards.[61] In this case, the passives also were said to be the "younger brothers" to the Spaniards. The Europeans, as the actives, asserted a hierarchical kinship connection with the defeated Maya, in this case the Itzá.[62] The warriors were degraded in the eyes of the people, as they were symbolically sodomized and placed in a dependent kin relationship to the Spaniards. The fear of losing a war was represented symbolically as the fear of being sodomized.[63]

Another fear was expressed in Maya religion and ritual. The Maya feared the wrath of their own gods; they saw the cosmos as unpredictable and harsh. The people had reason to fear the gods: these deities had destroyed many Maya leaders. The individual person was not important to the gods, who were willing to accept a person's blood in order to keep the society functioning.[64] The fear of the gods was symbolized as a fear of the unknown, and particularly a fear of sodomitic rape. Such rape asserted the power of the nobles over the gods while at the same time showing the ways in which the gods controlled all. The shaman, shown in this case to be male, made demands of the male god:

I cast a spell to forcibly cut and pound the lust of creation and the lust of the night. The body of wood and stone does not sleep, does not curl up. As I hurl stones at you, as I slap you with a log and a staff, you four gods, you four *bacabs,* my sign is submerged.[65] I am submerging/penetrating you with the genitals of your mother and the genitals of your father.[66] You are the lust of the women's children, the lust of the men's children. Amen.[67]

This text was intended to cure an individual, but, more important for our purposes, the ritual meaning was related to sacrifice.[68] The text placed the shaman in the position of the physical aggressor: he punished the gods by hurling stones at them and hitting them. Here the active partner was a violent partner, and the whole scene marked violence. The shaman became the sexually active partner by engaging in a forced sexual act with the god. This ritualized sex was necessary in order to engage in the cure. But the activity was suffused with violence and the god had little free will: The god was raped.

The word *chek*, which was used specifically to describe sexual intercourse, was used here to show how the shaman submerged and penetrated the god.[69] The curer then specified that he penetrated the god with the genitals of the god's parents. The cure itself required the sexual act represented by *chek*, and the context here demands a broad interpretation of the meaning of this term. The curer used the genitals of the mother and the father of the god in order to engage in sexual acts with that god. Note that an alternative translation for *cobol*, which I have translated as "genitals," was "prostitute," and the term also may have been associated with the active partner in sodomy.[70] With either translation, the rape was accomplished, but the translation which I believe to be the more likely one emphasized human body parts, a common way of referring both to the gods and to humanity in colonial Yucatec.[71] Such a sexual act represented the possibility of an "incestuous" sexual assault, legitimized in the ritual/religious sphere. The "incest" here was somewhat problematic, as the parents of the god were not presented as engaging in these sexual acts. Their genitals did engage in sexual acts with their child, but their bodies and "selves" did not. The free-floating genitalia, detached from the bodies of the gods, and attached to the body of the shaman, may make one think of the Lacanian notion of the phallus as a linguistic sign rather than a body part.[72] The legitimization of such a potentially incestuous relationship presented a strategy which empowered the shaman to rape the god. This shaman could do away with the disease only by using the powerful genitals of the parents of the god (the immense power of the free-floating genitalia again points to the Lacanian framework). Incest and sodomy themselves were maintained as parts of an important strategy legitimizing the nobles and the gods. The desire for the gods, represented as incest, had an important role to play in societal structures. It was through this desire that the shaman convinced the community that he had completed his task.

The male god, as a passive participant in this whole affair, appeared to have little power. But the rape may have shown the Maya people the intense power of the sacred, and the small amount of power reserved for humans. The sacred world developed all of the genitals used in these sexual acts. And it was only through the sacred that the shaman was able to engage in the various acts mentioned. The shaman was helpless until the gods were willing to help him. And they were: the gods (parents) were willing to assist the shaman in raping another god (son). The god was one of the most powerful: a *bacab* divided into his four parts.[73] The sacred power was perceived as overwhelming. If the gods could and would rape another god, then humans would stand little chance if they placed themselves in the disfavor of these gods.[74] The power of the sacred certainly was an important element in Maya society, and the rape of a god would have pointed to the unpredictability and harshness of that sacred world. The sodomitic incestuous desire was a cure through rape. But the disease was only created by the lust of the children of mothers and fathers, symbolizing the nobles themselves. Their lust needed to be controlled, and it was controlled by rape. The nobles were separated from the commoners (those "without mothers and fathers," those whose lust was unimportant).[75]

Perhaps the most important structural element here was the concept of penetration, a central part of Maya discourse. Penetration was associated closely with rituals related to warfare, disease, human sacrifice, and penis piercing. Each of these represented elements of Maya desire organized around a cultural matrix of activity and passivity. The homosexual rape represented in this text was connected ritually with penis piercing and human sacrifice. The penetration shown later in the document was structured around the Maya term, *pudz*. This term, which also translated as "to cut," was related to the knife the Mayan peoples used in ritual sacrifice.[76]

HOMOSEXUAL FANTASIES AND THE GENDERED STRUCTURE OF DESIRE

The gendered structure of homosexuality in Native American societies most commonly has been represented in the personage of the *berdache*, perceived alternately as a third gender, a forefather/mother to modern gay and transsexual identity movements, a hermaphrodite, a spiritual being that united the male and female aspects of the cosmos, a male entrance into the powerful female sphere of indigenous societies, a transvestite who freely chose to cross-dress, an old man who transvested himself in order to mark his inability to engage any longer in masculine pursuits, a slave forced to transvest himself, a commoner child forced to transvest himself and engage in the passive role in sodomy, or a young man forced to transvest himself in order to serve older nobles in the temples and palaces.[77] One might surmise, from all of these conflicting ideas regarding the *berdache*, that this figure represented different things to different societies, but there is scant evidence for such a conclusion.

While many of the analyses regarding the *berdache* have failed even to consider power relations in the indigenous societies, and even more of these analyses have failed to consider historical change and cultural differentiation, they have opened up a field of inquiry into indigenous gendered concepts of homosexual and transsexual activity.[78] Certainly transvestism played a role in many of these societies, but for the Maya of Yucatan no such role entered the indigenous language documents. While a transvested figure likely existed, the evidence shows no possible positive roles for such an individual.[79] For the Maya the more important concept was the "transsexualization" of the human body in a series of ritualized medical texts.[80] I relate this transsexuality to the possibility of either a third-gender subjectivity or a gendered structure for homosexual acts in preconquest and colonial Maya societies.

I return briefly to the aforementioned and cited quotation, from an extensive seventeenth-century ritualized medical text, the *Ritual of the Bacabs*, in which the god was raped. In that text the phallus became a free-floating entity which the shaman was able to grasp and attach to himself. That phallus, however, was not specifically a sign of the masculine. The detached genitalia included the *mother's* genitals as well as the father's. In this sense the phallus was reconfigured as the sign of libidinal power which was not necessarily attached to one gender.[81] Why did the shaman need both sets of genitalia in order to rape the god? What role did the mother's genitals play? The text does not allow definitive answers to these questions. Perhaps the mother's genitals were attached in some way to the son, the raped god. This would confirm the idea, stated by Trexler, that the passive male was feminized. But the narrative suggests that the active partner, the shaman, used the genitals of both the mother and the father. If both sets of genitals were attached to his body, this text would represent sexual acts that are not comprehensible to us.[82] If these genitals were not attached to his body, but rather simply were used by him in some manner, then he may have symbolized the metaphorical power of both the male and the female aspects of the cosmos to engage in acts of incestuous rape (again representing the unpredictability of the cosmos). In either case the text used the "concept" of genitalia to alter the bodily metaphors related to the shaman. Either he took on the genitalia of the god's father, the god taking on the genitalia of his own mother, or he took on the genitalia of both father and mother. In the first instance, the shaman's sign would have been changed into the sign of the male father god: his phallus would have been deified, and the son god's phallus would have been "transsexualized" into the phallus of his own mother. In the second instance, the shaman's phallus would have been "transsexualized" into the mixed-gender phallus, combining both the sign of the mother and the sign of the father. In either case, symbolic "transsexuality" played an important role in the text, representing much about Maya desires, fantasies, and fears as they related to the cosmos and the world of curing rituals.

The act of transsexualization may highlight both Maya tradition and Oedipal colonization.[83] Transsexuality was used in the texts in an effort to understand the place of libidinal power in the cosmological structure. This allowed the postconquest people to whom the text was directed to understand the context of the preconquest rituals. Even though they perhaps could not see those rituals, their imaginations and fantasies allowed them to understand the transsexualization of the phallus.

As the phallus floated in the open, the transsexual person as a singular figure would have presented the Maya with some conceptual problems. The phallus needed to be able to transsexualize the text by allowing all of the gods, ancestors, and shamans to move into a ritualized transsexuality. If transsexuality was to be associated with one individual identity, it would have lost its universalizing power. Allowing a person to transsexualize himself or herself, and conceiving this as a permanent identity located within the individual would have been problematic because the act of transsexualization had to remain an act, not an identity, in order to assert the libidinal position in the cosmos. Transsexuality in preconquest and colonial Yucatan was used as an element to empower certain deified figures and to disempower others.

This, of course, does not preclude a *berdache* or third-gender identity from being conceived in some related framework. However, the modern notion of a transsexual or transgender identity could not have existed in the same manner. In transgender communities in contemporary Western societies, people move across gender boundaries through both surgical and nonsurgical techniques.[84] More than occasionally, people in these communities question the boundaries of gender.[85] Several theorists have shown the radical potential of such a destabilization of gender categories.[86] And certainly the colonial and preconquest Maya concept of gender may be used to question the stability of gendered frameworks of power, since the Maya had a different established framework than the Spaniards.[87] However this may be, the differences were not such that the Maya failed to give importance to gender differentiation in power relationships. Nor could the Maya have conceived of transsexuality outside of their understanding of power. The Maya documents show that Maya imaginations presented transsexuality as a strategy for understanding cosmic power. For other elements of transsexuality to fall completely outside of that context would have been unimaginable.

Here I give one more example of the way in which transsexuality was used in the writing of these texts. This case does not involve male homosexual activity, but it stresses the importance of the principles outlined here. There is, as has been shown, a highly visible phallus in some of the ritualized medical texts. Diseases were personified in the *Ritual of the Bacabs,* leading to a symbolic gendering of the curing rituals. The phallus was represented in the cure and, as Lacan maintained for Western societies, this may have allowed for an entrance into the realm of symbolic power.[88] Note this one text (which is similar to several others in the *Ritual of the Bacabs*):

> Words for the enchantment of spiders:[89]
> First spider, second spider, third spider, fourth spider: first spider of wood, first spider of stone. For three days you were away with the bag of poison, Ah Uuc Ti Cab (He of the Seven Poisons). How did you acquire the poison on your back? For four days you existed beneath the garden.[90] The grain of your grandmother, the virgin Moon Goddess, the red Moon Goddess, the white Moon Goddess, is the sign on the back of the first spider of wood, the first spider of stone. How is the virgin needle? How is the virgin Moon Goddess, the white Moon Goddess, the red Moon Goddess? This is her sign, your penis.[91] Thirteen balls of dyed thread of the virgin Moon Goddess, the red Moon Goddess, the white Moon Goddess. What are the signs of your ugliness?[92] How am I to take them away? How am I to free them? How am I to untie them?[93] The vagina's mother with your penis: you are the first spider of wood, the first spider of stone. The four parts: how is my black cape? Is now when I am to kiss? How are the fourteen jars? How is my hail, the thirteen jars of my cold water? How am I to cool the pain of the first spider of wood, the first spider of stone? Spider! Spider! Spider! Spider! Amen.[94]

Among the modern Maya, the tarantula is a common and derogatory metaphor for the vagina.[95] As the spider was gendered female, women here were associated with a disease that was cured by the phallus (the poison itself, however, was gendered male). The gendering implicit in the early part of the text was a symbol for creation gone wrong. The spider was connected to a matrilineal line. It lived beneath the garden of the household (the garden itself has been gendered female from postclassic to modern times).[96] The grandmother's grain further gendered the spider, who hailed back to her grandmother, the Moon Goddess. The Moon Goddess represented the ritual matrilineal line of disease. She, through her own reproduction, placed her mark on the disease. She had significant control over the ritual, possessing the needle used to kill the spider (and pierce the penis).[97] The gendering of the disease represented some ritual fears. They stemmed perhaps from a fear of the power of women through their sexual desire and their ability to reproduce. For if women could reproduce humanity, they could destroy humanity by reproducing disease.

As the virginal needle entered the scene, it resembled the phallus and was possessed by the Moon Goddess. The needle was sacred and virginal, much like the Moon Goddess, and through this specifically gendered notion of the sacred, the Moon Goddess controlled a great deal. But the phallus then showed up as a disguised but still marked penis, first present and then disappearing. Either the spider or the Moon Goddess, both apparently gendered female, possessed the penis. The transsexuality of such a text was an assertion of its ritual power through the use of the floating phallus.

Transsexualization, this time female to male, was used as a strategy to understand a god. In this case the god was empowered to scare away the poisonous spider. As the text entered the central curing ritual, the vagina's mother (using a derogatory word for vagina) mixed with "your" penis ("you" was marked as the spider). The spider, gendered female, obtained a penis. The two together created the disease and perhaps the cure. The vagina's mother (and the spider's grandmother), the Moon Goddess, portrayed the matrilineal line through a gendered notion of fantasy and fear. And how did the shaman kill the spider? Apparently by raining some sort of hail on it. This represented "hail" coming from the phallus itself.[98] The blood and semen engaged in a phallic cure. The phallus was necessary in order for the goddess to have the power to get rid of the spider, and this phallus could be present in the matrilineal line only if it was placed on someone or something gendered female.

But another explanation is plausible, one that changes this particular notion of Maya transsexuality. This text and many others like it in the *Ritual of the Bacabs* represented both the cure (the removal of the spider) and the importance of the penis-piercing ritual. The needle, gendered female and possessed by the Moon Goddess, engaged in the ritual. The Moon Goddess had power over this ritual through her control over the needle and the colors red and white. As the penis was pierced, the curing began. The phallus was given great power connected with lineage arrangements, nobility, and the political structure. The pierced penis was in pain, but still placed the hail-water/blood on the spider, enchanting it to leave.

As I have shown elsewhere, the penis-piercing ritual often was used to assert the power of noble males by allowing them to engage in vision quests in which they communed with the gods.[99] In other cases it was used to present an offering to the gods so that the person making the offering could request certain things of the gods. Men felt a need to bleed from their genitals, likely as a way of harnessing the power of creation that women had developed through their similar ability to bleed from their genitals. The penis-piercing ritual was an attempt to bring forth, to give birth to, the gods.[100] Such a quest required measures that in essence transsexualized the individual into some sort of "intermediate gender." He was able to create life through his penis because he had harnessed the power of the male and female aspects of creation.

In this sense the "third gender" here was associated specifically with the masculine, not with a subjectivity aligned with the feminization of power. The penis-piercing ritual and the phallic symbolism found throughout much of the Mayan region symbolized a meaning for transsexuality that asserted masculinity. Such a meaning is vitally different than the ones often associated with the *berdache*.

The phallic transsexuality here crossed various barriers: female goddesses, people, and animals were transsexualized as they received male genitalia; male gods, people, and animals were transsexualized as they received female genitalia. But one must be careful not to impart to the Maya some transcultural, transhistorical, fetishization of particular body parts. Maya imaginations placed great importance on the harnessing of power through ritual celebration, and particularly through autosacrificial ceremonies. These events did not promote the actual exchange of body parts, only the symbolic exchange, which represented both desire (for community survival, for sexual domination) and power (over the cosmos and the gods: a power that the people knew never would entirely be theirs).

The Moon Goddess engaged in some type of (sexual?) act with the spider, apparently penetrating the spider in an effort to get rid of it. The Moon Goddess also may have penetrated the person to be cured and/or the curer. She must have possessed the phallus in order to engage in these acts. Yet she clearly was pictured as female, and never was pictured with a penis.[101] The passive partners were put in an asymmetrical relationship to the Moon Goddess. At the same time, the Moon Goddess was denigrated by the curer, suggesting that perhaps she was the passive partner to the active curer: She may have switched roles.

The vagina's mother used the penis to engage in the cure. The penis, associated with the spider, represented a sexual act which might be termed "lesbian." But no lesbian identity was shown in the text. The penis attained ritual power through its use as the phallus in (hetero)sexual intercourse. The rituals destabilized these categories of sexual desire. The free-floating phallus allowed for such a ritual destabilization.[102] However, one should not consider this to be a suggestion that Maya gender was somehow more free or equal than Western gender. Nor should one assume that homosexuality was accepted. As has been shown above, gender was a complex entity associated with power and desire. Homosexual acts that were described in the texts were symbolic of domination.

This and other rituals were based on a Maya notion of fantasy, fear, desire, and imagination. The ritual discourse demanded that the people imagine (or actually see) a situation in which the shaman let the blood of himself or others in order to commune with the ancestors and the gods. As the people imagined/saw this communication, they were told to desire this connection with the gods, and to desire the rule of the shamans, monarchs, lords, and nobles. In order to make the people understand the desire for this rulership, the text invoked sexual and gender fantasies. The people had to fantasize about sexual intercourse with and/or between the leaders, ancestors, and gods. Further, these fantasies only achieved completion as the people fantasized about the leaders, ancestors, and gods changing sexes/genders through the free-floating phallus.

Desire, imagination, fantasy, and fear related to politics, the cosmos, and warfare were connected closely with sexual desire. The symbolism of male homosexuality was used to assert both fantasy and fear. Fantasy and desire were always in these cases linked with control. The older noble fantasized sexual and pedagogical control over the younger. The younger noble may have desired sex with the older, but we have no records of these fantasies. The Maya historians feared their own ritual sodomization through loss in warfare. The Maya shamans demanded that the people fear the cosmos, and they represented this fear through incestuous sodomy. They symbolized their fears based on notions of homosexual rape. And the Maya shamans also demanded that the people fantasize about autosacrifice as a transsexualization of their desires.

THE MEANING OF THE HYBRID

Although many aspects of Mesoamerican social and cultural norms survived the conquest, and many of these attributes existed at the end of the colonial period, there was nothing in indigenous societies that was left untouched by colonization.[103] For the Maya, homosexual desire was part of the colonization process. One can see a series of changes based on differences between the various texts. The seventeenth-century and archaic *Ritual of the Bacabs*, along with the more archaic sections of the *Books of Chilam Balam*, asserted notions of spirituality and desire that were based on systems of fantasy, domination, and power that were unfamiliar to the early modern Spanish. The later parts of the *Books of Chilam Balam*, written in the eighteenth and early nineteenth centuries, along with other colonial documents, asserted a notion of sexual desire (and spirituality) based on concepts of conquest and contamination very similar to early modern Spanish ideas.

When the Spanish came to the Americas, they brought with them certain ideas that were embedded in European Christianity, among them the idea that individuals were responsible for their own actions and destinies. While Mesoamerican peoples did not believe that everything in one's life was left up to fate, they did think that the gods controlled the world and the cosmos in such a way that human action could have effects only within a broader framework controlled by the gods. In other words, while people could influence what happened to them, the greatest part of their destinies were preordained.[104]

After the conquest, this concept led to significant confusion and altered meanings in the Spanish/indigenous dialogue.[105] A central component of Christianity, sin, clearly was either misunderstood, or manipulated, or (most likely) both by the Mesoamerican peoples. They confessed to things that were not considered by the Spaniards to be sinful, and they resisted distinguishing the Spanish concept of sin from the Mesoamerican concept of divine unhappiness.[106] This misunderstanding led to confusion in the confessional and in life more generally. But, as Serge Gruzinski has noted, this confusion could have led to a position in which the Mesoamericans were able to hold onto a certain amount of power in the face of the onslaught of European ideologies.[107] The power of self-definition would have been an important, if fleeting, sense of empowerment. For, by the end of the colonial period, the Mesoamerican sense of self had changed to such a degree that misunderstandings of this type would occur significantly less often.[108] Late colonial confessional manuals were quite specific in this regard: "Have you sinned with a man thinking that you were with a woman?"[109] Such a concept of sin clearly connected with European thought of the time.

To understand the relationship between these changes in self-identity and Maya notions of homosexual desire, one needs to focus on changes in Maya concepts of ethnicity. Ethnic identity at the time of the conquest was based on several levels of identification: the local city-state, the lineage,[110] and the notion of broad differences between the Itzá and the Xiu. The historical texts extensively discussed the differences between the Itzá and the Xiu.[111] The Itzá most often were considered the despised outsiders, those of a different ethnic group, heavily influenced by central Mexico.[112] Parts of the *Books of Chilam Balam* were diatribes against the Itzá. The ethnic differentiation between the Itzá, the outsiders, and the insiders, the Xiu, was established carefully here.

A central role was reserved for sexual insults against the Itzá. In one case the Itzá were said to have stolen the anuses of children and committed sodomy with them.[113] In other cases homosexual sodomy, divided into active and passive roles, was used to assert the difference between the perceived Maya "self" and the "other," seen as someone with a Nahuatl name, thus influenced by central Mexico, and likely of Itzá descent. A certain preconquest era was said to have ended because of the misdeeds of two lords, *kak u pacal* and *tecuilu*.[114] *Kak u pacal* translated as "fiery glance." *Tecuilu* came from the Nahuatl *tecuilonti*, meaning "the active partner in the act of sodomy."[115] The insults treated these lords as inferior leaders who destroyed the society. The active partner in the act of sodomy was given a name from Nahuatl, perhaps signifying his role as an outsider and a conqueror from or influenced by central Mexico. This use of the outsider/insider dichotomy was a Maya tradition that invoked a particular sexual ideology related closely to the concept of sexual contamination: the idea that foreigners brought sodomy and other sexual acts considered illegitimate.[116] While it may seem that this was an early phenomenon, the sections that contain this information probably were written in the eighteenth century. At that time, ethnicity clearly was structured differently, and it was based on the local community.[117] In that situation the Maya writers still remembered the Itzá/Xiu distinction.

I argue that the Maya remembered these divisions because of the hybridity that was developed by the late colonial years. The mixture of Spanish and Maya ideas had created a hybrid structure that, within Spanish hegemony, developed a distinctly Yucatecan mixture. In that mixture, Maya people attempted to relate traditional creation rituals and notions of time with the Christian calendar and the concept that God created the world.[118] Yet the fundamentally different ideas of the power of the gods and of time were forced to bend to the will of Spanish hegemony. So the Maya could not view themselves as the descendants of the gods. Of course they could continue to do so in private, but the hegemonic culture and structures opposed these ideas. Yet the hybrid tradition allowed the Maya to maintain concepts that were similar to European ideas. One of these ideas was the relationship between sexual desire and warfare. Europeans and Mayas viewed conquest as a struggle to feminize the enemy. Yet the Maya did not appear to believe in the European idea of contamination. Homosexual sodomy was seen as part of the culture, not as a foreign imposition. As has been shown, the Spanish changed this view.

For the Maya at the time of the conquest, the difference between the active and the passive partner was central. The active partner was viewed symbolically as a paragon of masculinity: he was the conqueror, the winner in warfare. While he could be denigrated if he came from a hated group, his masculinity was affirmed by his conquest. When the discourse was related specifically to warfare, the evidence of a hierarchical active/passive dichotomy was very strong. A Chontal Maya town is named *Cuylonemiquia*, "the killing of the passive partner in sodomy."[119] Here space was used as a marker of sodomy, as well as a marker of war.[120] The active partner was the unnamed person who defeated the passive, Nahuatl-speaking group. In warfare the difference between the active and the passive sodomite was tantamount to the difference between the winner and the loser. Thus, in the above case, *Tecuilu* was the winner, the conqueror, the Itzá. The Chontal Maya town was perceived (at least symbolically) as the place where the Itzá were defeated.

Sexual insult, in both metaphorical and non-metaphorical language, was an important part of the *Books of Chilam Balam*. As I have shown elsewhere, the flower was a metaphor that represented the active/passive dichotomy. It symbolized warfare and bloodletting as well as sexual desire: any type of penetration could be part of the metaphor.[121] The flower in one text mentioned above symbolized the sexual acts that were performed ritually between the Spaniards and the backsides of the Maya. The flowers were presented as an important ritual element in an Itzá leader's name (his last name was Xochitl, Nahuatl for flower) and in the Maya text. The younger brothers lost their hearts and their spirits to their older brothers (the Spaniards), who then killed their flowers by symbolically engaging in anal intercourse with them.[122] The Maya fighters were defeated and sodomized: they were feminized effectively in a discourse that masculinized the winning warriors, the Spaniards. Sexual insults, often related to sodomy, presented and supported the theme of social death and destruction. The power mandated in these texts stipulated that control over one's sexual desires allowed one to be victorious. Those desires were required to be used in an active (and thus male) way rather than a passive (and thus female) way. The active partner was going to be the winner. So the difference between this concept and the Spanish idea of warfare was not great. The Spaniards also believed conquest to be associated symbolically with sexual acts. But the further association with sexual contamination was an idea that was new to the Maya during the colonial years.

The earlier and more archaic discourses regarding the rape of gods and the political concept of pederasty disappeared in later years. By the eighteenth century, the discourse that emerged was based on the idea that sodomy was sinful and that outsiders would contaminate the community.[123] Thus, by the eighteenth century, although some similarities with preconquest sexual ideas remained, the changes were pronounced.

MALE HOMOSEXUALITY, DESIRE, AND POWER

Spanish hegemony and hybridity led to some significant changes in late colonial Maya treatments of homosexual desire. This is not to say that the Maya during the preconquest era treated such desire and behavior as a positive or even acceptable thing. On the contrary, the vast similarities between Maya and Spanish notions of homosexual desire allowed for the hybrid creations. Nonetheless, a series of differences, related to different constructs of masculinity, desire, and power, emerged in the documents.

First, Spanish conquest ideology related contamination and developmental discourses of sodomy. In the contamination discourse, Spaniards associated sodomy with the "other" who, through infiltration, pushed the "self" into sodomitical acts. The developmental discourse argued that the least civilized societies had extensive sodomy, but that civilization destroyed such activity.[124] The documents contain little information about a Maya discourse of contamination, as such a discourse was not central to Maya conquest ideology. There was no discourse related to developmental theories of sodomy.

Maya conquest discourse, however, was centered around a portrayal of masculinity and power through the symbolic penetration of the defeated warriors by the victorious. Thus, when the Spanish conquered them, the Maya saw their own warriors as cowardly men who were sodomized and feminized by the Spaniards. This sense of masculinity, of course, also played a role in Spanish ideas. However, for the Maya, such a sense of masculine roles went far beyond what the Spaniards believed. Maya men were seen as the penetrators to such a degree that sacrifice was seen as a sign of masculinity. The sacrifice of another person or an animal showed that one was masculine. The sacrifice of one's own blood showed that the warrior was willing to be the feminine partner to the masculine gods, and at the same time assert his own masculine power.[125] The key was the element of penetration: this allowed the Maya men to declare their masculinity and their power.

In religion the Spaniards did not perceive any role for sodomy. The Maya, however, forcibly sodomized their gods in order to masculinize themselves and gain power from the gods. This, for the Maya, represented both the need for the shaman to have power in order for the world to survive, and the unpredictability of that power because of the harshness of the cosmos.

In noble politics, the Spaniards did not believe that pederastic relationships could teach aspiring nobles anything. They did know of other societies (various Arab societies, ancient Greece) which engaged in such relationships, but they considered these to be sinful. The Maya found such relationships, or at least the symbolism of them, to be important to the development of noble male youth.

Finally, regarding ritualized gender transformation, the Spaniards had no accepted role for such a structure. The Maya developed a concept which I have analyzed as the floating phallus. This allowed for the Maya to ritualize a metaphorical completeness, particularly in the penis-piercing ceremony. It also allowed them to use the concept of transsexualization in order to suggest desire and gain power.

By the eighteenth century, the Maya had been transformed. Sodomy was seen as sinful, and a discourse on sin was used in many Maya documents. The political and religious roles for forced sodomy and rape were no longer validated except in documents seen as archaic. Conquest and warfare were no longer factors in daily life. These factors show that Spanish hegemony had changed the power structures and the understandings of desire in Maya communities. But the Maya maintained some traditions. Underground rituals that were suggestive of transsexualization and rape continued to be practiced. More important, the discourse on sodomy had become a hybrid discourse.

While the Maya documents stressed sin, they also discussed the relationship between penetration and conquest. The hybridity meant that power relationships had changed. The ways in which they developed mental pictures of the world had changed, so the frameworks for understanding sexual desire necessarily changed. But the changes were based not simply upon Spanish hegemony, but on a much more complex interaction: the development of the hybrid phallus. It was this hybrid tradition that carried Maya culture forward past the colonial period and into the present day.

NOTES

1. See particularly Weeks, *Coming Out;* Foucault, *The History of Sexuality* (vol. 1); Halperin, *Saint Foucault.*

2. On hegemony, see Gramsci, *Prison Notebooks;* Stern, *Peru's Indian Peoples;* Kellogg, *Law and the Transformation of Aztec Culture.* For the purpose of this chapter, I have defined *hegemony* as "the power to assert discourses and create institutions which dominate the cultural sphere of any particular region."

3. See Burkhart, *Slippery Earth;* Sigal, *Moon Goddesses.*

4. Carrasco, *Inquisición y represión;* Perry, *Gender and Disorder;* Trexler, *Sex and Conquest;* Garza Carvajal, *Vir.*

5. Trexler, *Sex and Conquest,* 47–52. Note that Christianity's official condemnation of sodomitic activity contrasted with the notion of sodomy in popular culture. For official Christianity, the instigator (the "active" partner) was the primary person to blame for the act. In popular culture, the concept of "femininity" in a man was condemned, and the "passive" partner was considered the "feminine" one. This contradiction was played out in the courts of fifteenth- and sixteenth-century Italy and Spain, where, while the passive partner was condemned strongly, the active partner received more severe punishment; see Rocke, *Forbidden Friendships.*

6. The term *Christian* is used here as it was in early modern Spain. It refers to Catholics.

7. See Boswell, *Christianity, Social Tolerance, and Homosexuality.* The Church before the twelfth century does not appear to have condemned sodomy in the same manner, and the interpretation of the Sodom and Gomorra story certainly changed through time.

8. See Lavrin, *Sexuality and Marriage in Colonial Latin America.*

9. See Perry, *Gender and Disorder,* 123–27; Trexler, *Sex and Conquest,* 55–60. On Italian law, see Rocke, *Forbidden Friendships.*

10. Trexler, *Sex and Conquest,* 55–60. As Trexler readily admits, more research in the Spanish criminal archives is necessary.

11. See Gruzinski, "Las cenizas del deseo," and chap. 7 in this volume.

12. Carrasco, *Inquisición y represión;* Trexler, *Sex and Conquest,* 43–60.

13. Carrasco, *Inquisición y represión,* 166–220.

14. Ibid., 107–30.

15. See López Austin, *Cuerpo humano e ideología,* 2: 274. Note that López Austin translates the word *cuiloni* as "sodomite." Fray Alonso de Molina, the author of the most accurate and complete early colonial Nahuatl-Spanish dictionary, does not translate the word, but he does translate *cuilonitia* as "cometer pecado nefando." *Cuilonyotl* is translated as "pecado nefando, de hombre con hombre" (Molina, *Vocabulario,* part 2, 17). The *-tia* on the end of the first version is an agentive. The active partner is, as Molina says elsewhere (93; "el que lo haze a otro, pecando contra natura"), *tecuilonti. Cuiloni* is used in other cases to emphasize the role of the passive. Note also that the translation of *cuilonyotl* suggests, unlike the Spanish terminology, a linguistic differentiation between male/male and other types of sodomy. Of course, this could be an incorrect gloss by the friar. The quotation comes from Sahagún, *Florentine Codex,* 37–38. The

Nahuatl is "cuiloni, chimouhqui, cuitzotl itlacauhqui, tlahelli, tlahelchichi, tlahelpul, tla-camiqui, teupoliuhqui auilli, camanalli, netopeoalli, tequalani, tetlahelti, teuiqueh, teiacapitz-tlahelti, cioaciuhqui, mocioanenequini, tlatiloni, tlatlani, chichinoloni, tlatla, chichinolo, cih-cioatlatoa, mocioanenequi."

16. See Klor de Alva, Nicholson, and Quiñones Keber, *The Works of Benardino de Sahagún*.

17. See Trexler, chap. 2 in this volume.

18. Trexler, *Sex and Conquest*, 131–33.

19. Some historical/religious oral texts that recalled the Toltecs of central Mexico suggested this. Brasseur de Bourbourg, *Histoire des nations civilisées*, 2: 67, 77, 173. Cited in Bleys, *Geography of Perversion*, 122.

20. I, of course, do not mean to suggest that the Maya of the colonial period are writing an accurate account of preconquest Maya views.

21. Gordon, *Book of Chilam Balam of Chumayel*, 106–7. All references to the *Book of Chilam Balam of Chumayel* (hereafter, *CBC*) are to the facsimile in this edition. All quotations also are cross-referenced to the Roys and Edmonson (*Heaven Born Mérida and Its Destiny*) editions; Fontes Rerum Mexicanarum, *El Libro de Chilam Balam de Tizimín Reproducción*, 9v. All references to the *Book of Chilam Balam of Tizimín* (hereafter, *CBTi*) are to the facsimile in this edition. Also see Edmonson, *Ancient Future*.

22. *CBC*, 79; *CBTi*, 6r.

23. De la Garza, *Relaciones Histórico-geográficas*, 1: 165.

24. Díaz del Castillo, *Historia verdadera*, 7–8. See Sigal, "Politicization of Pederasty."

25. Farriss, *Maya Society*, 287–93.

26. See Restall, *Maya World*, 170–73.

27. Rugeley, *Yucatán's Maya Peasantry*.

28. See Lockhart, "Encomienda and Hacienda"; Patch, *Maya and Spaniard*.

29. See Hunt, "Colonial Yucatan"; Restall, *Maya World*.

30. Restall, *Maya World*, 148–65.

31. Ricard, *Spiritual Conquest of Mexico*.

32. Gibson, *Tlaxcala; Aztecs*; Farriss, *Maya Society*; Lockhart, *Nahuas after the Conquest*.

33. For similar analyses that go beyond the change vs. tradition paradigm, see Farriss, *Maya Society*; Gruzinski, *Man-Gods*, and *Conquest of Mexico*; Kellogg, *Law and the Transformation of Aztec Culture*.

34. Fondo de Cultura Económica, *Códice de Dresde*.

35. See Sigal, *Moon Goddesses*, 130–42.

36. For linguistic evidence of this, see Sigal, *Moon Goddesses*, 138–39.

37. I first proffered this analysis of the pederastic political rituals in an earlier article ("The Politicization of Pederasty").

38. See, for example, *CBC*, 36; *The Book of Chilam Balam of Tusik* (hereafter, *CBTu*, a photographic copy of which is located in the University of Washington Archives), 17r–17v; Roys, *Book of Chilam Balam*, 94; Edmonson, *Heaven Born Mérida*, 168–169.

39. Solís Alcalá, *Diccionario Español-Maya*, 151 and 365, translates *zuyua* as "confusion," or "figurative language."

40. Roys, *Book of Chilam Balam*, 98; Edmonson, *Heaven Born Mérida*, 168.

41. The *Books of Chilam Balam* gave great importance to the shadowy presence of the *halach uinic* ("dignitary, leading person, true person"), often simply translated as "governor." *Batab* ("governor") was a far more common term in the colonial documents, clearly speaking of the leader of a local community. Nancy Farriss and Philip Thompson both argue that the *halach uinic* was some sort of regional ruler. Matthew Restall states that the *halach uinic* was probably a *batab* of a powerful community (Thompson, "Tekanto in the Eighteenth Century"; Farriss, *Maya Society*, 148–51; Restall, *Maya World*, 61–83). Restall's evidence and my own have shown that the *halach uinic* most often was a member of a very powerful lineage in a particular region (Sigal, "Politicization of Pederasty"; Restall, *Maya World*, 61–83; *CBC*, 87). It is likely that the

halach uinic, through intermarriage, established several dependent communities. As in central Mexico, Yucatan appears to have been headed toward amalgamation at the time of the conquest (see Lockhart, *Nahuas after the Conquest,* 20–28; Restall, *Maya World,* 13–19).

42. Girls did not face the same testing, for they did not play a direct role in the political hierarchy.

43. *Kik* is "blood"; *kikel* is "semen."

44. Contemporary informants, while they have some knowledge of the "language of Zuyua," claim to have no direct knowledge of the relationship of semen and blood to the rituals. Perhaps this is something that they would not share with an outside observer, but more likely it is an element that has been lost through the centuries of Christianization.

45. See Sigal, *Moon Goddesses,* 150–82.

46. For an explanation of the idea of a phallic signifying economy, see Lacan, *Feminine Sexuality,* 74–85.

47. Similar ceremonies in the *Ritual of the Bacabs* showed blood and semen as representative of the phallus. While blood could have been gendered female, and often was gendered as such, in these ceremonies blood emanated from the penis and allowed for a connection between men and the gods. See Sigal, *Moon Goddesses,* 161–73.

48. On warfare, see Sigal, *Moon Goddesses,* 130–41.

49. See Dover, *Greek Homosexuality;* Foucault, *The History of Sexuality* (vol. 2).

50. See Herdt, *Guardians of the Flutes,* 255–94.

51. From *ex,* which, although it appears in colonial-era documents, is only translated in modern dictionaries. This term developed into "trousers" in the postconquest era. See Barrera Vásquez, *Diccionario Maya* (hereafter, *DM*), 921. Roys translated the term as a preconquest notion, "loin-cloth" (Roys, *Book of Chilam Balam,* 94).

52. *CBC,* 36; Roys, *Book of Chilam Balam,* 94; Edmonson, *Heaven Born Mérida,* 183–84: "mehene xen cha ten a uex yn uui u booc uaye y nach u booc ce u booc yn uexe . . . u booc yn yubake pay num u boc . . . tu ɔu muyal le . . . ua halach uinice chi be yume bin yn tales cij u than hex u boc yex lic u katice u pay num u booc tu ɔu caane lay pome thabbil elil u cah hex yax pakab chi lic u katice lay muxbil cacau cho u uae."

53. See Keuls, *Reign of the Phallus,* 275.

54. The younger male had power, as the smell from his pants created pleasure for the elder male. The younger male gained power by having some limited control over the decision of whether or not to provide his own body for the elder male's pleasure, much as men and women gained some power through control over their bodies and sexual desires. For examples, see Silverblatt, *Moon, Sun, and Witches;* and Behar, "Sexual Witchcraft."

55. See Burns, "Language of Zuyua."

56. Roys states that the name could mean "hollow stiff tortoise shell" (Roys, *Book of Chilam Balam,* 96). One can see the potential meaning of the metaphor. Edmonson (*Heaven Born Mérida,* 187) translates it as I do.

57. *Armadillo* is repeated with two different terms. Edmonson translates the second term as "armadillo meat." Roys translates it, using the *yx,* as "female armadillo" (*CBC,* 38); see Roys, *Book of Chilam Balam,* 96; Edmonson, *Heaven Born Mérida,* 187: "mehene ca a tales ten hun tul noh xib lay ma kalan u botonil u ha bone hom tochac u kabae cay bacac be yume hex lic u katice lay ybache yx ueche."

58. Lacan, *Feminine Sexuality,* 85.

59. *CBC,* 79, 105–7; *CBTi,* 6r, 9v; Scholes and Roys, *Maya Chontal Indians,* 91.

60. *CBC,* 107.

61. *CBC,* 105–7.

62. Trexler (*Sex and Conquest,* 81), looking at this same passage, asserted that the Maya "showed their rear ends" to the Spanish conquerors. While the implication is correct, Trexler was relying on an older translation.

63. The analysis here obviously owes a lot to Trexler (both *Sex and Conquest* and chap. 2 in

this volume). I've known Richard Trexler since I participated with him on a panel in 1992, and I wish to thank him here for aiding me in my analysis of these relationships.

64. See Clendinnen, *Ambivalent Conquests;* Sigal, *Moon Goddesses.* Also see, on the similar situation related to the Nahuas, Hassig, *Aztec Warfare;* Gruzinski, *Man-Gods,* and *Conquest of Mexico;* Clendinnen, *Aztecs.* On the Andeans, who had some similarities, but who do not appear to have seen the cosmos as so ruthless, see MacCormack, *Religion in the Andes.*

65. From ɔam *chektahech,* I have derived "submerge" ("penetrate"). The whole phrase was translated as such in the colonial dictionaries. What's more, both ɔam and *chek* had sexual connotations: ɔam was connected with the idea of impregnating someone, while *chek* was a word describing sexual intercourse. Apparently there is some type of metaphor at work here, related to the submersion of the penis into any sort of receptacle.

66. Arzápalo Marín translated "tu ca cobol a na tu ca cobol a yum" (which Roys and I have translated as "the genitals of your mother and the genitals of your father") as "into the prostitute of your mother, into the whore of your father." He is interpreting genitals as a metaphor for prostitution.

67. Manuscript of *El ritual de los Bacabes,* hereafter abbreviated *RB,* 122 (from the photographic copy at the end of Arzápalo‑Marín's text); Roys, *Ritual of the Bacabs,* 42; Arzápalo Marín, *El ritual de los Bacabes,* 357–58: "tin can xot cuntah tin can max cuntah u col chab u cool akab ma uen ci ma coy la ci uinicil tun uinicil te tumenel tin chim tex tah lah tex tu cal ual tu cal xol cex can tul ti ku cex can tul ti bacabe ɔam tun yn uayasba ca tin ɔam chektahech tu ca cobol a na tu ca cobol a yum cech u cool ale u cool mehene Amen."

68. This was true for many of the texts of the *Ritual of the Bacabs.* For examples, see *RB,* 7, 8, 28, 45, 116, 120.

69. See Archivo General de la Nación, Mexico City (*Inquisición*), 1187, 2, 6–161.

70. *DM,* part 1, 88–89, 324, 876.

71. See Sigal, *Moon Goddesses,* 150–73.

72. Lacan, *Écrits,* 1–8; Butler, *Bodies That Matter.*

73. The four *bacabs* themselves represented the world. See Morley, Brainerd, and Sharer, *Ancient Maya,* 465–66.

74. This idea was reiterated many times in writings related to the epidemics after the conquest. See De la Garza, *Relaciones Histórico-geográficas.*

75. See Sigal, *Moon Goddesses,* 58–59; *CBC,* 3.

76. *DM,* 678–79.

77. See Williams, *The Spirit and the Flesh;* Roscoe, *Living the Spirit, The Zuni Man-Woman,* "How to Become a Berdache," and *Changing Ones;* Gutiérrez, "Must We Deracinate Indians to Find Gay Roots?"; Trexler, *Sex and Conquest,* and chap. 2 in this volume; Horswell, chap. 1 in this volume.

78. The female to male "berdache," a less observed figure, had some similar and some different roles; see Whitehead, "The Bow and the Burden Strap"; Blackwood, "Sexuality and Gender."

79. There are hints of such a role in the Spanish sources, but no information in indigenous or Spanish-language documents over which the Maya had some influence (although see Williams, *The Spirit and the Flesh,* 142–47). Walter Williams went to Yucatan and placed a chapter on the Maya in his book, which was about the *berdache* in Native American societies in the area now known as the United States. Williams failed to consider possible differences between the Maya, a long-established sedentary society which had, from late preclassic to early postclassic times, developed significant urban areas, and the primarily nonsedentary societies (with no settled populations, much less urban areas) that made up the bulk of his research. Moreover, Williams took his experiences, which can best be described as very abbreviated field work encounters with members of two Maya communities, and applied these experiences to what he perceived as Maya history from before the Spanish conquest. Williams makes a series of arguments regarding both early modern Spain (132–40) and Yucatan of the same period (136,

140, 142–43) which can be understood only in the context of a historical analysis of gender, desire, and power. For example, Williams declares that he can find some elements of contemporary Maya society that remain unchanged from preconquest times. His evidence is based on a perceived lack of homophobia in these societies. He fails to consider the fact that the Maya of Yucatan and Chiapas engage in a great amount of sexual "joking" in everyday conversations (Bricker, *Ritual Humor;* Burns, *An Epoch of Miracles;* Hanks, *Referential Practice*). Moreover, the homosexual identities that Williams claims to find suggest just the opposite of his analysis. He finds a hairdresser (147) who is known to be, and accepted as, gay. He finds another effeminate man (145–47) who also is accepted as gay. Male hairdressers in the United States often are stereotyped as gay and accepted as such. Effeminate men in both Mexico and the United States often are considered gay. The argument that these two figures are accepted in the Maya societies suggests a very positive attitude. As admirable as these values are, they also are thoroughly modern and betray significant Western influence.

80. While the *ix pen* (literally, "she, the fornicator," this word was translated in the colonial dictionaries as "sodomite") could conceivably have represented a berdache-type figure, this word does not appear in any of the documents other than colonial dictionaries. While its existence in these dictionaries certainly suggests that there was some sort of role and word for an "effeminate" male, this does not tell us anything more about identity or values.

81. See Butler, *Bodies That Matter,* for her analysis of the "lesbian phallus," a privileged sign that may be attached to the lesbian body. Note here that I am not saying that the phallus itself is or ever was attached to any *body*. The phallus was a part of the shaman's power and a part of the power of the parental deities. It was in some way attached to their identities, but not necessarily to their bodies.

82. One thinks of the unaltered, intersexed/hermaphroditic individual raping a man, but the text is too unclear to assume this to be the case.

83. Oedipal colonization here refers to the historical sense of an Oedipus complex theorized by Freud and amplified by Lacan. The Spanish may or may not have been affected by this concept, and they may or may not have brought it over from Europe. See Butler, *Bodies That Matter.*

84. See Garber, *Vested Interests,* 93–117.

85. See Bornstein, *Gender Outlaw.*

86. See Butler, *Gender Trouble* and *Bodies That Matter.*

87. See Clendinnen "Yucatec Maya Women and the Spanish Conquest"; Sigal, *Moon Goddesses.*

88. Lacan, *Feminine Sexuality,* 74–85.

89. *Siyan* is interpreted as *sian,* "enchantment." While *siyan* itself could have meant "story," the texts which used this term all suggested some sort of enchantment. Here the curer attempted to enchant the spider. One could easily use the other translation, "Words of the story of spiders."

90. Pun on *yamtunil,* from *amtun,* meaning "garden." It also could have meant "spider of stone."

91. The phrase *a uach,* "your penis," was used throughout these texts as a double entendre. In a different context, *ach,* "penis," could also have meant "sting." Roys (*Ritual of the Bacabs,* 53) translates it as such.

92. "Ugliness" is from *kas,* written here as *ka.* Roys (*Ritual of the Bacabs,* 159) translates the term as "gall" or "bitterness." Arzápalo Marín (*El ritual de los Bacabes,* 384) does not translate the term.

93. Arzápalo Marín (*El ritual de los Bacabes,* 384) interprets this section differently. To him, the shaman was attempting to decipher the signs.

94. *RB,* 157–60; Roys, *Ritual of the Bacabs,* 53–54; Arzápalo Marín, *El ritual de los Bacabes,* 383–85: "u thanil u siyan am lae hunil am cabil am oxil am canil am yax am te yax am tun ox kin bayanech tu chemil u cab ah uuc ti cab tij tun bacin a chah u cabil a pach can kin yanech yalan u

yamtunil u mukay a chich ti suhuy ix chacal ix chel sacal ix chel u uayasba u pach yax am te yax am tun he tun bacin u suhuy puɔ tun bacin suhuy ix chel sacal ix chel chacal ix chel la bacin u uayasba a uachoxlahun uol u bon kuch suhuy ix chel chacal yx chel sacal yx chel la tun bacin u uayasba a ka sam tun bacin yn colob sam tun bacin yn lukes sam tun bacin yn chochob fel u na ta uach cech yax am te yax am tuncan heb tun bacin yn ekel nok la tun bacin tin ɔuɔci he tun bacin canlahhun ꝑul tun bacin yn battil ha oxlahun ꝑul yn sissala la tun bacin tin siscunci u kinam yax am te yax am tun am am am am Amen."

95. See Hanks, *Referential Practice,* 121–22.

96. Ibid., 110–12; Restall, *Maya World,* 124–30.

97. The "needle" was the sting-ray spine.

98. Note that the Maya also make fun of Christianity by appearing (through repetition) to stutter. After all, the *am,* "spider," is not that different from the sacred term, "amen." Maybe the narrative takes as its ritual strategy an attempt to make fun of Christianity.

99. No doubt the visions were brought on by the pain and the loss of blood. Noble women pierced their tongues. See Schele and Freidel, *Forest of Kings;* Sigal, *Moon Goddesses,* 152–56.

100. See Sigal, *Moon Goddesses,* 161–73.

101. Ibid., 94–128.

102. On the free-floating phallus and the phallus as a sign, see Lacan, *Feminine Sexuality,* 83. On the "lesbian" phallus, see Butler, *Bodies That Matter,* 72–88.

103. See Farriss, *Maya Society.* On the similar situation for the Mexica of Tenochtitlan, see Kellogg, *Law and the Transformation of Aztec Culture.*

104. Burkhart, *Slippery Earth;* Gruzinski, *Man-Gods;* León-Portilla, *Aztec Image.*

105. See López Austin, *Cuerpo humano e ideología;* Burkhart, *Slippery Earth;* Gruzinski, "Individualization and Acculturation," and *Conquest of Mexico;* Clendinnen, *Ambivalent Conquests;* Sigal, *Moon Goddesses.*

106. Burkhart, *Slippery Earth;* Gruzinski, *Man-Gods.* For some specific Maya examples, see Sigal, *Moon Goddesses,* 58–61, 220–21.

107. Gruzinski, "Individualization and Acculturation."

108. Gruzinski, *Man-Gods,* and "Individualization and Acculturation"; Klor de Alva, "Nahua Colonial Discourse"; Sigal, *Moon Goddesses.*

109. "ɔocan va a kebanchahal yetel uinic tan a tuclic y chuplal yanech?" From *Modo de confesar en lengua Maya Tixcacal Cupul,* ms., photographic reproduction located in the Tozzer library, 1803, 247; University of Pennsylvania Library, bound as last part of *Colección de Platicas Doctrinales y Sermones en Lengua Maya* (by various authors, copied in Mérida, 1868).

110. Restall, *Maya World,* 13–19.

111. See Munro Edmonson's explanation in *Ancient Future,* xvi–xx.

112. Coe, *Maya,* 144.

113. *CBTi,* 6r.

114. *CBC,* 79.

115. Fray Alonso de Molina translated *tecuilonti* as the active partner in sodomy. The passive partner was translated as *cuiloni* (Molina, *Vocabulario,* part 2, 16, 93).

116. For information on the way that Europeans used this tradition, see Bleys, *Geography of Perversion;* Trexler, *Sex and Conquest.*

117. See Restall, *Maya World.*

118. There are many examples of this. For a particularly poignant one, see *CBC,* 60–63.

119. Scholes and Roys, *Maya Chontal Indians,* 91.

120. Trexler, *Sex and Conquest,* 74.

121. See Sigal, *Moon Goddesses,* 49–52.

122. *CBC,* 106. The nahuatl *xochitl* translates as "flower." On the flower as a metaphor for sexual desire and warfare, see Hassig, *Aztec Warfare;* León-Portilla, *Aztec Image;* Sigal, *Moon Goddesses,* 49–52.

123. On sin and sexual activity, see Archivo General de la Nación, Mexico City (*Inquisición*), 1187, 2, 6–161; Cogolludo, *Historia de Yucatán*, 1: 331–35; *Documents of Tabi*, located in the rare manuscript room of Tulane University's Latin American Library, 33.

124. See Bleys, *Geography of Perversion*.

125. Sigal, *Moon Goddesses*, 130–41.

WORKS CITED

Arzápalo Marín, Ramón. *El ritual de los Bacabes*. Mexico: Universidad Nacional Autónoma de México, 1987.

Barrera Vásquez, Alfredo, et al. *Diccionario Maya*. 2d ed. Mexico: Editorial Porrúa, 1991.

Behar, Ruth. "Sexual Witchcraft, Colonialism, and Women's Powers: Views from the Mexican Inquisition." In *Sexuality and Marriage in Colonial Latin America*, ed. Asunción Lavrin. Lincoln: University of Nebraska Press, 1989.

Blackwood, Evelyn. "Sexuality and Gender in Certain Native American Tribes: The Case of Cross-Gender Females." *Signs* 10 (1984): 27–42.

Bleys, Rudi C. *The Geography of Perversion: Male-to-Male Sexual Behavior outside the West and the Ethnographic Imagination, 1750–1918*. New York: New York University Press, 1995.

Bornstein, Kate. *Gender Outlaw: On Men, Women, and the Rest of Us*. New York: Routledge, 1994.

Boswell, John. *Christianity, Social Tolerance, and Homosexuality: Gay People in Western Europe from the Beginning of the Christian Era to the Fourteenth Century*. Chicago: University of Chicago Press, 1980.

Brasseur de Bourbourg, Charles Etienne. *Histoire des nations civilisées du Mexique et de l'Amerique-Centrale durant les siècles antérieurs à Christophe Colomb*. 4 vols. Paris: A. Bertrand, 1857–59.

Bricker, Victoria. *Ritual Humor in Highland Chiapas*. Austin: University of Texas Press, 1973.

Burkhart, Louise M. *The Slippery Earth: Nahua-Christian Moral Dialogue in Sixteenth-Century Mexico*. Tucson: University of Arizona Press, 1989.

Burns, Allan. *An Epoch of Miracles*. Austin: University of Texas Press, 1983.

———. "The Language of Zuyua: Yucatec Maya Riddles and their Interpretation." In *Past, Present and Future: Selected Papers on Latin American Indian Literatures*, ed. Mary H. Preuss. Culver City, CA: Labyrinthos, 1991.

Butler, Judith. *Bodies That Matter: On the Discursive Limits of "Sex."* New York: Routledge, 1993.

———. *Gender Trouble: Feminism and the Subversion of Identity*. New York: Routledge, 1990.

Carrasco, Rafael. *Inquisición y represión sexual en Valencia: Historia de los sodomitas (1565–1785)*. Barcelona: Laertes, 1985.

Clendinnen, Inga. *Ambivalent Conquests: Maya and Spaniard in Yucatan, 1517–1570*. Cambridge: Cambridge University Press, 1987.

———. *Aztecs: An Interpretation*. Cambridge: Cambridge University Press, 1991.

———. "Yucatec Maya Women and the Spanish Conquest: Role and Ritual in Historical Reconstruction." *Journal of Social History* 15, no. 3 (1982): 427–42.

Coe, Michael D. *The Maya*. London: Thames and Hudson, 1987.

Cogolludo, Diego López de. *Historia de Yucatán*. 3 vols. Campeche: Comisión de Historia, 1954.

De la Garza, Mercedes, et al., eds. *Relaciones Histórico-geográficas de la Gobernación de Yucatán*. 2 vols. Mexico: Universidad Nacional Autónoma de México, 1983.

Díaz del Castillo, Bernal. *Historia verdadera de la conquista de Nueva España*. Madrid: Quinto Centenario, 1989.

Dover, K. J. *Greek Homosexuality*. New York: Vintage Books, 1978.

Edmonson, Munro. *The Ancient Future of the Itza: The Book of Chilam Balam of Tizimín*. Austin: University of Texas Press, 1982.

————. *Heaven Born Mérida and Its Destiny: The Book of Chilam Balam of Chumayel.* Austin: University of Texas Press, 1986.

Farriss, Nancy M. *Maya Society under Colonial Rule: The Collective Enterprise of Survival.* Princeton, NJ: Princeton University Press, 1984.

Fondo de Cultura Económica. *Códice de Dresde.* Mexico City: Medio Siglo, 1983.

Fontes Rerum Mexicanarum. *El Libro de Chilam Balam de Tizimín Reproducción.* Graz, Austria: Akademische Druck, 1980.

Foucault, Michel. *The History of Sexuality.* Vol. 1. *An Introduction.* New York: Vintage Books, 1978.

————. *The History of Sexuality.* Vol. 2. *The Use of Pleasure.* New York: Vintage Books, 1985.

Garber, Marjorie. *Vested Interests: Cross-Dressing and Cultural Anxiety.* New York: Harper, 1992.

Garza Carvajal, Federico. *Vir: Conceptions of Manliness in Andalucía and México, 1561–1699.* Amsterdam: Amsterdamse Historische Reeks, 2000.

Gibson, Charles. *The Aztecs under Spanish Rule.* Stanford, CA: Stanford University Press, 1964.

————. *Tlaxcala in the Sixteenth Century.* New Haven, CT: Yale University Press, 1952.

Gordon, G. B., ed. *The Book of Chilam Balam of Chumayel.* Philadelphia: University of Pennsylvania Museum, 1913.

Gramsci, Antonio. *Selections from the Prison Notebooks.* New York: International Publishers, 1971.

Gruzinski, Serge. "Las cenizas del deseo: Homosexuales novohispanos a mediados del siglo XVII." In *De la santidad a la perversión o de la porqué no se cumplía la ley de Dios en la sociedad Novohispana,* ed. Sergio Ortega. Mexico City: Editorial Grijalbo, 1985.

————. *The Conquest of Mexico: The Incorporation of Indian Societies into the Western World, Sixteenth–Eighteenth Centuries.* Cambridge, U.K.: Polity Press, 1993.

————. "Individualization and Acculturation." In *Sexuality and Marriage in Colonial Latin America,* ed. Asunción Lavrin. Lincoln: University of Nebraska Press, 1989.

————. *Man-Gods in the Mexican Highlands: Sixteenth–Eighteenth Centuries.* Stanford, CA: Stanford University Press, 1989.

Gutiérrez, Ramón A. "Must We Deracinate Indians to Find Gay Roots?" *Out/Look* 1 (1989): 61–67.

————. *When Jesus Came, the Corn Mothers Went Away: Marriage, Sexuality, and Power in New Mexico, 1500–1846.* Stanford, CA: Stanford University Press, 1991.

Halperin, David M. *Saint Foucault: Towards a Gay Hagiography.* New York: Oxford University Press, 1995.

Hanks, William F. *Referential Practice: Language and Lived Space among the Maya.* Chicago: University of Chicago Press, 1990.

Hassig, Ross. *Aztec Warfare: Imperial Expansion and Political Control.* Norman: University of Oklahoma Press, 1988.

Herdt, Gilbert. *Guardians of the Flutes: Idioms of Masculinity.* New York: McGraw-Hill, 1981.

Hunt, Marta. "Colonial Yucatan: Town and Region in the Seventeenth Century." Ph.D. diss. University of California–Los Angeles, 1974.

Kellogg, Susan. *Law and the Transformation of Aztec Culture, 1500–1700.* Norman: University of Oklahoma Press, 1995.

Keuls, Eva C. *The Reign of the Phallus: Sexual Politics in Ancient Athens.* Berkeley and Los Angeles: University of California Press, 1985.

Klor de Alva, J. Jorge. "Nahua Colonial Discourse and the Appropriation of the (European) Other." *Archives de Sciences Sociales des Religions* 77 (1992): 15–35.

Klor de Alva, J. Jorge, H. B. Nicholson, and E. Quiñones Keber, eds. *The Works of Bernardino de Sahagún: Pioneer Ethnographer of Sixteenth-Century Aztec Mexico.* Austin: University of Texas Press, 1988.

Lacan, Jacques. *Écrits: A Selection.* New York: W. W. Norton, 1977.

―――. *Feminine Sexuality: Jacques Lacan and the école freudienne.* Ed. Juliette Mitchell and Jacqueline Rose, trans. Jacqueline Rose. New York: W. W. Norton, 1982.

Lavrin, Asunción, ed. *Sexuality and Marriage in Colonial Latin America.* Lincoln: University of Nebraska Press, 1989.

León-Portilla, Miguel. *The Aztec Image of Self and Society: An Introduction to Nahua Culture.* Salt Lake City: University of Utah Press, 1992.

Lockhart, James. "Encomienda and Hacienda: The Evolution of the Great Estate in the Spanish Indies." *Hispanic American Historical Review* 49 (1969): 411–29.

―――. *The Nahuas after the Conquest: A Social and Cultural History of the Indians of Central Mexico, Sixteenth through Eighteenth Centuries.* Stanford, CA: Stanford University Press, 1992.

• López Austin, Alfredo. *Cuerpo humano e ideología.* 2 vols. Mexico: Universidad Nacional Autónoma de México, 1980.

MacCormack, Sabine. *Religion in the Andes: Vision and Imagination in Early Colonial Peru.* Princeton, NJ: Princeton University Press, 1991.

Molina, Alonso de. *Vocabulario en lengua Castellana y Mexicana y Mexicana y Castellana.* Mexico: Editorial Porrúa, 1992.

Morley, Sylvanus G., George W. Brainerd, and Robert J. Sharer. *The Ancient Maya.* 4th ed. Stanford, CA: Stanford University Press, 1983.

Patch, Robert W. *Maya and Spaniard in Yucatan, 1648–1812.* Stanford, CA: Stanford University Press, 1993.

Perry, Mary Elizabeth. *Gender and Disorder in Early Modern Seville.* Princeton, NJ: Princeton University Press, 1990.

Restall, Matthew. *The Maya World.* Stanford, CA: Stanford University Press, 1997.

Ricard, Robert. *The Spiritual Conquest of Mexico.* Berkeley: University of California Press, 1966 [1933].

Rocke, Michael. *Forbidden Friendships: Homosexuality and Male Culture in Renaissance Florence.* New York: Oxford University Press, 1996.

Roscoe, Will. *Changing Ones: Third and Fourth Genders in Native North America.* New York: St. Martin's Press, 1998.

―――. "How to Become a Berdache: Toward a Unified Analysis of Gender Diversity." In *Third Sex, Third Gender: Beyond Sexual Dimorphism in Culture and History,* ed. Gilbert Herdt. New York: Zone Books, 1994.

―――, ed. *Living the Spirit: A Gay American Indian Anthology.* New York: St. Martin's Press, 1988.

―――. *The Zuni Man-Woman.* Albuquerque: University of New Mexico Press, 1991.

Roys, Ralph. *The Book of Chilam Balam of Chumayel.* Norman: University of Oklahoma Press, 1967.

―――. *The Ritual of the Bacabs.* Norman: University of Oklahoma Press, 1965.

Rugeley, Terry. *Yucatán's Maya Peasantry and the Origins of the Caste War.* Austin: University of Texas Press, 1996.

Sahagún, Bernardino de. *The Florentine Codex: General History of the Things of New Spain. Book 10: The People.* Ed. Charles E. Dibble and Arthur J. O. Anderson. Santa Fe: School of American Research and University of Utah Press, 1961.

Schele, Linda, and David Freidel. *A Forest of Kings: The Untold Story of the Ancient Maya.* New York: William Morrow, 1990.

Scholes, France V., and Ralph L. Roys. *The Maya Chontal Indians of Acalan-Tixchel.* Norman: University of Oklahoma Press, 1948.

Sigal, Pete. *From Moon Goddesses to Virgins: The Colonization of Yucatecan Maya Sexual Desire.* Austin: University of Texas Press, 2000.

―――. "The Politicization of Pederasty among the Colonial Yucatecan Maya." *Journal of the History of Sexuality* 8 (1997): 1–24.

Silverblatt, Irene. *Moon, Sun, and Witches: Gender Ideologies and Class in Inca and Colonial Peru.* Princeton, NJ: Princeton University Press, 1987.

Solís Alcalá, Ermilo. *Diccionario Español-Maya.* Mérida: Editorial Yikal Maya Than, 1949.

Stern, Steve J. *Peru's Indian Peoples and the Challenge of the Spanish Conquest: Huamanga to 1640.* Madison: University of Wisconsin Press, 1982.

————. *The Secret History of Gender: Women, Men, and Power in Late Colonial Mexico.* Chapel Hill: University of North Carolina Press, 1995.

Thompson, Philip. "Tekanto in the Eighteenth Century." Ph.D. diss. Tulane University, 1978.

Trexler, Richard. *Sex and Conquest: Gendered Violence, Political Order, and the European Conquest of the Americas.* Ithaca, NY: Cornell University Press, 1995.

Weeks, Jeffrey. *Coming Out: Homosexual Politics in Britain from the Nineteenth Century to the Present.* London: Quartet Books, 1977.

Whitehead, Harriet. "The Bow and the Burden Strap: A New Look at Institutionalized Homosexuality in Native North America." In *Sexual Meanings: The Cultural Construction of Gender and Sexuality,* ed. Sherry B. Ortner and Harriet Whitehead. Cambridge: Cambridge University Press, 1981.

Williams, Walter L. *The Spirit and the Flesh: Sexual Diversity in American Indian Culture.* Boston: Beacon Press, 1986.

CHAPTER FOUR

Political "Abomination" and Private Reservation: The Nefarious Sin, Homosexuality, and Cultural Values in Colonial Peru

WARD STAVIG

In 1513 Spanish forces under Balboa took a very significant step in the journey of expansion, encounter, and conquest that would shortly extend the European world and its values beyond the circum-Caribbean region and on into Peru and the heart of the Inca empire. As Balboa and his men crossed Panama, more than the "discovery" of the Pacific was at hand, for in this crossing, as described by Peter Martyr, many of the attitudes, perceptions, actions, and subsequent discourse over homosexuality and sodomy—commonly referred to at the time as the "abominable" or "nefarious" sin—were made manifest. Encountering indigenous men attired in female dress who engaged in "nefarious" acts, the Spaniards "threw some forty of these transvestites . . . to the dogs." Richard Trexler, in his stimulating and controversial study that deals with this topic, *Sex and Conquest*, notes that this was "the first record of Spanish punishment of sodomy on the American continent."[1]

While Balboa's actions reflected values that had been honed in Spain, especially in actions and propaganda dealing with Moors, the New World encounter added further weight and immediacy to discussions and policies related to sexual practices that varied from condoned Iberian Christian norms. The message of Balboa and other Spaniards who arrived later was clear. They would not tolerate notorious sexual behavior, including attire or comportment, that to them smacked of sodomy or homosexuality. Leaving aside for the moment more complicated and subtle readings of these Spaniards' actions, such as perceptions of participants and notions of power and sex, the incident in Panama is also revealing for what it purports indigenous views to have been. Peter Martyr wrote,

When the natives learned about it, . . . they spit upon those they suspected to be guilty of this vice. They begged [Balboa] to exterminate
them, for the contagion was confined to courtiers and had not yet spread
to the people. Raising their eyes and their hands to heaven, they gave
it to be understood that God held this sin in horror, punishing it by
sending lightning and thunder, and frequent inundations which destroyed the crops. It was likewise the cause of famine and sickness.[2]

One needs to ask whether this account or similar aspects from the rather
limited number of other early European accounts are rooted—at least to
some degree—in indigenous values and practices, or whether they are almost
totally European fabrications as the Spaniards "read" their values into these
early interactions and observances of New World peoples. If these words do
mirror indigenous statements, do they come from the mouths of a terrified
population—from fears and suspicions of a people witnessing the rigors and
horror of Spanish "justice"—or do they reflect cultural realities? Or should
we see these accounts of Balboa's march to the Pacific as another lesson in the
way that early chroniclers and histories often tell us much less about indigenous peoples than they do about the Europeans? What these chroniclers
and accounts reveal about indigenous peoples and their values and practices
is at least as debatable as the Spaniards' "readings" of their own values and
practices. We also need to ask whether in the late colonial period—when
some two centuries already separated indigenous peoples from their pre-
Columbian ways, and during which the Church and state sought to bring
them into the Euro-Christian fold through teaching, repression, and subtle
and not-so-subtle coercion—values expressed so long before (assuming for
the moment their validity) still reflected indigenous values in the eighteenth
century. Behind all this are the complicated issues of ethnicity and identity,
for, of course, the indigenous world is most complex and reflects this profu-
sion of attitudes, beliefs, and values.

This chapter takes up perceptions, issues, and values related to homosexuality and sodomy among indigenous peoples in the Andean highlands
and coastal regions of what was once the Inca empire and the relationship of
these values to European beliefs and norms after the encounter. In the first
parts of the essay I cast the net broadly, trying to understand the all-too-little
documented heritage of these themes, while the final section focuses on an
official accusation of homosexuality brought by indigenous villagers in a rural
region of eighteenth-century Cuzco. This "window" into life in rural Cuzco
is quite revealing due to the attitudes expressed and the manner in which the
case was adjudicated. I make no claim that this is a representative case, but
neither was it specifically selected for what it did say. Rather, it was the one
such case dealing with the subject of homosexuality I encountered in the

region and time frame that I researched.[3] It is notable for what it reveals about villagers in one ordinary community and the equally ordinary priest and religious personnel who heard and evaluated the accusations, denials, and clarifications. Whether it is also notable for being the only case is something I cannot answer.

The extremely personal nature of most sexual behavior, including homosexuality, has long contrasted with the public concern and debate that has been waged over such private matters. In Western tradition the Old Testament established codes of conduct and provided didactic stories such as that of Sodom and Gomorrah in which the weight of God's punishment fell on those who transgressed these codes, especially when transgressions became public or were openly tolerated or embraced. If we are to believe some of the most well known of the early records from the Andes, at least from the time of the Inca a similar struggle took place in that part of the world, which pitted the empire of Tawantinsuyu against its enemies and those with differing values over issues related to what the Spanish lumped together as homosexual behavior. The Incas are reported to have imposed their sexual values on those whom they subjugated, just as they imposed sexual codes and values on their own people. For most people in Europe and in the Andean sierra the Incan values, as reflected in the European accounts, largely confirmed societal norms on both sides of the Atlantic. However, in Tawantinsuyu and its periphery there were people, sometimes even societies, who adhered to sexual practices that differed from Inca norms and who were vulnerable to the values of the dominant society.

The coming of the Spaniards to the New World and their subsequent political-religious domination textured Andean values with those of Europe, but many of their values appear to have been quite similar (although this similarity was certainly exaggerated, if not fabricated, by certain authors). Following on the heels of the Spanish conquistadors, European friars and priests sought to remold the crown's new Andean subjects into European Catholic form. Through programs as heavy handed as extirpation and the destruction of mummified ancestors to efforts as sympathetic as an understanding word and the promise of salvation, the religious sought to bring New World "merinos" into the Christian flock. Sexual behavior outside Iberian norms caused considerable consternation, and public awareness could bring not only disapproval but legal punishment by Church or state. In cases of sodomy and homosexuality, men and women were even subject to the death penalty for living lives not in accord with Spanish laws and customs.

Despite Ibero-Inca denigration, at the level of individual or private actions and in certain circumstances even at the governmental level, homosexuality and sodomy were not always dealt with so rigorously, but were sometimes addressed in an understanding, if not exactly humane, manner. This suggests a certain sense of ethical relativism on the part of those who became privy to the perceived cultural-legal transgressions, or perhaps a distance between law and practice. By the eighteenth century, the *naturales* (a term commonly used in the colonial period for indigenous peoples) in highland regions like rural Cuzco had long operated under value systems, Indian and Spanish, that publicly derided sodomy and homosexuality but privately may have exercised a degree of tolerance or at least turned a blind eye to such behavior if it was not notorious. The emotions and attitudes revealed by reactions to intimate conduct that deviated from conventional norms provide a "window" through which the values of colonial Andean society can be observed and analyzed. Likewise, they allow us to better understand the position and plight of those whose lives put them outside the public norms of their neighbors.

The attitudes and values reflected in the documents reveal a most complex world. Spanish values and those of the peoples of rural Cuzco were not always distinguishable. Some had become intertwined, while others paralleled each other despite the differences between the societies. Thus, in the later colonial period, it is very problematic to speak of "indigenous values" and "European values" as if in peoples' everyday lives these could be clearly separated, especially in areas such as attitudes, religious values, and personal behavior.

This was particularly true of sexual values, for they were one of the main focuses of the European cultural assault that sought to "Catholicize" and "Europeanize" the Spanish crown's indigenous subjects, just as Tawantinsuyu had sought to impose its ways in the decades prior to Pizarro's arrival. For the Spanish priests and friars, confession was an important part of this process, as the Church used the tools available to it in the effort to religiously "remake" indigenous peoples. Confession and its concomitant-penitence "were the tools to correct errors and mold consciences into proper doctrinal observance."[4] Using the Sixth Commandment, priests probed the sexual behavior of indigenous peoples, and "confession became a means of instructing the Indians in norms of sexual behavior."[5]

The confessors sought to uproot or control not only such common transgressions as fornication, adultery, and masturbation, but also behaviors that were considered to be much graver, including incest, sodomy, bestiality, and homosexuality. For instance, one confessional manual included the following questions which were directed at women: "Have you agreed to men sleeping with you utilizing other than your natural vessel [vagina]? . . . [Have you had relations with] a male dog? with a male four-footed animal? with whatever male living thing, which is called an animal?" And males were asked about their nefarious activity as well as such things as "if they had touched or been touched" by other males.[6]

The degree to which the peoples of rural Cuzco, and other Andean peoples, accepted or absorbed the Church's teachings varied and often involved a very personal process between indigenous people and their priests and friars. However, "there was always a gap between religious canons and the actual behavior of people."[7]

> In the post-conquest world most *naturales* became Christians and in late colonial Cuzco indigenous peoples considered themselves to be believers, Catholic Christians. However, their conversion and the depth of their devotion to Christian values [were] tempered by their continued adherence to Andean beliefs as native peoples accommodated Catholicism to their spiritual and cultural world. The result was a mixture, a syncretic intertwining and blending, of Andean and European religions and beliefs. Syncretism provided indigenous peoples with a means to help them cope with, and adjust to, values from two worlds which, in turn, allowed them to better contend with colonialism.[8]

Thus, though in many aspects of their intimate lives indigenous and European values were in conflict, when it came to homosexuality, sodomy, and other sexual practices, there was apparently considerable overlapping of attitudes. This included more tolerance for private behaviors than might have been expected, considering the legal statutes that prevailed in colonial society.

SODOMY AND HOMOSEXUALITY—
THE HISTORICAL DEBATE

In the period extending from the sixteenth century until very recently, few would have debated the notion that sodomy and homosexuality were behaviors held in disrepute by the Incas and the highland villagers subject to them and that, in terms of the values related to these sexual practices, little changed with the coming of the Spaniards. The legal punishments and cultural castigation for these acts meant that such behaviors usually remained hidden behind closed doors or were engaged in most discreetly. However, it has been equally certain that homosexuality and sodomy were accepted aspects of human sexual expression in some pre-Columbian Andean societies, particularly in the northern coastal region of the Inca empire. In the canon of thought that emerged from the sixteenth century it was argued that before the arrival of the Spanish the Incas had begun to suppress homosexuality and other sexual practices that did not meet with their approval in regions that came under the control of Tawantinsuyu.[9] Indeed, the generally reliable and perceptive chronicler Pedro de Cieza de León noted that "the abominable sin was practiced in some of the villages of the district of Pueblo Viejo, as well as in other lands where there were evil people." He argued that this was as it was in "the rest of the world," but "they [the Inca] abhorred those who were guilty of it."[10] However, Cieza de León also interjected a disturbing notion into this canon, for he reported that under the Inca "abominable" practices may have continued in religious ceremonies and that "if the Incas, by chance, had some knowledge of such proceedings in the temple, they may have ignored them . . . [for] to abandon . . . [them] would have been as bad as death itself, to those who were born in their practice."[11]

In the *Royal Commentaries of the Incas*, Garcilaso de la Vega, influenced by and catering to Spanish law and morality in seeking to glorify the Inca past, embraced and expanded "Incan" attitudes against homosexuality. He wrote that when the Incas conquered the region of the old Mochica and Chimú cultures on the northern coast of Peru, where anal intercourse was practiced, the Inca ordered

> that the sodomites be sought out with great care and when found burnt alive in the public square, not only those proved guilty but those convicted on circumstantial evidence, however slight. Their houses should be burnt and pulled down, and the trees in their fields pulled up by the roots and burnt so that no memory should remain of so abominable a thing, and it would be proclaimed as an inviolable law that henceforward none should be guilty of such a crime, or the sin of one would be visited on his whole town and all the inhabitants would be burnt just as single ones were now being burnt.[12]

If Garcilaso's comments were accurate, one should disabuse oneself of any notion that only men were being executed. Moche ceramics contain representations of male-female sodomy, as well as male sodomy and some instances in which the receptive or "passive" person seems to be female but in which genitalia are not clear, and such relations seem to have been common and culturally accepted in the northern coastal cultures of Peru.[13]

Even if Inca rulers generally took a hard line in opposition to sodomy, it is clear that there did exist a certain degree of tolerance and acceptance. Cieza de León, while affirming the Incas' negative attitude toward sodomy, indicated that punishment, but not death, was used to castigate those who engaged in the practice.

> Never was it said of any of them that they were guilty of the aforesaid sin (sodomy), but, on the contrary, they despised those who used it, looking down on them as vile and contemptible for glorying in such filth. Not only did they themselves not indulge in this, but they did not even allow anyone whom they knew to practice it to enter their homes or palaces. Aside from this, it seems to me that I heard it said that if it

came to their knowledge that anyone had committed this sin, he was so severely punished that he was pointed out and known to all.[14]

Prior to the coming of the Spanish, however, homosexual sodomy played a part in certain religious ceremonies, and this practice continued into the early colonial period. Cieza de León, seeming to contradict himself, commented that, in the Inca realm,

It is considered certain that, in the shrines and temples where conversation was held with [the devil], he let it be known that he would consider it a service if certain *mozos* [boys; young men] were attached to the temples from childhood, so that, at the time of sacrifices and solemn feasts, the chieftains and other men of rank could indulge in the cursed sin of sodomy.[15]

Father Domingo de Santo Tomás informed Cieza de León of two cases he had punished:

In each important temple or house of worship they have a man or two, or more, depending on the idol, who go dressed in women's attire from the time they are children, and speak like them, and in manner, dress, and everything else imitate women. With these, almost like a religious rite and ceremony, on feast (days) and holidays, they have carnal, foul intercourse, especially the chiefs and headmen. I know because I have punished two, one of them . . . in the province of Conchucos, near the city of Huánuco, the other in the province of Chincha, where the Indians are subjects of His Magesty. And when I spoke to them of the evil they were doing, and upbraided them for the repulsiveness of the sin, they answered me that it was not their fault because from childhood they had been put there by the caciques to serve them in this cursed and abominable vice, and to act as priests and guard the temples of their idols.[16]

While on the road to Cuzco from the Lake Titicaca region, Cieza de León came across "two of those Indians who had been put in the temple" coming from Colla (the region where the accusation of homosexuality I shall deal with was made).[17]

Father Calancha, apparently believing that in the preencounter era only male-male sodomy had been practiced, observed that, with the suppression of homosexual sodomy by Spaniards in the northern region of Peru in his time (the early seventeenth century), the people are "not free of this contagion, the wife being the accomplice. If as gentiles the accomplices were males, today [as Christians] they use matrimony to cover the treason done to nature, robbing from generation what they give to sensuality."[18]

So what were the attitudes of the Incas and the commoners in the empire toward homosexuality and sodomy? How did they respond when confronted with behavior that was either overt or which provoked suspicions of these sexual practices? The answers to these questions remain very unclear. It seems that at least ritual religious relations were an accepted, or at least tolerated, aspect of life for certain members of the elite and their partners, but in reality we know very little. Outside the temple the situation is even more opaque. Early chroniclers and observers provide conflicting testimony or nuances of what they had seen or heard. Richard Trexler argues that documentation for legal punishment of homosexuality and sodomy is weak. He states that "there is no credible evidence that the Incas punished by law homosexual behavior or transvestism. The fabled Incas were not, as Garcilaso would have it, haters of sodomy."[19] However, there were plenty of comments to the effect that homosexuality and sodomy were looked down upon, and there were suggestions of punishment. This punishment, if not an outright invention, came from somewhere, either from law or from public or official disapproval. Trexler, who acknowledges that Cieza de León "was not particularly an apologist for the Inca," notes that the chronicler discussed the Incas' shaming of people involved in such practices in the "Cuzco heartland."[20] He dismisses the comments of some Europeans, such as the chronicler known only as the "Anonymous Jesuit," as lacking historical credibility, since the material was recorded so many years after the fateful day in Cajamarca when the Inca fell captive to the Spanish. Garcilaso de la Vega is also seen as tainted, being considered an Inca apologist. These observations may well be correct, but from this distance their prejudices and knowledge are no less certain than any of our own.

Trexler argues that these authors, and others like Acosta, are trying to build a case for their assumption of the civilized—in sixteenth- and seventeenth-century understandings of the term—nature of the Inca and for the corrupting influence of the less civilized peoples, mainly lowlanders like those in the northern coastal or jungle regions, who were reputed to practice sodomy and to openly tolerate homosexuality. In keeping with the then "current" notions of civilization, Spaniards assumed that as people became more civilized, they left behind "uncivilized" practices such as sodomy. Garcilaso's efforts were to glorify his people and, from the point of view of Trexler, "to rescue the race of his mother from the imputation that the *orejones* [Inca nobility] were women."[21] While it is true that Garcilaso certainly did glorify the past, and other writers may have forced their notions of civilization onto the Inca, could it not also be that the Inca had developed attitudes similar to those of the Spanish—with the exception of the religious context of homosexuality and sodomy—and started to impose their values on conquered peoples who condoned and publicly practiced what they did not believe to be proper, just as the Spaniards did? Admittedly, this scenario may be no more valid than Trexler's, but in assuming the mantle of devil's advocate it seems as reasonable to consider this option as to reject the work of so many early observers, even with their personal and cultural biases.

In sum, recent analyses like that of Trexler question the attitudes toward and repression of homosexuality and sodomy under the Inca that many had taken as given on the basis of writings such as those of Garcilaso. Without probing very deeply, contradictions emerge, and, at least in the religious context, it is apparent that older generalizations don't hold up. Likewise, during the colonial period, comments about the "abominable" or "nefarious" sin persisted. There appears to have been considerable cultural-regional variation, as in northern Peru, where Calancha noted the persistence of male-female sodomy well into the seventeenth century.[22] Women typically were not seriously considered as potential lovers of one another and, except for the inquiries of an occasional priest, little attention was given to lesbianism. While the issue is far from settled, for highland men—outside the religious context, which was rapidly suppressed or went underground—Cieza de León's words have an air of authenticity when he says that "sinners of this kind were not to be found, except as happens in every place, that there was one, or six, or eight, or ten and these secretly practiced this vice."[23]

THE IBERIAN HERITAGE

Sixteenth-century Spanish attitudes toward male homosexuality were deeply rooted not only in Spanish morality, but in prejudice and propaganda against the Moors. Spanish law dealing with sodomy from the century or so before the sailing of Columbus, while acknowledging homosexuality and sodomy as a social reality, expressed cultural contempt—part of a process of "otherizing"—for a practice the Spanish had come increasingly to associate with foreigners.[24] The value-laden discourse over this subject became a source of Spanish pride. The laws relating to sodomy that prevailed in the period of the encounter had been refined in the previous centuries. The *Siete Partidas*, developed in the thirteenth century and made law in Castile in the mid-fourteenth century, provided for the castration and stoning to death of the active partner, while minors under fourteen and nonconsenting passive partners were exempted. Under Ferdinand and Isabella, the law was changed to burning.[25]

The modern scholar Francisco Guerra, though overstating the power of the law to alter or deter behavior, summed up the legal-cultural position of sodomy under Spain as follows:

> Sodomy under Spanish law was a most serious offense, second only to heresy and crimes against the person of the king. Those found guilty

were burnt, and proof of their crime was easily accepted from testimonies or circumstantial evidence. The text of the law was indeed a most formidable deterrent against sodomy and bestiality. Behind all this was Spanish hate of Arab morals.[26]

Spaniards like the poet Quevedo held in esteem the antisodomy aspect of Spanish morality in male-female relations and used it to chide others. For instance, when Quevedo wished to deprecate the Genoese, he wrote, "[A]nd we order that those [women] who have a Genoese for a lover may have a Spaniard as another, without jealousy of the first, because each of them works in a different area."[27] A few years later, however, this seventeenth-century author expressed a concern for changing sexual morality and sexual relations between men when he wrote, "Honoured were the Spaniards when they could call the foreigners sodomites and drunkards. . . . Then [in Spain] there was no sodomite . . . all of them [the Spaniards] were inclined to women."[28]

Sodomy was considered to be a crime against both king and God. After its establishment, the Inquisition handled many of the accusations of nefarious behavior, and in at least two New World cases the accused Spaniards were burned to death.[29] Native peoples were subject to punishment for anal intercourse, but they were answerable to the Inquisition for only a very brief period. Before the official establishment of the Holy Office in Peru in 1570, the bishops were responsible for maintaining Catholic morality, and by 1575 the Spanish king had already had a change of heart concerning *naturales* and the Inquisition. In that year Philip II issued an edict that freed indigenous people from the rigorous scrutiny of the Inquisition and returned their supervision to the control of the bishops for they were "so new to the faith, so frail a people, and of so little substance." "They [Amerindians] were not considered to be in the category of *gente de razón* . . . in the same way as were Europeans, Creoles and mestizos, and their conversion was considered to be too recent for them to attain the same knowledge and comprehension of the Faith."[30]

In matters such as sexual offenses, not being considered *gente de razón*, and therefore not being considered the equals of others in colonial society, could work in favor of native peoples. It removed them from the purview of the Inquisition, freeing them from the religious flames that could consume *gente de razón*. The Church continued to prosecute cases that came to its attention through denouncement, notorious behavior, and sometimes through suspicion, but emphasis was placed on altering beliefs and behavior through public teachings and private instruction rather than punishment. The Catechism approved by the Provincial Council of Lima in 1583 (1584 edition), written in Spanish, Quechua, and Aymara, reads as follows concerning the sixth commandment:

Question. Who breaks the Sixth Commandment, which is, Not to
fornicate?

Answer. He who commits hideousness with the wife of another man,
or with an unmarried woman and much more if it is with another man,
or with a beast. And also who enjoys dishonest words or contacts with
himself or another. And such depravities are punished by God with
eternal fire, and many times in this present, with serious diseases of
body and soul.[31]

A seventeenth-century confessional manual listed questions to be asked of
women that included interrogatories such as, "Have you sinned with another
woman, like yourself? . . . When you engaged in this abominable sin, were
you thinking about married men? unmarried men? the priest? the friars? your
male kinfolk? those kin of your husband?"[32]

Religious instructors and confessors also argued that God would visit social and political decline, natural disasters, disease, mental illness, and eternal damnation upon sinners in this world, but they also sometimes let it be
known that sexual offenses such as sodomy carried a civil penalty. In the sermons of the *Tercero Cathecismo y Exposición de la Doctrina Christiana*, printed
in 1585, civil punishment was mentioned, but in a manner that suggests that
fear of legal punishment was used to strengthen religious admonitions. The
Church did not threaten denouncement to civil authorities, for this would
have undermined their efforts. These sermons incorporated Inca beliefs
concerning sin and disease and mixed them with Christian warnings about
mental and physical ailments. Sermon 23 is particularly important in understanding efforts at the transmission of sexual beliefs between Europeans and
Indian cultures.

Sermon XXIII. Of the Sixth Commandment. In which it is taught
how much adultery angers God and how he punishes it, and also how
fornication with an unmarried woman, even on a single occasion is a
deadly sin, and of the other manners of lewdness because of which
God punishes the Indian nation. . . . God punishes also this sin with
diseases; what do you think is the *Bubas* malady but punishment for
this sin? . . .

Above all these sins is the sin we call nefarious and sodomy, which
is for man to sin with man, or with woman not in the natural way, and
even above all these, to sin with beasts, such as ewes, bitches, or mares,
which is the greatest abomination. If there is anyone among you who
commits sodomy sinning with another man, or with boy, or with a
beast, let . . . [it] be known that because of that fire and brimstone fell
from heaven and burnt the fine cities of Sodom and Gomorrah and left
them in ashes. Let it be known that they carry the death penalty under

the just laws of our Spanish kings. Let it be known that because of this
the Holy Scriptures say that God destroys kingdoms and nations. Let
it be known that the reason why God has allowed that you the Indians
should be so afflicted and vexed by other nations is because of this vice
sodomy that your ancestors had, and many among you still have. And
let it be known that I tell you from God's command that if you do not
reform all your nations will perish, and God will finish you, and will
eradicate you from the earth. This is why my beloved brothers cry your
great sins, and ask mercy of Jesus Christ, that I turn to tell you that
God will finish you, and he is already doing so if you do not reform.
Take away drunkenness and feasts which are the sowing ground of these
abominable vices, remove the boys and men from your beds, do not
sleep mixed up like pigs, but each one of you by himself, do not sing or
say dirty words, do not entice your flesh with your hands because this
is also a sin and deserving death and hell.[33]

The Church used these lessons in the effort to rid indigenous peoples of
beliefs and practices that clashed with Church doctrine and to instill the values of Catholic Spain. Unlike other, more ethereal, teachings that missionaries and priests strove to inculcate, most precepts dealing with sexual morality must have been somewhat easier for *naturales* to comprehend. However,
it did not necessarily follow that indigenous peoples would think these precepts wise or adopt them. This was a very uneven process that depended,
among other factors, on the strength and persistence of local beliefs and the
skill, vigilance, and acceptance by the community of the local priest.[34] Face-
to-face relations between parishioners and their priests were important. Individual priests varied greatly in the way they dealt with their congregations
and the way they sought to extend Christian values. Some priests considered
sexual offenses to be serious, while others did not. Yet others despaired of
changing, or thought it not worth the effort to try to change, the sexual behavior of Indian commoners.[35] However, sodomy and homosexuality were
different, in that cultural prohibitions, as well as Spanish if not Inca law, in
both the Andean sierra and among the Europeans, placed these forms of sexual activity outside public parameters. But how did ordinary indigenous villagers react when they came face-to-face with what they thought to be overt
homosexual behavior?

THE NOT-SO-NEFARIOUS WORLD OF YANAOCA
In 1773 the behavior of individuals in the community of Yanaoca (Canas y
Canchis, Cuzco) aroused suspicions of homosexuality among villagers who
informed the local priest of their concerns. According to the accusers, Lucas
Tayro, the sexton, had "scandalized the community and the surrounding ter-

ritory with his infamous, horrible and ruinous behavior with notorious harm to his person and to his accomplice and to the many [people] that observe the outrage of his vile commerce."[36] Clearly, public expressions of homosexual behavior were not to be tolerated in the village. The supposed accomplice of Tayro was Don Ramón Moscoso, a Spanish cacique (leader or head of an *ayllu* or community, who was traditionally indigenous, also known as a *curaca*) and tribute collector who was married to a female *curaca* of noble indigenous heritage. Another villager, the organist of the church, was also implicated, but little mention was made of the organist, and Tayro escaped from jail, leaving the Spanish cacique to face the charges alone. Community members testified that Moscoso had provided Tayro with clothes and that during the fiesta of Corpus Christi he had "furiously wrested the Indian from the side of a woman with whom he suspected that he (Tayro) had been unfaithful." A Spanish witness stated that he had heard villagers mention that Don Ramón Moscoso "was in illicit friendship with . . . Lucas Tayro." Moscoso was also accused of not frequenting the marriage bed with his wife. His wife made no documented comments about their relations, but she testified that she had never seen her husband and Tayro having sexual relations. She had, however, once found Tayro by her husband's bed, but he had been dressed.[37] In his defense Moscoso argued that as cacique (*curaca*) he was obliged to devotedly care for the people of the community and that his treatment of Tayro was different only because Tayro was keen, polite, and "de bellas propiedades" (of beautiful properties [features]). While comments such as "de bellas propiedades" might draw suspicion, according to the cacique the charges against him were "vague and without merit."

The priest of the community, his curiosity piqued by what he first perceived as bisexuality, suggested that Moscoso might be a hermaphrodite— "one of those monsters of the human race that combine in his person the two sexes and, using both, with his wife he has been a male and with his accomplices he has been . . . (the) woman." Had the crime Moscoso committed been adultery or sodomy, wondered the priest? Upon reflection, however, he reasoned that there had never been a hermaphrodite who functioned perfectly as both sexes, so a doctor was called in to examine the cacique. It was found that Moscoso was a man, an "hombre integramente dotado de partes, genitales muy perfecto." The doctor also examined the anus and found the area inflamed and disfigured in a way that, according to the physician, "some attribute . . . to his depraved perversity."

The case was submitted to wider Church review, and those involved, sensitive to the Black Legend (the propaganda promoted by other European states that Spain, Spaniards, and the Catholic Church were brutal and backward, especially in religious persecution and the treatment of colonized peoples), noted that in places like Scotland and Paris it was not very long ago that people like Moscoso were burned, although the Church did not plan to impose the harsh civil penalty, death by fire, if the cacique was found guilty. Instead, he would be excommunicated. In the end it was decided that the evidence was not conclusive enough to "impose the full weight of the serious punishments," the depositions not presenting more than presumptions and suspicions. Those hearing the case ruled that "we ought to absolve and we absolve" Don Ramón Moscoso.[38]

Besides revealing an almost scientific inquiry into the evidence by the priest that stands the Black Legend on its head, the case also demonstrates public morality. The people of Yanaoca were scandalized by the public indiscretion of prominent individuals in the community and they denounced them, an action commensurate with (at least perceived) indigenous and Spanish teachings. It is possible that the accusation was, in reality, an attack on Moscoso—a Spaniard, cacique, and tax collector—but this is unlikely, since in the original complaint only the name of the sexton was given. Moscoso, as well as his wife, sided with indigenous forces in the great 1780 upheaval known as the Túpac Amaru rebellion; they were supported by the community at that time and in other problems concerning the community, which casts further doubt on the validity of the "Spaniard, cacique, tax collector" explanation. While the civil law provided for the conviction of sodomites and homosexuals on circumstantial evidence, the accused was found not guilty despite the testimony. Even if the accused had been found guilty, it was made clear that any punishment would have been more lenient than the harshness the law provided for.

Thus, while the law and the public morality of Cuzco villagers, Spaniards, and the Church condemned homosexuality, in this case the law and the Church were circumspect in their judgment. It was the public behavior that had attracted the censure of the villagers. As long as community values were not threatened and behavior was discreet, the intimate life of others might remain their private concern. However, even then their privacy was at the discretion of those who were aware of their actions. Men and women who transgressed public morality were vulnerable to being denounced and prosecuted. Thus, in the late colonial period, law and culture put sodomites and homosexuals in a difficult and dangerous position.

For those like Moscoso and Tayro, who were accused of behavior that their neighbors and the law viewed as a serious transgression of societal norms, these were anxious moments. Having been thought to have engaged in intimate behavior not in accord with public morality, they faced a fate that might bind them to a stake with the flames of public condemnation consuming them alive.

We most likely will never be able to say with any degree of certainty whether the values of this village stemmed from Inca or pre-Inca times in the Andean sierra, or if they reflected a system of values that were at least influenced if not instilled by Europeans in the encounter of two worlds. But we do know that empires and conquerors—Incas and Spaniards—often tried to influence or alter behavior, to make the "other" more like themselves. This most intimate or personal realm was no different.

NOTES

1. Trexler, *Sex and Conquest,* 82, 146. Trexler also comments that the "active partners" apparently were not thrown to the dogs (82), which is important to his argument about power and dominance.

2. Trexler, *Sex and Conquest,* 146.

3. The materials for the chapter come from research on the peoples who lived in the provinces of Quispicanchis and Canas y Canchis in Cuzco. As students of the Andes know all too well, what happened in this case does not necessarily reflect what happened in other Andean areas, let alone what transpired in different eras.

4. Lavrin, "Sexuality in Colonial Mexico," 48–49.

5. Harrison, "The Theology of Concupiscence," 139.

6. Ibid., 143–46.

7. Lavrin, "Sexuality in Colonial Mexico," 48.

8. The literature on syncretism, or religious resistance, is extensive. One might begin by looking at articles in two issues of the journal *Allpanchis* (Cusco, 1982): 16, no. 19 (*El Cristianismo Colonial*), and 17, no. 20 (*Religion, Mito y Ritual en el Perú*); MacCormack, *Religion in the Andes* (see especially chap. 6), and "Pachacuti"; Spalding, *Huarochirí* (see especially chap. 8); Arriaga, *Extirpation of Idolatry.* For a useful typology, see Klor de Alva, "Spiritual Conflict."

9. Bestiality also appears to have been represented. See Larco Hoyle, *Checan,* 34. In *Sexual Behavior in Ancient Peru,* Federico Kauffman-Doig indicates that much of the artistic evidence relating to bestiality, particularly between men and llamas, has been "destroyed by 'cultured' persons, due to a mistaken patriotism, in an effort to erase proofs that showed the presence of a practice considered as abominable" (53–54). For other references to the subject of bestiality in the Andes, see two works by DeNegri: "Una suerte zoocrástica," and "Zooerastia la llama señorita," 46–47 (see Kauffman-Doig, "Bibliografía").

10. Cieza de León, *Travels,* 78–80.

11. Ibid., 78–80.

12. De la Vega, *Royal Commentaries,* 162. While the basic account of Garcilaso is supported by others, one should be wary of claims of execution on the basis of circumstantial evidence. It may well be true and would be in keeping with Inca practice, but it is also very similar to Spanish law. The 1581 edition of the *Recopilación de leyes,* vol. 2, fols. 197v–198v, book 7, title 21, stated concerning circumstantial evidence in sodomy cases, "We order that if it happens that such offense cannot be proved in perfect and completed matter, but is proved and found in very near and contiguous acts to the conclusion of such, in a way that the offender could finish this harmful error, he shall be taken for the true performer of such an offense, to be judged and sentenced to suffer the same penalty in the same way and manner as a man who has committed the said offense with full perfection as previously stated (burnt)"; cited in Guerra, *Precolumbian Mind,* 222. Garcilaso could well have read this law and it could have influenced his memory or interpretation as he and other observers saw similarities between Inca and Spanish customs. Antonio de la Calancha in his *Crónica moralizada,* book 3, chap. 2, parag. 13 (1638), 556 makes a comment very similar to that of Garcilaso (also see Guerra, *Precolumbian Mind,* 189), but perhaps he was influenced by Garcilaso. See also Rowe, "Kingdom of Chimor": "The north coast

people were much addicted to sodomy, practicing it both with men and women. The Incas regarded it as an abominable vice and tried to stamp it out by destroying the family and property of guilty persons" (49).

13. See Larco Hoyle, *Checan*, 110; and Guerra, *Precolumbian Mind*, 256. Larco Hoyle maintains that 95 percent of the Mochica erotic art depicting sexual intercourse was of the variety represented what the Spanish referred to as the "nefarious or abominable sin." But Guerra, after analyzing the art in *Checan*, found sodomy represented in 75 percent of the art depicting sexual intercourse. Guerra, in his book *The Precolumbian Mind*, concluded that "[t]he archeological specimens reproduced by Larco Hoyle fall within the following categories: 24% erotic representations of the human penis; 4% erotic vessels representing the human vulva; 11% representations of normal coitus; 5% figures showing male masturbation; 31% heterosexual sodomy or anal coitus between man and woman; 3% homosexual sodomy between men; 1% homosexual relations between women; 14% oral copulation or fellatio; 6% bestiality or coitus between human and animal." P. H. Gebhard, not taking into account doubtful cases of anal intercourse such as those in which "body positions suggest anal coitus, but the genital organs are hidden, or not clearly modeled," found sodomy in only 21 percent of Mochica pottery (P. H. Gebhard, "Motivos sexuales en la cerámica peruana prehistórica," *Fascinum*, no. 7, 8, 9, 10, as cited in Kauffman-Doig, *Sexual Behavior in Ancient Peru*, 38). Trexler in *Sex and Conquest* suggests that the "women" were in fact men such as those found in temples dressed as women (111–13).

14. Cieza de León, *Incas of Pedro Cieza de León*, 178–79.

15. Trexler, *Sex and Conquest*, 108. In the first part of *The Travels of Pedro de Cieza de León*, the translator and editor, Clements Markham, just notes that chapter 14 is unfit for translation (230).

16. Cieza de León, *Travels*, 314. In *Sexual Behavior in Ancient Peru*, Kauffman-Doig contradicts the anti-homosexual attitudes of the Incas. He cites the chronicler Pachacuti in reference to the reign of Tupac Yupanqui: "Many young men were raised who were not to know women; these afterwards served the warriors in battle." However, as Kauffman-Doig readily admits, the "reference is . . . somewhat confused" (90).

17. Cieza de León, *Travels*, 314–15.

18. Calancha, *Crónica moralizada*, as cited in Trexler, *Sex and Conquest*, 138.

19. Trexler, *Sex and Conquest*, 156–57.

20. Ibid., 148–50.

21. Ibid.

22. Calancha, *Crónica moralizada*, book 3, chap. 2, parag. 13 (1638), 556, as cited in Guerra, *Precolumbian Mind*, 189, n. 17.

23. Cieza de León, *Travels*, 179.

24. Guerra, *Precolumbian Mind*, 221–26. For instance, he states that in Spain stories circulated that for Arabs a pilgrimage to Mecca was not complete unless they had intercourse with a camel.

25. Trexler, *Sex and Conquest*, 45–47.

26. Guerra, *Precolumbian Mind*, 221–22. The laws pertaining to sodomy in force during the conquest and colonization of the New World had been issued by King Ferdinand the Catholic and Queen Isabella of Castile at Medina del Campo on 22 August 1497 and ratified by Charles V and Philip II of Spain. For law pertaining to sodomy, see the *Recopilación de leyes*, 1581 edition, vol. 2, fols. 197v–198v, book 8, title 21.

27. Guerra, *Precolumbian Mind*, 227; see also Quevedo, "Pragmaria que han de guardar las hermanas comunes," 813.

28. Guerra, *Precolumbian Mind*, 227.

29. Ibid., 223–24.

30. Herring, *History of Latin America*, 177; and Boxer, *Church Militant*, 85.

31. Lima, Concilio Provincial, *Doctrina Christiana y Catecismo* (Lima, 1584), 4, 81, 84, as cited in Guerra, *Precolumbian Mind*, 240.

32. Harrison, "The Theology of Concupiscence," 146.

33. Lima, Concilio Provincial, *Tercero Cathecismo y exposición de la Doctrina Christiana, por Sermones* (Lima, 1585), 4, 81, 215 f., as cited in Guerra, *Precolumbian Mind,* 241–42.

34. For a discussion of the issues of the transference of Christian beliefs and practices to Peru, see MacCormack, "Heart Has Its Reasons." The debate over the use or avoidance of pre-conquest words, symbols, and ideas is of particular interest. MacCormack argues that in the long run the missionaries chose to force conversion, avoiding Andean parallels in their teaching, and their impact was lessened for having taken this path.

35. Boxer, *Church Militant,* 90. In late-sixteenth-century Pernambuco, Brazil, Boxer noted that "anal intercourse, whether homosexual or heterosexual, was the single most commonly confessed sin. But the Inquisitors do not seem to have been greatly concerned about the sexual mores of the lowest servile colored classes, regarding them as quasi- or non-persons, whose spiritual salvation was problematical and of little importance anyway."

36. Biblioteca Nacional del Perú (BNP), 1773, C992, *Criminal contra don Ramón Moscoso, vecino del pueblo de Yanaoca y Lucas Tayro, indio del mismo pueblo, sobre el ilícito comercio con que escandalosamente vivían.* All subsequent quotations in this narrative are from this source. Yanaoca was a *doctrina* and should have had a priest, but the suspects were denounced to the priest of Checa. Since no mention was made of a priest in Yanaoca, we must assume that the *doctrina* was temporarily without the services of a priest.

37. It is an interesting comment by the wife, who appears to assume that being undressed was the normal state for engaging in sex, a practice that was still not widespread in Europe at the time. Perhaps the testimony only meant to indicate that Tayro had been fully clothed instead of partially undressed. Kauffman-Doig (*Sexual Behavior in Ancient Peru*) indicates that in the ceramic art from the much warmer north coast "generally, the woman but rarely the man copulates naked; he is generally wearing a breech clout, which is loosened for the act, or he is represented as fully dressed" (35). In the much colder sierra, complete nakedness during sex seems less likely.

38. Biblioteca Nacional del Perú (BNP), 1773, C992, *Criminal contra don Ramón Moscoso.*

WORKS CITED

Arriaga, Pablo José de. *The Extirpation of Idolatry in Peru.* Trans. L. Clark Keating. Lexington: University of Kentucky Press, 1968.

Boxer, C. R. *The Church Militant and Iberian Expansion, 1440–1770.* Baltimore: Johns Hopkins University Press, 1978.

Calancha, Antonio de la. Crónica moralizada del orden de San Agustín en el Perú. Barcelona, 1638.

Cieza de León, Pedro de. *The Incas of Pedro Cieza de León.* Trans. Harriet de Onis. Norman: University of Oklahoma Press, 1959.

———. *Travels of Cieza de León, Second Part (Chronicle of Peru).* Ed. and trans. Clements R. Markham. New York: Burt Franklin, n.d. (originally published by the Hakluyt Society).

De la Vega, el Inca, Garcilaso. *Royal Commentaries of the Incas.* Trans. Harold V. Livermore. Austin: University of Texas Press, 1966.

DeNegri, M. A. "Una suerte zoocrástica en el Perú de ayer y hoy." *Revista del Cuerpo Médico* 9, no. 4 (1979).

———. "Zooerastia la llama señorita de la altura." *Equis* 84 (1977): 46–47.

Guerra, Francisco. *The Precolumbian Mind.* New York: Seminar Press, 1970.

Harrison, Regina. "The Theology of Concupiscence: Spanish-Quechua Confessional Manuals in the Andes." In *Coded Encounters: Writing, Gender, and Ethnicity in Colonial Latin America,* ed. Francisco Javier-Cevallos-Candau et al. Amherst: University of Massachusetts Press, 1994.

Herring, Hubert. *A History of Latin America.* 3d ed. New York: Alfred A. Knopf, 1968.

Kauffman-Doig, Federico. *Sexual Behavior in Ancient Peru.* Lima: Kompaktos, 1977.

Klor de Alva, J. Jorge. "Spiritual Conflict and Accommodation in New Spain: Toward a Typology of Aztec Responses to Christianity." In *The Inca and Aztec States, 1400–1800,* ed. George Collier, Renato Rosaldo, and John Wirth. New York: Academic Press, 1982.

Larco Hoyle, Rafael. *Checan: Essay on Erotic Elements in Peruvian Art.* Geneva: Nagel, 1965.

Lavrin, Asunción. "Sexuality in Colonial Mexico: A Church Dilemma." In *Sexuality and Marriage in Colonial Latin America,* ed. Asunción Lavrin. Lincoln: University of Nebraska Press, 1989.

MacCormack, Sabine. "'The Heart Has Its Reasons': Predicaments of Missionary Christianity in Early Colonial Peru." *Hispanic American Historical Review* 65, no. 3 (August 1985).

———. "Pachacuti: Miracles, Punishments, and Last Judgment: Visionary Past and Prophetic Future in Early Colonial Peru." *American Historical Review* 93, no. 4 (October 1988): 960–1006.

———. *Religion in the Andes.* Princeton, NJ: Princeton University Press, 1991.

Quevedo, Francisco de (Gómez). "Pragmaria que han de guardar las hermanas comunes." In *Quevedo: Satíricos, Picarescas, Políticas, Burlescas, Filosóficas, Ascéticas, Crítico Literaria, Poéticas.* Madrid: EDAF, 1972.

Recopilación de leyes de los reynos de las Indias, mandados imprimir y publicar por la Ma. Católica del Rey D. Carlos II. Facsimile ed. Madrid: n.p., 1943.

Rowe, John. "The Kingdom of Chimor." *Acta Americana* 6, nos. 1 and 2 (1948): 26–59.

Spalding, Karen. *Huarochirí. An Andean Society under Inca and Spanish Rule.* Stanford, CA: Stanford University Press, 1984.

Trexler, Richard C. *Sex and Conquest: Gendered Violence, Political Order, and the European Conquest of the Americas.* Ithaca, NY: Cornell University Press, 1995.

CHAPTER FIVE

Tales of Two Carmelites: Inquisitorial Narratives from Portugal and Brazil

DAVID HIGGS

Over the last thirty years social historians have become increasingly con-scious of the elements of invention and fiction found in official records which survive from the past.[1] The same point can be made regarding the re-liability of the records of the activities of the Portuguese Inquisition in Brazil, which are preserved in the National Archives of Portugal. An example would be the dispute over the reliability of the evidence amassed by the Inquisi-tion about the continuing Judaic practices among seventeenth-century Por-tuguese, known as New Christians, descendants of forcibly converted Jews, where a Portuguese, gentile intellectual argued that many accusations were invented pretexts for confiscations, and a French professor of Jewish history held that, on the contrary, the evidence was accurate and had been carefully double-checked.[2]

Similar considerations exist for writers appraising trials for sodomy. The archive of the Portuguese Inquisition contains a remarkable body of trials, investigations, and denunciations for the abominable sin, the *pecado nefando* ("nefarious sin"; also sometimes written *nefando pecado*). These trials are of-ten complete, containing initial denunciations, the drawing up of a grid of questions to be asked of witnesses, the confession of the accused, if made, a family genealogy, and sentencing, with a record of differing opinions among inquisitors. However, the scholar is confronted with the problems of voice and evidence and the assumptions of those who controlled the compilations, which are implicit in such documents. Such concerns still exist in the twenty-first century.[3] Trials for sodomy held long before late-nineteenth-century theories of medicalization became current pose other challenges to interpre-tation. Sin and the devil were considered realities in Portuguese Inquisition documents drawn up hundreds of years ago in interrogations taken from in-dividuals under severe conditions of stress and sometimes in torture sessions.

Not only were the trials conducted in close conformity with style manuals and using a "technical" vocabulary to describe the penis, anus, and ejaculations of those involved, but also the scribes often transcribed the oral testimony of witnesses from more colloquial terms into their formal jargon of male member, posterior vase, and scattering seed. When confessions were made in trials after interrogations about sodomy in a macho culture, men often were reticent to admit to taking the receptive (*paciente*) role or enjoying it. Sometimes the storytelling structures in these "true" confessions would be at variance with the testimony of others who were questioned. The Inquisitors constantly exhorted the accused to make truthful and full confessions. However, in some fortunate cases, the historian can gain a better view of circumstance, situation, and self-representation from internal evidence within a trial, or by using additional sources from other enquiries.

Here I want to examine in detail two such instances in which the Portuguese Inquisition investigated ordained sodomites.[4] António Soares was tried in Lisbon in the first half of the seventeenth century and exiled to Brazil. The second individual, Padre Madre de Deus, was investigated in Rio de Janeiro at the end of the eighteenth century but was not arrested despite the unanimity among witnesses. Both were Carmelite friars, and both lived in the convent, which was constructed early in the seventeenth century and which today is the Faculdade Candido Mendes on the Praça 15 in Rio de Janeiro, close to the harbor. This building was one of the most imposing in the city during the seventeenth and eighteenth centuries. A number of Carmelite friars who lived there were commissioners of the Inquisition (*comissários*), and thus, in a limited sense, the convent was the seat of the Inquisition in Brazil, since there was no tribunal sitting in Portuguese America, and all Brazilians who were tried had to be shipped to Lisbon. It was also an area of intense street life on the Rua Direita, today Primeiro de Março, and the area was still marked in a contemporary study as an area for gay cruising.[5]

SOARES (INQUISITION OF LISBON TRIAL DOCUMENT 6919)

Padre Frei António Soares, Old Christian (that is, of purely gentile descent), and professed Carmelite friar, was born in January 1609 in Lisbon into a wealthy family, and in that city he had an active sexual life with other males prior to his initial sentence by the Inquisition when he was twenty-two. Three years later, in 1634, he was exiled to Brazil, whence he returned to Portugal in 1649, after fifteen years. After various appeals he was allowed to remain in Portugal. In the detail of the accusations against him and in his confessions we find evidence that reveals much about a seventeenth-century sexual identity.

In his confession Soares, son of Francisco Soares, who lived in Lisbon in the district called Cotovia,[6] said that he had first been sodomized at age fourteen by a Dominican priest at the Benfica convent on the outskirts of Lisbon. Although he had been in the Dominican novitiate at the time, he subsequently joined the Carmelites. António was twenty-one years old in November of 1630. At the start of his trial documentation, various extracts of other interrogations were transcribed, starting with that of a seventeen-year-old student who said that eleven months earlier, under some trees outside a house belonging to the father of António, they had taken down their breeches and António took up position to penetrate him but that he broke away for fear that they were visible to passers by, and no semen was ejaculated. The second witness was a fellow Carmelite, aged twenty-six, who said that three years previously, in the novice's house, the younger António urged him to engage in sodomy and that he had put himself on all fours on António's bed and was sodomized. This friar, Manuel Correia, added that during the following two years they repeated the act, with each one taking receptive *and* insertive roles ("sendo cada um ora agente ora paciente").[7] This precision about exchanging receptive and insertive acts over a long period of time on two hundred occasions put this sexual activity clearly outside any claim of impulsiveness or occasional transgression.

A third extract was from an elite witness, António de Figueiredo Falcão, who had the habit of Christ and also was a nobleman of the royal household and son of a former official of the Madrid council. He recalled a time three years earlier at the home of Soares when they had laid on the floor and engaged in masturbation until Soares partially penetrated him, but that he had become unwilling and pulled away, saying this was foolishness (*parvoíce*), but that Soares had tried to insist and had an orgasm against Falcão's buttocks as he sought to reenter him. This behavior, said Falcão, showed the intent of Soares.

Another accusation came from a thirty-year-old married man, also of high social rank. Miguel d'Abreu, of the secretariat of the Crusade Bull, testified that some fifteen months later, an occupant of the Carmelite convent, brother Cosme, lent his cell to António Soares so that Soares could masturbate there with Abreu. Cosme locked them inside and stayed outside. Although Abreu was ten years older and married, he and Soares were friends and had previously masturbated each other ("a fazer molicies um ao outro"), whereupon António suggested that they might commit the "sin from behind," and Abreu mounted him. When he felt an orgasm was coming, he withdrew to ejaculate outside of Soares's anus. He claimed further that when Soares mounted him, he had, when he felt ejaculation was imminent, withdrawn himself.

These details were to underline that the most heinous element in sodomy, the spilling of seed in the anus, had not taken place. In short, in recounting sexual incidents which included mutual masturbation and anal penetration, he insisted that no ejaculation had occurred within his anus. He added that António and Manuel were notorious among the other friars as a sexual couple. Seventeen additional extracts from other trials and depositions showed that António Soares had an active sexual life in the Carmelite convent, prior to his arrest on 29 November 1630. One of the charges against him came from a Dominican, son of a *familiar* (arresting officer) of the Inquisition, who when fifteen had been sodomized for the first time in the novice house at Benfica and, a week after the event, had complained about it. Most of the accusations came from individuals who were under twenty at the time of the sexual acts, and none were over thirty save the single married man. The accusations show a high level of homosexual activity among novices.

The confession of António Soares is very long, and, given his range of sexual partners, who all seem to have been of some social standing, it merits close attention, coming from a time when voluntary written or printed sexual autobiography about homosexual behaviors was unheard of. It began with his first experience of sodomy, when Frei João de Sãnto António sodomized him, "and he, as a youngster, not understanding the gravity of the said sin, consented easily" ("e ele como menino não entendendo a graveza da dito pecado consentiu facilmente"). This Dominican Friar João was, at the time of the confession, studying theology in Coimbra; that is, António knew where the friar who deflowered him was seven years later, but it was only when he was himself arrested that he accused João, and he added that they had sex two or three times more. Soares went on with a string of numbers, including a Joseph, who was also a novice at Benfica, with whom he admitted to reciprocal sodomy to orgasm, while not remembering clearly who initiated their acts.[8] When António talked about Manuel Correia, he said their relations had begun four years previously at the Lisbon Carmo. Manuel was then a novice but was at present a priest: earlier he had been a young musician (perhaps a chorister) of the Royal Chapel. In António's version of events, the older Manuel propositioned him and sodomized him first but then offered himself to be sodomized by António. This subsequently went on so frequently that he could not recall how many times. There was attention to detail of age, as in the case of the groom whose name he had forgotten but who did not yet have any beard when he sodomized him two years earlier at his home.

This António Soares case seemed to somewhat perplex the Inquisitors. The confession of hundreds of sexual acts and many partners put Soares outside of any imagery of penitence. It can be read as a statement about a clearly queer identity in seventeenth-century terms by the Inquisitors in April 1631. They accepted that he might have been traveling to Lisbon from Coimbra to

confess when he was taken into custody, and that he was a minor and an ecclesiastic, and hence not eligible for capital punishment, but added that he
was extremely dissolute and that he had tried in the Inquisition cell with unheard of daring to rape one or more of the three men with him, and that he
went about saying scandalous things which might bring the Holy Office into
disrepute.[9] His sentence of life imprisonment on bread and water was thus
to be heard in the Inquisition in the presence of some members of his Order
and other trustworthy individuals, but he was not sentenced to parade in the
public auto-da-fé. In 1634 the provincial of the Carmelites petitioned that
Soares be exiled to Brazil, and the Inquisitors pointed to the serious disor-
ders arising from his bad behavior in the Inquisition prison. The suggestion
was that he should be detained in the Carmelite monastery of São Barello in
São Paulo in Brazil.

The second phase of the life of António Soares began when he arrived at
the Rio convent, noted as being very ill from a spar falling on him on the ship.
The Superior in Rio, Frei Martinho Moniz, gave in 1635 a series of reasons
why António had not been sent to São Paulo: the convent there was small
and did not have a cell, and the brothers did not follow the rule there with
the same care as was the case in big religious houses, and he added that there
were no ships going there because of "enemies" (meaning the Spanish) and
that it was very dangerous to go so far by canoes. He added that Soares
showed great penitence and humility and that all this caused him to request
that Soares remain in Rio. In 1644 António Guerra, Provincial da Ordem de
Nossa Senhora do Carmo, said that Soares had spent ten years in Brazil for
his crime when aged seventeen, and that now he was very sick and debilitated
with open ulcers, having been bled many times for grave sicknesses, so that
the doctors have ordered him to leave Brazil in order to save his life. Further
enquiries were ordered on 31 March 1644, and in June he was ordered to
leave Bahia, where he then was, to go to a Carmelite convent in Portugal in
the Algarve (Lagoa).

The pathetic picture of the sick and penitent Soares takes on a different
hue when the reader of the trial reaches the letter written from Bahia on 29
November 1644, from the visitor to the calceate Carmelites who had arrived
with Letters Patent from the provincial general of the Carmelites in Rome.
The visitor noted that Soares had never fulfilled his penances: he had not
gone to São Paulo, and thanks to the protection of Moniz he had gone into
business in Rio and had amassed a substantial fortune and had become extremely powerful among the friars.[10] He had even become Prior, despite the
decree of Urban VIII and the sentence of the Holy Office. The visitor ordered Soares to appear before him in Bahia to see if he could "cure" such a
lost soul. Soares had sent false documents to Rome and had bribed various
people. As for his sexuality, "The truth is that he is convicted of carrying out

filthinesses with youths, and as for the same kind of sin for which he was exiled there are violent presumptions against him with three accomplices with whom he shut himself up for long periods, sometimes in the convent and sometimes outside of it."[11] He added that three others had complained of being propositioned. He had ordered Soares to come to Bahia but reported in a letter of 29 November 1644 that Soares had fled to Lisbon and was doing business there. We cannot know whether this Frei Luís de Mertola, Comissário Geral do Carmo do Brasil, had any personal animus against Soares. •

Discussions of the Soares case were taking place in Lisbon in the year of the auto-da-fé in which six incorrigible sodomites (*devassos*) were put to death. They continued for the next five years, during which Soares had returned to Portugal and then gone back to Brazil and then returned. Correspondence from the Rio Carmelites said that Soares was irreplaceable for business interests of the Order. What emerged was that he was still being accused of sodomy with younger partners, but that he had become so powerful because of his mercantile activities that no punishments were enforced against him.

On 11 June 1650, he was in Portugal and resided in the convent in Evora, and he gave considerable alms. In the light of information received from the Evora Inqusitors, the provincial vicar of the order granted a permit to Soares to reside in the Camarate convent, although with the reservation that he could not come to Lisbon save with explicit license from the Inquisitor General. Camarate was in the municipality of Loures, some nine kilometers from Lisbon, and was the site of a Carmelite convent built in 1602, which existed until 1834.

Soares in 1650 was thirty-eight years of age and rich, having spent almost eighteen years in exile in Brazil. Later in June, Lisbon Inquisitors said that they had two witnesses from Rio to say Soares had been involved in the crime against nature but that he had been shipped in an English vessel, and they did not ask the only other Portuguese passengers on board, a man and his wife, what was "murmured" about him. Also, once in Lisbon, he lived in his father's house, but the Inquisitors stated that it did not seem appropriate to ask the menservants who worked there about Soares. He had returned to the heart of the city of his youth, Lisbon, saying his father was old and ill. His sentence and subsequent permits were supposed to keep him out of the central city in both Rio and Lisbon. Instead he had stayed in the biggest city of colonial Brazil and when enquiries were made at Camarate, the reply was that he was in a property of his father next to the convent of Spode in the place known as Cotovia in the Bairro Alto of Lisbon. Most of the extant evidence of a self-identifying, gay sexual subculture of individuals who called themselves *fanchonos* in the seventeenth-century Portuguese world arose from those cities.[12] In July 1651 Soares was permitted to come to Lisbon because his uncle was sick, and in August, Soares was said to be so sick that he needed the medical talents available to him in Lisbon at the Carmo convent.

By 1651 the almost-forty-year-old Carmelite Frei António Soares had a number of stories running through his life, all derived from the primary conflict of the religious interdiction of his self-perception as a person whose sexuality defined him. The second story was his unsatisfactory penitence and obedience as seen by the Inquisition. The third was his continuing activity as part of a prosperous Lisbon commercial family's transatlantic business. He apparently was active in business as long as he was in a position to do that, that is, resident and effectively able to deal with shipments arriving in a port.

Shortly before his fortieth year, he wrote a brief summation of his bad health situation, perhaps from sexually transmitted diseases, though he did not say that, to the Inquisitor General. This spoke of the passage of twenty-two years since he was first penitenced by the Holy Office, of eighteen bleedings of the feet, and asserted that the need to ask the Inquisition for a permit each time he had to come to Lisbon caused great mortification for him and *for his relatives* (my emphasis), and he asked to have his penances lifted so that he could look after his health, without any desire to vote in the deliberations of his order. He was given permission to come six times annually to the city but not to exceed eight days residence: this was dated 3 November 1650, and signed by the Inquisitor General.

Obviously, a powerful young man with his order and his family on his side did not go for execution like the incorrigible old priest in 1645, Sanches de Almeida. This was despite the great amount of sex he had, and also the scattered evidence that he was still engaging in male-male sodomy in Brazil. At present we do not know whether he renewed his campaign to return to the Lisbon convent or contented himself with six annual visits to the city. The interest of the case is that it mixes together explicit confession of egalitarian sex among bourgeois and grand bourgeois partners from a young age (emphasis on both top and bottom and swapping roles), his continuation in those sex practices into his thirties at least, and his competence at business. From the age of forty, we do not now know about the remainder of his life.

COUTINHO (INQUISITION OF LISBON TRIAL DOCUMENTS 15035, 16888)

The second Carmelite to be investigated by commissaries of the Inquisition, Frei Thomé da Madre de Deus Coutinho, was not arrested or interrogated directly. We do not hear his own commentaries, nor do we know if he knew he was being investigated. Instead we have two *sumários*, summaries of evidence gathered about him, which have different call numbers in the Lisbon manuscript documentation.[13] From these we can see how slave boys discussed the important figure in the monastery who sodomized them, the circumstances under which they were forced to submit, and the statements of fellow Carmelites.

Carmelites together with Jesuits, Franciscans, Benedictines, and Mercedários were active in the religious life of colonial Brazil. Their Rio convent was at the heart of the old city near the main docks. In May 1783 the rivalries and unedifying behavior of monks and friars at the time of a capitular meeting had led to an order from the Queen, Maria I, to reform them. In 1785 the Viceroy Luiz de Vasconcellos e Souza (1779–90) decreed a "general visitation and Reform" to be carried out by the Bishop of Rio de Janeiro, formerly an Inquisitor in Evora, Dom José Joaquim Mascarenhas Castello Branco (1774–1805). The Carmelites of Rio were under great pressure to reform various laxities which had crept into their conventual life. There was a turbulent period in the life of the convent for some fifteen years. The Carmelite who was accused of sodomy in the 1790s had taken part in the "Reform" of the order.[14] The Viceroy in 1784 had noted the delicate topics of the relations of the friars with slaves of both sexes. Fourteen friars were known in 1785 to have had sexual relations with slave women, and some had had children by them.[15]

No mention of the sexual behavior of Coutinho appeared in the documents of the Reform or the Carmelite archives in Brazil, but the Inquisition documents in Lisbon revealed how fellow Carmelites used the denunciation of the *pecado nefando* to try to discredit Coutinho. Those documents were considered in Lisbon when D. José Maria de Melo, bishop of the Algarve, had taken up the post of Inquisitor General on 7 January 1790, retaining it until 1818. During the reign of Queen Maria, accusations of sodomy, while recorded for both Portugal and Brazil, were few, and no Brazilian was arrested to stand trial in Lisbon during the period 1777–1807.

The name of Frei Thomé da Madre de Deus Coutinho, Presidente da Província, was often heard during the first years of the Reform. He collaborated with the bishop and the Viceroy, although he was not an architect of the investigations.[16] He confronted the leaders of various factions among the friars after an imposing procession surrounding the bishop had proclaimed the investigation and named him as president of the Carmelite Province and Padre Mestre Doutor Frei Fernando de Oliveira Pinto as the secretary of the Reform. Both men were born in Minas Gerais. Between 1785 and mid-1791, Coutinho held a leading position in the Reform. The bishop ordered the cells of some of the Carmelites to be searched and turned up money and various other evidence of broken vows. The bishop was severe, making strong criticism of the earlier, inefficacious Reform of 1780–81.[17]

Coutinho was noted as being extremely rigorous in applying disciplinary procedures. In 1787 Frei João de Santa Thereza Costa wrote to the reformer bishop about the punishments and violence ordered by Frei Thomé. Other letters in the same year deplored the imprisonment of eighteen friars; some of them were whipped, and some were put on bread and water. Others had to take part in humiliation rituals at the refectory. Five friars ran away. This is not the place to present all the evidence collected by Francisco Filho, but enough has been cited to show that many of Coutinho's fellows at the Carmo detested him.

One friar, Frei Felipe de Jesus Maria, was whipped and fed on bread and water because Coutinho suspected him of being responsible for freeing a slave that Coutinho had locked in a room. This raises a theme which is certainly germane to the accounts of the slave boys who recounted how the friar sodomized them in his cell with the door locked. Other friars complained of the vituperations of Coutinho during his homilies and of his passionate nature. Perhaps the denunciations against Coutinho for sodomizing the slave boys were orchestrated, but they were also probably well founded. If he had not antagonized the other friars with his excesses, the sodomy would never have come out, but the terms of the Edict of the Faith, which called for those who knew of sodomy to denounce it, became a stick with which to strike back at Couthino in the hands of opposing friars who were being reformed.

The Frei Thomé de Madre de Deus Coutinho who used the occasion of giving a French lesson to proposition a young novice was almost certainly the same Friar Thomé whom a shoemaker neighbor of the convent pointed out as one who was said by other monks to be a reader of Voltaire in a community which was thought to be traditional in its outlook.[18] He was also said to be behind the search into the goods owned by the friars, having suggested that the special pastoral letter of the bishop be read in each of the parishes of Rio and its surroundings, accusing the Carmelites of cheating in not giving up personal property and threatening with excommunication those faithful who did not pass on information they had.[19] If it was the public perception that Coutinho was causing this much trouble for his fellows, the venomous accusations that he sodomized slave boys are not surprising.

Filho devoted a section of his thesis to Coutinho (86–90). The president of the Province was deposed in 1791 on the order of Resende: he had been in charge from 16 February 1785 to the beginning of 1791. Then he was replaced by Padre Mestre Frei João de Santa Thereza Costa, who had denounced him in 1787. Coutinho was officially dismissed by March of 1792. He seems to have angered the Viceroy by his violence against a mentally unbalanced friar who had disobeyed Coutinho's orders and was consequently given a severe beating. The *Annaes do Rio de Janeiro* provide the outline of the story leading to the demotion of Coutinho, who was sent to the convent's farm at Macacú. The investigations may have provided additional evidence leading to the sudden demotion of Coutinho. Subsequently he was sent to the hospice at Itú, but after further petitions he was allowed to reside at the convent of Angra dos Reis on the beautiful Ilha Grande. He apparently died there some time between 1803 and 1806.

The campaign against Coutinho dated from a denunciation by two brothers, well written, which transparently derives from the malice engendered by the friars' quarrel over the Reform. The denunciation also provides a further insight into the disgrace which befell him. The interesting thing was the revelation of the commonplace sexual use of slave boys.

THE DENUNCIATIONS

Two brothers who were Carmelites wrote a denunciation on 1 December 1787, in which they claimed Coutinho was sodomizing slave boys (IL 15035). The younger brother, who had recently joined the Carmelites and was a chorister, claimed that Coutinho propositioned him during a French lesson and that because of this he stopped learning the language. They made the denunciation in order to obey the Edict of the Faith and avoid excommunication for failing to denounce a sin of which they had knowledge.

A few days before writing the denunciation, the brothers were talking with two other friars, and they spoke about the public and irreligious behavior of Coutinho, who made "luxurious" use of some slave boys belonging to the community "by the unaccustomed way" (*via desusada*). A slave boy of about seventeen who was sweeping a dormitory overheard them, and they asked him gently, without bribes, if he had been the object of Coutinho's attentions. He said he had been sodomized two or three times. One of the friars reminded them that sodomy was to be denounced and, "bringing the Edict we saw the obligation we had to denounce the case" (IL 15035). Another slave said he had been propositioned but refused. The friars went on to say that sodomy was spreading among the slaves, who sodomized each other:

> I heard the said slave José Teixeira say that he and the other slaves named here, Raimundo nicknamed "navel-to-navel" [*por alcunha embigado*—perhaps a reference to intercrural intercourse?], Inocêncio, Fulgêncio, Anastasio, nicknamed Donato, joined to carry out the same abominable sin of sodomy with a younger boy called Gaspar, son of our slave José, the barber, and that it was the said Inocêncio who used the said Gaspar from behind. (IL 16888)

The denouncers continued that they heard that Gaspar's father had gone to complain to the Reverendo Padre Mestre Doutor Presidente da Casa Frei Anastácio Furtado de Mendonça, asking him to send Gaspar to the farm where his mother was, in order not to "*see him lost*" (my emphasis: "o não ver perdido") because the Padre Presidente da Província had already lost his other son, Máximo. ("Lost" here perhaps meant "made a habitual homosexual of" his other son.) Mendonça, surprised, promised him that Gaspar should be sent to the farm.

Another denunciation, written days after the first, was included, this time by Frei João da Trindade Costa, who claimed that, passing by the door of Coutinho, he heard the voice of Raimundo, who was between twelve and thirteen years old (from his later interrogation, it seems he was more like fifteen in 1787), saying that it was too painful for him, as he had already been taken five times that day, and that Raimundo was inside the cell and slept in the friar's cell, "which is notorious" (IL 16888). The denouncing friars were thus identifying younger boys who were said to be sodomized by Coutinho and who also participated in sexual activity with other adolescent slave boys where the older sodomized the younger.[20] Their testimony thus delineated a homoerotic set of relationships inside the Carmelite convent. This information was sent to Lisbon.

Under the signature of inquisitors Alexandre Jansen Moller and António Veríssimo de Larre dated 13 March 1789, a Rio comissário was ordered to carry out investigations. This Bartolomeu da Silva Borges was then quite elderly and was a long-time resident of Rio with a wide clerical acquaintance. His father, a Portuguese immigrant, had been a familiar of the Inquisition who requested the post in 1716 from Rio, where he was a shopkeeper. Borges had an uncle who was a familiar, while the son of another brother was a comissário. The commission of March 1789 was returned from Rio with the completed enquiries by Comissário Silva Borges, dated 1 December 1789 (IL 15035).

The enquiry heard various friars, like Padre Estevão da Trindade, fifty-eight, Rio-born, and a Carmelite friar, who all said that it was public knowledge in the convent that Coutinho sodomized Raimundo and Gaspar. Another priest, Frei Jeronymo Velasco, added that Coutinho often masturbated with the slave boys ("com a propria mão usou muitas vezes do pecado de molicies"; IL 15035), although masturbation was not among the offenses listed on the Edict of the Faith to denounce to the Inquisition.

Gaspar's father, José Felix, the illiterate, Brazilian-born, mulatto barber and slave of the friars of the Carmelite convent, who was fifty-six, testified that he had heard in person from the slave boys Raimundo and José that Coutinho was sodomizing his son. He said that on various occasions he "chastised" his son to tell him the truth until Gaspar admitted that Coutinho violently sodomized him. The barber had gone to the Prior of the convent to complain, and that was why all three boys were sent to the country estate, "in order to heal some great evil which is public among the monks and slaves of the Convent" (IL 15035). His testimony was signed with a cross.

At the end of the witness statements there was a wrap-up letter, written in wobbly handwriting, from the Rio *comissário,* Borges, dated 5 December 1789. He explained that he had not questioned some witnesses from the monastery who were now dead, or absent, or overseas. Frei José was in Santos, and he had decided that it was injudicious to get the boys back from the farm, since they were unlikely to understand the need for secrecy. He then added his *ad hominem* assessment of Coutinho as being of deceitful double character, and said that his sodomizing the boys was notorious among friars and laymen. He wrote that Coutinho was a friar who often lived outside the convent and who had exhibited disorderly behavior as long ago as when he was a chorister. Borges wrote that he had long known members of Coutinho's family and was sorry that Coutinho did not conduct himself with the honor which characterized some of his close relatives.

The record of this enquiry brought about a stinging rebuke from the promoter in Lisbon, dated on 23 June 1790, in which the *comissário* was reproved for his failure to follow instructions and for his subjectivity in his comments. He was warned of the care he should take in making the enquiries he was asked to undertake, in which he was not to be a judge but only a simple and faithful executor of what he was ordered to do. In the long interval required to carry correspondence two ways across the Atlantic, Silva Borges had died, and it was another *comissário* in Rio who carried out the second commission and who actually questioned the slave boys. Their testimony was fairly laconic. Two said that they had gone to Coutinho's cell, that he locked the door, and took down their breeches, and sodomized them on the bed. The youngest slave, Gaspar, whose father had beaten him until he confessed to being sodomized by Coutinho, now denied that anything had been done to him. He did say that he ran errands for Coutinho and that the other boys in the convent said that he was the priest's catamite (IL 16888).

We cannot now ever know who was lying and who was telling the truth in these depositions. The prosecutor in Lisbon thought there was clearly a case against Coutinho and asked that he should be arrested on the uniform evidence of Frei José dos Serafins, a calceate Carmelite, as well as the slaves, and because of his scandalous public reputation. At the same time he pointed out that the main evidence came from unacceptable witnesses: "[I]n the depositions of the three creoles José, Gaspar and Raimundo who cannot make legal proof and as clear as is required in law because of the many and serious reservations that in them are found such as that they are accomplice witnesses, singular, minors and slaves . . ." (IL 16888).

In the time-honored way of priestly cover-ups of scandal, the investigation was simply ordered closed by the Inquisitors in Lisbon on 18 November 1795. Religious authorities in Spanish America were equally complicit in preventing the punishment of some notorious sodomites in the hierarchy in the twenty years at the turn of the sixteenth and seventeenth centuries, as revealed in a fascinating study reporting the investigations of a prominent theologian in the Andes who was also a Visitor General to the entire bishopric of La Plata.[21]

CONCLUSION

The interesting thing here is the revelation of the homosexual use of slave boys, which, in the lay community, was perhaps often not seen as an opposite choice to heterosexuality but as a genital practice. For monks and friars, sodomy with slave boys was a potential sexual outlet as much as was the sexual commerce with slave women by friars who were colleagues of Coutinho.
• The early European settlers imported many African slaves to work on sugar plantations in the area of Rio and elsewhere. Many of these slaves, both female and male, were used sexually by their masters. In Olinda, Pernambuco, in 1593, a twenty-one-year-old son of a slave-owner confessed to an Inquisitor that although *already* (my emphasis) sleeping with women ("usando já de mulheres") at fourteen years of age he had also sodomized once each two of his father's young slaves, one younger than he and the other of the same age, stating significantly that this was in the house. He stressed that both of these African slaves from Guinea were receptive, and stated regarding one that, "penetrating him with his virile member in the back vase of the said negro [he] achieved within him as if he was a woman." The motive of his confession to the Inquisitor was perhaps to assuage his conscience but perhaps also to avert possible accusations from former male slave sex partners.[22] His stress on the fact that he was already "using" women at age fourteen was intended to put all such behavior in the category of youthful exuberance. One hundred years after the Coutinho enquiries, Pires de Almeida, writing in Rio in 1906, made allusions to the reputation of friars for "uranism" with black boys, who provided satisfaction to the tonsured as well as sustaining among themselves a "scandalous libertinism."[23]

Both cases revealed aspects of the sexual behaviors in the Portuguese-Brazilian world in a convent setting which remained age-structured; that is, the insertive partner sought out younger, not fully mature, males. Soares was exiled from the city of Lisbon, where his behavior was scandalous, and the failure to take action against him when he returned also preserved discretion. Neither was Coutinho arrested and shipped to Lisbon for trial, despite the evidence of the enquiries.

The trial and the summaries remind us of the layered appreciation of what may lie behind the documentation available in Lisbon. The Soares trial took place at the epicenter of the Counter-Reformation; it also coincided with particular storms within the Portuguese elite over the restoration of Independence from Spain in 1640. The Inquisitor General who set the tone at the time, D. Francisco de Castro, bishop of Guarda, had been installed on 20

May 1630, ten years before the end of the Spanish hegemony.[24] He was in office until his death. Of the sodomites who appeared in autos-da-fé during the entire existence of the Inquisition, the largest contingent, sixty-six, appeared in the 1640s, compared with seven in the previous decade, although the Inquisition was also then directed by Castro.[25] Such a striking change in sentencing during the first years of the reign of the Braganza king, when many partisans of the Spaniards were still unsure of the long-term outcome of the Portuguese revolution, points to political motivations in the surge of homophobia.[26]

In the case of Coutinho, the bitter disputes over the Reform of the Carmelites provide a "political" backdrop to the investigation of his sexual behavior at the end of the eighteenth century. The decline of the numbers of Carmelites in Rio was sharp: from 182 friars in 1780, it decreased to 49 in 1803, and by 1840, it was down to about 19.[27] Perhaps the Carmelites had a worse reputation in colonial Brazil than the Franciscans for failing to live up to their vows of chastity. It might even be that young homosexuals, or perhaps those who did not wish to marry, were especially drawn to profess as calceate Carmelites. Perhaps sexual activities between novices were not uncommon, as much in the seventeenth as in the eighteenth centuries. However, in the seventeenth-century case of António Soares, his fellow Carmelites in Brazil and indeed in Portugal obviously did all they could to shield him from punishment. In the eighteenth-century case of Coutinho, his fellow Carmelites ganged up on him by revealing his intrusion into the sexual system among adolescent male slaves.

NOTES

1. For example, see Cobb, *Police and People*, 3–81; Davis, *Fiction in the Archives;* Iacovetta and Mitchinson, *On the Case.*

2. Salomon, "Portuguese Inquisition."

3. Maynard, "On the Case of the Case," 65–87.

4. This chapter presents additional research on the Carmelites beyond the brief references to them in Higgs, "Rio de Janeiro."

5. Parker, *Beneath the Equator,* 131, map 5.2.

6. "Cotovia" was formerly an area overlooking the lower town in Lisbon and included the terrain where the Polytechnic School stands. Another name for the same area was Monte Olivete. See Caeiro, *Os conventos de Lisboa,* 38.

7. Arquivo Nacional da Torre do Tombo (Lisboa), Inquisição de Lisboa (hereafter, ANTT, IL), Proc. 6919.

8. The testimony follows: "Ambos sós se cometeram um ao outro para o pecado de sodomia e não se lembra qual deles foi o primeiro que falou, e consentindo ambos desceram as calças e logo ele confitente meteu seu membro viril no traseiro do dito frei Joseph e tendo com ele copula sodomitica derramou dentro dele semente. E logo virando-se e sendo o dito frei Joseph agente e ele confitente paciente meteu seu membro viril no traseiro dele confitente e dentro nele derramou semente" (ANTT, IL, Proc. 6919).

9. The prosecutor deplored the persistence of Soares in his sexual behavior, which included trying to force himself on a cell-mate: "que atento a grande disolução do Reu nest pecado abomi-

navel cometido por ele até nos lugares ao culto divino dedicados, e há pouco esperança que se pode esperar de emenda neles, pois preso nos carceres secretos em uma casa tão pequena em companhia de três homens com atrevimento não ouvido intentou cometer por força o tal delito; era indigno de favor e merecia toda aquela pena que não fosse de morte natural maiormente que conforme informação (posto que extrajudicial) indúvitavel da qual se tem noticia nesta Mesa, o Reu dentro nestes carceres sempre procedeu como homem desalmado e desbocado dizendo coisas em grave prejuizo de terceiros, umas evidentemente falsas e outras mui inverosimeis, e se lá fora se tiver noticia delas causariam grande escandalo e resultaria disso não só detriments da República mas do mesmo Santo Oficio o que suposto a todos excepto o deputado António Correia pareceu que o Reu oiça sua sentença na Sala desta Inquisição na forma costumada diante sós de alguns teligiosos de sua mesma ordem e dos oficiais do Santo ofício e que tenha reclusão perpetua irremisivel em os carceres secretos, e se confesse cada mes e comungue nas quatro festas principals jejue (jeiuasse nas quartas e sextas feiras) . . . a pão e agua toda a vida e tenha sua discipline nos tais dias e que em caso que por algum justo motivo se lhe alivie a dita reclusão adiante ele não possa em algum tempo tomar ordens nem ter voz activa ou passiva e sirva nos Ofícios mais humildes do mosteiro em que foi posto e o deputado António Correia declarou que em tudo se conformava com os mais votos excetos no tocante á reclusão porque lhe parecia mais conveniente para o reu poder cooperar [?] com as obrigações todas de cristão que fosse a reclusão em um convento de religiosos reformados e a todos que vai este processo ao conselho e assistiu pelo ordinário de sua comissão o Chantre João Bezerra Jacome e que encorreu em confiscação de todos os seus bens por que de direito pertencesse. [six signatures of Inquisitors]" (ANTT, IL, Proc. 6919).

10. "Das penitências que trouxe nenhuma coisa tem cumprido porque não foi para o convento de São Paulo em cujo carcere vossas ilustrissimas lho comutou o carcere perpétuo da inquisição. Ficou-se em o Rio de Janeiro que é porto de mar onde com cartas de recomendação do mestre frei Martinho Moniz que lá e ca é poderoso na Ordem se deu á mercancia de tal modo que ajuntou muitos mil cruzados além disto se desmandou em tudo o genero de vícios e se faz tão poderoso que não há quem possa com ele" (ANTT, IL, Proc. 6919).

11. "A verdade é que ele está convencido de exercitar torpezas com moços e no que toca a mesma especia do pecado que veio degredado tem violentas presumpções contra si com tres complices com que se fechava mui devagar, ora fora do Convento, ora no Convento, e sendo reprehendido nunca se quis emendar, os que se queixam de ser por ele cometidos são mais três ou quatro, e porque eu neste convento da Bahia alcancei notícia de tudo isto o mandei vir" (ANTT, IL, Proc. 6919).

12. See Mott, "Pagode português."

13. ANTT, IL, Proc. 15035 and Proc. 16888; hereafter cited parenthetically in the text as IL 15035 and IL 16888.

14. My thanks to William de Souza Martins, doctoral candidate at the University of São Paulo, for drawing to my attention the study by Francisco Filho, "A reforma da província carmelitana fluminense," 190. He also gave me the reference to the call number of the document in the National Archives in Rio de Janeiro (ANRJ), códice 1064, Devassa feita pelo escrivão da Ouvidoria Geral do Carmo, da Relação da Cidade do Rio de Janeiro, contra os frades do Convento de Nossa Senhora do Carmo da mesma cidade, 1783, 1 vol.

15. See Filho, "A reforma," 49, and the report by Luiz de Vasconcellos e Souza, "Negocios ecclesiasticos; Filho, "A reforma," 54.

16. Filho, "A reforma," 34.

17. Ibid., 67.

18. ANTT, IL, Proc. 411.

19. Lisboa, *Annaes do Rio de Janeiro,* 7: 108–12, 158–78.

20. One can note a modern U.S. study of sexual abuse of boys which showed that "boys at highest risk of being raped are under 13, are non-white, rank low on the socioeconomic ladder, are products of broken homes and are not living with their fathers. The average age was 10" (Philp, "Sexual Abuse of Boys," A9).

21. See Spurling, "Honor, Sexuality, and the Colonial Church."

22. ANTT, IL, Proc. 14326.

23. "[E]specialmente no que se refere ao uranismo praticado em nossos conventos sobremodo acrescido pelo contingents africano e seus descendentes, que serviam de pasto aos tonsurados senhores, e entretinham entre si escandalosa libertinagem." See Almeida, *Hygiene Moral,* 62–63.

24. I am grateful to Pedro Marcelo Pasche de Campos for the gift of his unpublished working paper, "Entre a Fé e o Poder," in which he points to the prosopography of the leading figures in the Inquisition hierarchy and their role in setting policy.

25. Higgs, *Queer Sites,* 114, table 5.1.

26. Borrillo, *L'Homophobie,* passim.

27. Filho, "A reforma," 21.

WORKS CITED

Almeida, Pires de. *Hygiene Moral: Homosexualismo (A Libertinagem no Rio de Janeiro); Estudo sobre as perversões e inversões do instincto genital.* Rio de Janeiro: Laemmert, 1906.

Borrillo, Daniel. *L'Homophobie (Que sais-je?).* Paris: Presses Universitaires de France, 2000.

Caeiro, Baltazar Matos. *Os conventos de Lisboa.* Sacavém: Distri Editora, 1989.

Cobb, Richard. *The Police and People: French Popular Protest, 1789–1820.* Oxford: Clarendon, 1970.

Davis, Natalie Z. *Fiction in the Archives: Pardon Tales and Their Tellers in Sixteenth-Century France.* Stanford, CA: Stanford University Press, 1987.

Filho, Francisco Benedetti. "A reforma da província carmelitana fluminense (1785–1800)." Unpublished Mestrado diss. São Paulo: History Department of the University of São Paulo, 1990.

Higgs, David, ed. *Queer Sites: Gay Urban Histories since 1600.* New York: Routledge, 1999.

———. "Rio de Janeiro." In Higgs, *Queer Sites.*

Iacovetta, Franca, and W. Mitchinson, eds. *On the Case: Explorations in Social History.* Toronto: University of Toronto Press, 1998.

Lisboa, Balthazar da Silva. *Annaes do Rio de Janeiro.* 8 vols. Facsimile of 1834 edition. Rio de Janeiro: Editora Leitora, 1967.

Maynard, Steven. "On the Case of the Case: The Emergence of the Homosexual as a Case History in Early Twentieth-Century Ontario." In Iacovetta and Mitchinson, *On the Case,* 65–87.

Mott, Luiz. "Pagode português: A subcultura *gay* em Portugal nos tempos inquisitoriais." *Ciência e cultura* 40 (1988): 120–39.

Parker, Richard. *Beneath the Equator: Cultures of Desire, Male Homosexuality, and Emerging Gay Communities in Brazil.* New York: Routledge, 1999.

Pasche de Campos, Pedro Marcelo. "Entre a Fé e o Poder: Um estudo sobre os Inquisidores Gerais Portugueses." Unpublished paper, Niterói, 1996.

Philp, M. "Sexual Abuse of Boys Kept under Wraps." *Toronto Globe and Mail,* 3 December 1998, A9.

Salomon, H. P. "The Portuguese Inquisition and Its Victims in the Light of Recent Polemics." *Journal of the American Portuguese Cultural Society* (summer–fall 1971): 19–28.

Spurling, Geoffrey. "Honor, Sexuality, and the Colonial Church: The Sins of Dr. Gonzalez, Cathedral Canon." In *The Faces of Honor: Sex, Shame, and Violence in Colonial Latin America,* ed. L. L. Johnson and Sonya Lipsett-Rivera. Albuquerque: University of New Mexico Press, 1998.

Vasconcellos e Souza, Luiz de. "Negocios ecclesiasticos no Brazil colonial: Relaxacão dos frades do Carmo e reforma ineficaz." *Revista Trimensal do Instituto Historico e Geographico Brazileiro* 51, parte 2 (3º e 1º trimestres, 1888): 115–55.

CHAPTER SIX

Crypto-Sodomites in Colonial Brazil

LUIZ MOTT

Translated by Salima Popat

The objective of this chapter is to discuss, on the basis of the records of the Holy Office of the Inquisition in Lisbon, the extent to which there was space in colonial Brazil for the crystallization of a diversified gay subculture, given the imposition of the ideological canons of the heterosexist morality dominant in the Judeo-Christian tradition. Using the life story of a sodomite from Pernambuco in the northeast of Brazil, imprisoned by the Portuguese Inquisition in 1595, I question the teaching of Michael Foucault that "sodomy was a forbidden type of act *and the author was a mere juridical subject* [my emphasis],"[1] concluding that at least three hundred years before the medicalization of the homosexual persona we can notice the emergence of a gay subculture in the New World.

If we take this life story to illustrate the specific case of Brazilian sexuality, we can clearly detect three cultural matrices that shaped not only ideas and performative limits, but also the diverse colorings of the sexual cultures of Brazil's Latin American neighbors. The hegemonic matrix of Western sexuality is Judeo-Christian morality, whose pillars lay fixed mainly in the *Tábuas da Lei* in Leviticus, the *Epístolas Paulinas,* the medieval confessionals, and the Catholic catechism promoted by the Council of Trent.[2] From its origin, this hegemonic matrix has never been accepted peacefully, but has always been contested by the numerous sexual heresies that have survived all Western history, and, in the case of the Portuguese, especially after the great voyages and the close contact of the metropolis with the native people overseas, has suffered uncontrollable foreign influences. In the Brazilian case, as is well known, the hegemonic matrix was strongly disrupted, especially by contacts with the indigenous sexual culture, notably the indigenous people of the Tupinambá tribe, and by the sexual anarchy of the African slaves, mainly those from Guinea and the Kingdoms of Congo-Angola and Benin. I use the term *anarchy* purposely, as emphasized by Gilberto Freyre, "[T]here is no slavery without sexual depravity."[3] And although some African ethnic groups practiced a very repressive sexual morality in the New World,[4] what prevailed were the practices imposed by white males and their followers that inspired the saying, "Below the Equator there is no sin!" Thus developed a sexuality more liberal, heterodox, and sadistic than that practiced in the European metropolis.[5]

Thus, with the syncretization of these three sexual matrices as a backdrop and tropicalist neosexuality as an example, we delve into indiscreet documents left by serious inquisitorial scribes to see what happened behind the curtains in Colonial Brazil as related to the abominable and nefarious sin of sodomy.

THE VISIT OF THE HOLY OFFICE IN PERNAMBUCO

In a radiant land lives a sad people.
—Paulo Prado, *Retrato de Brazil*

21 September 1593—the time of sugar cane processing in New Lusitânia.[6] On this day, the Investigator Hector Furtado de Mendonça arrived at the Port of Recife. He brought with him two years of experience in the arduous task of Investigator of the Holy Office of the Bahia de Todos os Santos and its provinces, where he had heard more than 120 confessions and more than 200 denunciations of deviations of faith and morality. He was met by the governor of Pernambuco, D. Felipe de Moura, and the vicar of the Jurisdiction, father Diogo do Couto. Upon his arrival the most important locals were present: the Lins, the Holanda, the Albuquerque, and, beside the politicians, the regular and secular clergy, the good men of the village, and the people in general. The Inquisition was the most feared beast of the colonial period, and at the simple proclamation, "In the name of the Holy Office of the Inquisition!" every Christian had to obey the orders, let themselves be imprisoned, surrender their horses or their belongings to all those who held the feared and envied title of prosecutor or commissioner of the *Monstrum Horribilem*.[7]

A month after his arrival, on 24 October, the twentieth Sunday after Pentecost, the Investigator solemnly reestablished the Inquisition in Olinda, posting on the doors of the Cathedral of Salvador and the Church of San Pedro Martír, Corpo Santo e Nossa Senhora do Rosário da Várzea do Capibaribe, the *Edict of Faith and General Monitor of the Holy Office,* forcing all Christians, under the threat of excommunication *ipso facto incurrenda,* to denounce or confess everything known that "any person had done, said and committed against the Holy Catholic faith and against its beliefs and the teachings of the Holy Mother Church of Rome."[8] Coincidentally, San Pedro Martír (1202–1252), killed with a blow to the head given by an atheist, was the patron of the Holy Inquisition—and his presence as a patron of the first church of this captaincy reveals the respect that the colonizers of Pernambuco had for the Holy Tribunal of Faith.

At this time, although Salvador da Bahia was the administrative headquarters of Portuguese America, New Lusitânia led the progress and development of the colony, making Olinda the leading city in the Portuguese-American world, having under its jurisdiction more than fifty good sugar mills in full production.[9] With a population of about three hundred Christians and sons of Christians in 1528, the captaincy at the end of the sixteenth century had about eight thousand whites, two thousand domesticated Indians, and ten thousand African slaves.[10]

Olinda, the headquarters of the captaincy, with its irregular and rough topography, spread itself around two basic poles: the Governor's Square and the Church of Salvador. The city also had a House of Customs, three convents, four churches, and more than ten streets. In 1584, ten years prior to the arrival of the Inquisitorial Inspector, the Jesuit Cardim described the headquarters of the state in the following way:

> Located in an eminent place, with a great view of the sea and the land, [Olinda] displays rows of houses made of stones, bricks and roofing tiles, with its beautiful church matrix of three naves, surrounded by several chapels, sheltering more than two thousand inhabitants between the villages and its outskirts, with much slavery from Guinea—around two thousand slaves.[11]

The elite, "people of honor," displayed luxury not always compatible with the tropical heat: The women and their children wore "all kinds of velvets, damasks and other silks, and in this there is much excess." More excesses were practiced by the landed elite, proprietors of the sixty-six sugar mills in Pernambuco that ended up producing harvests of up to two hundred thousand *arrobas* (1 arroba = 32 pounds) of sugar. "Dignified men . . . buy thoroughbreds for from 200 to 300 cruzados, and some had three, four expensive horses, enjoyed parties and banquets . . . and drank annually 50 to 80 thousand cruzados of wine from Portugal." And the chronicler ends with an exclamation of disapproval: "In Pernambuco one finds more vanity than in Lisbon!"[12] Years later, Brandônio proudly said, "Olinda is a small Lisbon."[13] Pernambuco was to be known as the New Lusitânia.

It is in this land recently occupied by Christians, but already marked by deviations from the faith and morality taught by the Holy Mother Church, that the Investigator would examine the lives and customs of its population, hearing, in the twenty-two months that he stayed, a total of 209 denouncers in the captaincies of Pernambuco and Itamaraca, 54 in the neighboring captaincy of Paraíba, and more than 61 confessions from the residents of the same region,[14] whose private deviations as announced to the Holy Inquisition were divided among the following categories: 90 blasphemies, 87 heretical propositions, 62 Jewish practices, 36 acts against religion, 34 bigamies, 17 sodomies, 16 Lutheran (Protestant) practices, and 8 witchcrafts, totaling 350 occurrences.[15] While many of the heretical propositions and dissonant words, as well as dozens of blasphemies, dealt with the question of sexuality, the truth is, in this region, the deviations of the sexual morality are relatively few if compared with the sins against the faith, since the accusations of bigamy and sodomy together represent only 14.5 percent of the total records—and sodomy itself does not reach 5 percent of the total.

If we compare this finding with the confessions of guilt in the first and second Inspections of Bahia, described by Sônia Siqueira,[16] we would initially have to agree with Rudolpho Garcia in stating that "there are not as many sexual sins against nature in the denunciations and confessions in Pernambuco as there are in those of Bahia."[17] However, further study of other Inquisitorial sources among the records found in the Torre de Tombo allows us to analyze such differences and conclude that in New Lusitânia there were proportionally even more crypto-sodomites than in the Bahia de Todos os Santos. Thus, during the colonial period, the reality was the same as that observed by contemporary gay visitors: in Pernambuco, the homosexuals are more closeted than in Bahia, "but they certainly exist!"

A behavioral regularity, though, was observed in Bahia as well as in Pernambuco: although in the Monitoring Office a list of crimes that should have been denounced to the Investigator did not contain an explicit mention of sodomy, it seems that the "nefarious sin" (*pecado nefando*) was what culprits most feared, insofar as, in Salvador as in Olinda, the first colonizers who appeared at dawn at the Investigator's door to self-denounce as soon as the grace period opened were precisely two sodomites: in Salvador, the priest Frutuoso Alvares; in Olinda, Antônio Rodrigues, resident of São Lourenço.

HOMOSEXUALITY IN THE COLONIAL IMAGINARY
Sodom means betrayal, Gomorra rebellion.
—Sermon delivered at an auto-da-fé, 1645

Many of the first inhabitants of Pernambuco were somewhat familiar with homosexuality, at that time called by scholars *pecado nefando* (nefarious sin) and *pecado contra natura* (sin against nature); and by the people, *somitigaria* (sodomy), *mau pecado* (evil sin), *velhacaria* (libertinism), and *fanchonice* (faggotry). In the Iberian Peninsula since the Middle Ages, the people called *sodomitas* (sodomites) either *fodincu* (active) or *fodidincu* (passive), depending on the position assumed in the *peccattum nefandum*. They also used the root word *somitigo* (sodomite), a term current in Portugal and in the more archaic parts of Brazil, used as a synonym for *avaricious,* perhaps resulting from a corruption of or association with the word *Semitic,* since Semites were the main victims of the *Monstrum Horribilem.* The most current expression was *fanchono* (faggot), generally reserved for the more flamboyant homosexual that we assume today to be the equivalent of a *bicha* (queen), or like a *bicha louca* (crazy queen), but who was crucially different from the *sodomita.* The *fanchono* did not necessarily practice the crime of *sodomia perfeita* (penetration of the anus by the penis, with ejaculation), limiting himself to kisses, hugs, and *molices* (mutual masturbation) with partners of the same sex. Since the sixteenth century, the people had used the term *fazer as sacanas* (licentious sexual acts), including under this denomination the most common of the *molices,* the *punheta* (masturbation), and the much previously practiced *coxeta* (friction to ejaculation between the thighs), which the Inquisitors and even today's legislators refer to as the *copula intra femura* (i.e., between the thighs).[18]

More than once I noticed in the Inquisitorial documentation that sodomy was much more present in the imaginary, in the collective memory, and in the daily lives of the first Pernambucans than I had imagined, due to its condition as "the most shameful, filthy and dishonest sin, the most upsetting before God and the world, because only speaking with men about this sin, without any other act, it is so upsetting that the air cannot suffer it, but naturally is corrupted and loses its natural virtue."[19] Even while being a *peccatum horribilem* and one of the greatest moral taboos of all Christianity, sodomy, besides being cited and discussed by the settlers, was the subject of frequent commentaries and jokes, especially when a *fanchono* made a gracious appearance in the neighborhood. In the interior of Itapicuru, in the seventeenth century, we have a record that "the residents used to blabber about a mulatto *fachono.*"[20]

Despite the Pauline religious decrees that "these things not even be mentioned among you," the people did not resist the temptation to converse about and even cite cases which had the "Greek love" as a theme. Here's an example: Estevão Cordeiro, thirty-one years old, farmer, resident of the Cornijo plantation complex, in the district of Santo Amaro, confessed that "while talking with some of the neighbors, he does not remember the time nor the purpose, he said that in Rome, women walked around with their breasts bare and the Holy priests gave forgiveness to the men who slept carnally with them, with the intention of distracting the men from committing the *nefarious sin.*"[21] In describing this uncommon picture, this new Christian was simply ratifying one of the most repeated assertions in the secular and ecclesiastic conversations about the "nefarious sin": that it was most fair to call sodomy an Italian vice, since Italy, and Rome particularly, were considered the European version of Sodom and Gomorra. Until the eighteenth century in Minas Gerais, it was said that "to fornicate the Italian way" was synonymous with anal intercourse.[22] And the belief that Italy was the capital of sodomy so permeated the Iberian imaginary that the records of the Lisbon Inquisition show that some *fanchonos* cited the names of Roman cardinals and even Popes as deep-rooted lovers of boys—with good reason, since in the *Encyclopedia of Homosexuality*, in the article entitled "Gay Clerics," the following appear as lovers of the same sex: João XII (938–964), Benedito XI (1021–1050), João XXIII (+1419), Xisto IV (1419–1482), Pio II (1405–1464), Paulo II (1417–1471), Julio II (1443–1513), Leão X (1475–1521), and Julio III (1487–1555).[23] Note also that among accused sodomites who arrived at the Holy Office of the Inquisition, if there were any who were known to have lived or simply passed through Italy, the Inquisitors would immediately pressure them with more deceitful questions, since the suspicion of having practiced the Italian vice was strong.[24]

According to Foucault, the West, apart from developing what he called *scientia sexualis* (sexual science), engages in extensive discussion of sex, especially regarding whether it is to be blessed or damned. Nevertheless, everything leads us to believe that the author of the *History of Sexuality* once more exaggerated this generalization, since such perverse fixation is not exclusively our privilege, as the first chroniclers registered that the Tupinambá spent hours talking about that kind of filth. Also, in Islamic countries such as Morocco and Algeria, there exist testimonies that jokes frequently applauded within male circles are the ones with the theme of *camelot*—the gay villain.[25] In the colonial northeast of Brazil, homosexuality was present not only in memories, but also in the histories and perhaps even among the *folia dos fanchonos* (group of faggots) in diverse places and for prolonged periods, for there was at least one sodomite body present: visible, within reach of those less proper and those more daring. If Goethe repeated that "[h]omosexuality is as old as humanity itself," I affirm that homosexuality has been present in Brazil since its prehistory, being vividly practiced by Amerindians—existing even very close to Pernambuco in the neighborhood of Paraíba, a type of "gay campus"—nudist by tribal tradition, but homoerotic by choice. This was the famous *Bay of Betrayal*, whose original name, *Acejutibira*, signified "*cajual* [fruit that produces the cashew] of the *tibira* [passive sodomite]"— the same root word, *tibira*, that the Tupinambá called Baltazar da Lomba, the most effeminate sodomite of all colonial northeast history, when they saw him wash clothes and mix dough like a woman.[26]

A few examples establish the presence of homosexuals at the very beginning of Brazil's colonization: If I am not mistaken, the first person exiled by the Portuguese Inquisition to Brazil was the sodomite Estevão Redondo, servant of the governor of Lisbon, who arrived in New Lusitânia in February of 1549, his name being recorded in the *Book of the Exiled* with the stamp of the governor, D. Duarte d'Albuquerque Coelho.[27] Considering the lengthy involvement of young Redondo with the nefarious sin, although I do not support the contemporary popular opinion that "this path (homoeroticism) has no return," I note without fear of contradiction that not even the enormous shame of having been publicly sentenced in an auto-da-fé, nor the painful journey across the Atlantic, nor even banishment "forever" in this land of savage Indians and African slaves, was sufficiently strong to "cure him" of his homosexual orientation. In fact, as a general rule, many of those sentenced by the tribunal of the Holy Office of the Inquisition frequently relapsed into "the love that dare not speak its name." Estevão Redondo is indeed the first gay European known to set foot in the New World, and Pernambuco, the land that prides itself in being the cradle of *machos*, must feel the shame of being the place where the first *fanchono* in the history of Brazil appeared. Consequently, from the time of its origin, the state counted among its number the presence of one public and notorious homosexual, so notorious as to become generally known among those suffering the condemnation of the exiled.

The second gay that I have discovered in this region is mentioned casually throughout an accusation against the sailor Bastião Dias, resident of Boa Vista of Olinda, who was accused by the mulatta Lionor Fernandez, *mulher do mundo* (woman of the world), of having disrespected the Vicar Francisco Teixeira with "bad and hurtful words," shouting to all those who would listen that "it is worse to confess a man's or woman's sins to the *fanxono* than to the said priest." The end of the accusation clarified what interests us: "He declared further, having been questioned by the Inspector, that 'the fanchono is a Black who frolics in this village,' whom they commonly call the drunk, whose nickname is known to be the said *fanxono*."[28]

The reader should not be surprised that a *fanchono* lived freely and openly in his merrymaking in the New Lusitânia. In Lisbon, in the same century, a few steps away from the shady, secretive prisons of the Holy Office of the Inquisition, lived a certain Rafael, a *fanchono* from the island of Madeira, "who had effeminate speech, was a *fanchono*, any man who saw him would lose himself, and he was a good lay!" Another individual to be compromised was Manoel Maricas, the innkeeper in Coimbra, "so infamous of the vice that he was given the name of Maricas (fag). He tempted travelers to commit the abominable sin of sodomy, and more than a convict, he seemed incorrigible in the vice." A final individual to have a name identifying his nefarious behavior was Pantalião da Costa, nicknamed Menino Puto (Boy Whore), "who paid other boys to stick his hand in their flies and kiss them."[29] In Bahia, another Afro-Brazilian who fooled around with his master made a fool of himself dancing with a pot on his head. "The whole city knew him to be a sodomite," even though he did not carry the degrading nickname of *fanchono*. He was denounced to the Inquisition together with other mulattos, since it was rumored in Salvador that "one sucked the other."[30]

If for the *fanchono das folias* (group of faggots) of Recife we do not have available information about lustful intimacies, for Baltazar da Lomba, evidence is abundant that he was indeed a sodomite, that he was incorrigible, and moreover, the most effeminate of all the homoerotics registered in the history of the northeast. Not even the first transvestite of Brazilian history, Francisco Manicongo (Bahia, 1591), was so effeminate as this controversial Portuguese, who arrived in Paraíba in 1570, before he was fourteen years old. From the time of his arrival, he had assumed the posture, the facial expression, and the professions traditionally exclusive to the fragile sex: "He usually sews, weaves and mixes dough like a woman"; and more than this, whether by physical weakness or predilection, only God knows, he became the most famous *fudidinculo* (passive) of the state with a notorious image. He only gave himself to the Indians of the land: "[S]erving himself to the Indians from the villages he passed, Baltazar de Lomba, as a female, claim[ed] to be their wife and they called him *tibira*—which means *passive sodomite*." Although he lived most of his nefarious existence in the neighboring town of Filipeia da Nossa Senhora, during the Inspection of New Lusitânia, Baltazar de Lomba assisted in Pernambuco, always "serving as a soldier," that is, employed in the house of whomever contracted his domestic services.[31] Such examples prove our thesis that, despite the draconian legislation and the canons of the Holy Mother Church against the abominable sin *contra naturam*, ultra-effeminate or publicly recognized homosexuals circulated with a certain freedom in the Brazilian colony.

More tragic and astonishing should be, however, the stories known to few residents of Pernambuco, witnessed elsewhere, of sodomites who were imprisoned and condemned to death. When the official Furtado de Mendonça inaugurated the Inspection in New Lusitânia, more than one hundred sodomites had already been caught by the Courts of Lisbon, Coimbra, and Évora. Certainly many of the Brazilian settlers who stood in the midst of the curious crowds that gathered at the autos-da-fé knew that many other *fanchonos* had already been publicly whipped or exiled to distant lands, and that at least a dozen of them had been "committed to Secular Justice," a merciful euphemism utilized by the Inquisitors for those condemned to death by fire.[32]

Among those who remembered the cruel genocide of the *filhos da dissidência* (children of dissidents) was the black woman Joana Afonso, from São Tomé, herself an outcast exiled to Brazil, condemned by the king's justice for the crime of adultery. In her hearing of the accusation before the Board of the Inspection, she declared that around 1570, in her homeland, many men were arrested for sodomy and many more were burned for it and others exiled. Salvador Romeiro (now a resident of Pernambuco) was also arrested, and before his imprisonment it was publicly known by everyone on the island that he was a sodomite and that he did not sleep with his wife and slept with other men; this was stated publicly when the Supreme Judge Salema imprisoned him in the kingdom.[33]

Therefore, our first colonizers were aware that sodomy sometimes was treated by the powerful as the gravest of crimes, having led some of their contemporaries to prison, exile, and even the fire. This harsh treatment, however, had been a thing of the metropolis, since in this new colony below the equator, newly converted Christians and *fanchonos* lived very freely and relatively peacefully until the Reverend Inspector began his Inquisitorial work.

THE ROOTS OF HOMOPHOBIA IN THE NORTHEAST

Viado must die![34]
—Popular saying in present-day northeast Brazil

Besides the perceptible presence of homosexuality in the imaginary of many Portuguese-Brazilian settlers and of a few homosexuals publicly identified in the daily life of the colony, the reader should not repeat the mistake of contemporary foreign gays, who imagine present-day Brazil to be a tropical paradise for homosexuals. Do not conclude, therefore, that the draconian legislation coexisted peacefully with tolerance vis-à-vis the practitioners of this "wicked sin." There is conclusive evidence that homophobia was most cruel in the populated enclaves of this virgin land. We can see that it was precisely in this primordial formation of the Brazilian people that the roots of our exacerbated contemporary machismo infiltrated the national ethos. I believe that the conjunction of two historical factors, one contingent, the other essential, may explain why in the New World the Iberians became so much stronger in their male chauvinism and our Lusitanian patriarchs even more authoritarian than they were in the Old Continent.

The first explanation has to do with the famous saying most heard, repeated, and tastefully assimilated by the many who crossed the ocean on their way to what Laura Mello e Sousa has called "the Atlantic inferno": "*Ultra Equinotialem non pecari*" ("Below the equator, there is no sin").[35] The greatness of the land, the secrecy of the woods, the tempting nakedness of the *cunhãs e pias* (Tupi for "boys and girls")—much more lustful than Europeans, who had been repressed for centuries by the fear of the fire of the inferno—contributed to the development here, more than in the old metropolis, of a sexual practice that was not only more free, intense, and diverse,[36] but also so popular and casuistic, that if the Inquisition had not interfered in time, I suppose that it might have emerged as formal heresy. Ronaldo Vainfas, in a chapter entitled "Norms of Fornication," has synthesized better than anyone not only the manifestations of the desires of men, but also the rules of licit sexuality.[37]

The many dissonant propositions of the colonists about sexual matters, when they wrote freely about whether it was sinful to sleep with an Indian, a black, or a public woman, call attention to the *heterosexualizing* emphasis of this discourse. Though modern, revolutionary, and heterodox, this discourse served clearly as justification for and support of the only sexual orientation permitted and blessed by the owners of moral power: heterosexuality.

When the youngsters Manuel de Viseu, Bastião Luiz, Antônio Marques, and many other colonists of the northeast said repeatedly, when they weren't working in the field or daydreaming while in the hammocks on their verandas, that "it was not a mortal sin to sleep carnally with a single woman (or with an Indian, or with a black woman, or with a woman of the world, etc.) paying her for her work,"[38] they were directly stimulating heterosexuality, since all other erotic performances—masturbation, bestiality, homosexuality—received the status of *mortal sin*. The tailor Cristovão Martín, a new Christian, goes even further in his praise of heterosexuals, in declaring loudly and clearly, "It is in the service of God to take a woman,"[39] making a virtue of what the *Catechism of Trent* confirmed to be a grave sin, deserving of a penalty enforced by the Episcopal authority. When the merchant Sebastião Pereira conversed about daily life with Father Antônio in Rua Rocha in the village of Recife, "They ended up talking about a married girl whose husband is away, how she was dissolute and dishonest and used her body wickedly, sleeping with whomever would ask her; Bastião said then that she did very well since whomever does not have enough of that cannot go to paradise";[40] in other words, he defended the venereal acts between male and female. Even if those acts included the grave sin of adultery, they became a kind of indulgence or passport to eternal life. So strong was such a belief that the debauched carpenter Pero Gonçalves said without shame, "Fornicate, fornicate until it is enough, for in the land of the king, no one has ever gone to the inferno for fornicating" (instead of the word *fornicar* [to fornicate] written here, he used the vulgar Portuguese word [*foder*, to fuck], for virtuous [*honestidade*] words were not written, or so stated the notary of the Inspection).[41] Fornication between a man and a woman, of course!

I conclude this anthology of heretical propositions praising heterosexuality with this symptomatic expression of the sailor Gonçalo Francisco, a

single youth just beginning to grow a beard, traveling by boat from Recife to Olinda and from Olinda back. . . . [I]t happened that in the said path to Varradouro, the said sailor took a Brazilian black woman and the accuser told him to let go of the black woman, then the said sailor answered: Be quiet, that whomever does not sleep with women in this world will sleep with the devil in the other, and the accuser reprimanded him for saying such a thing, and he replied that he had already heard that from other men.[42]

This document is a crucial piece to confirm our affirmation that heterosexuality was compulsively imposed *manu militari et inquisitori* (by military and Inquisitorial force), reinforced by laws, verses, prose, and sayings that worked as an antidote to the persistent and generalized homoerotic temptation. Just as the above-mentioned Pope conceded great indulgences to the men who, to avoid the "Italian vice," would kiss the bare breasts of Roman prostitutes, here in the New World, as implied in this last document, it was commonly accepted that only by intensive practice of heterosexuality could one avoid the harsh punishments painted in the Sistine Chapel and in other churches, where one could see nightmare devils sticking their entire hands or sharp spears in the anuses of defenseless *sucubbi*—immediately identified with the *donzeloes* or *fanchonos* who in life did not follow the teachings of this flaming sailor who at the reef of Olinda besieged and sexually possessed many *brasilas and guineas* (popular words for Indians and Africans) who had fallen prey to his net.

DAY-TO-DAY HOMOPHOBIC REPRESSION
The repression of the sodomites is not a myth. It was the daily bread of a difficult pleasure.
—Rafael Carrasco, *Inquisición y represión*

I defend the hypothesis that machismo in the colonies reveals itself more virulently and the patriarchy more aggressively than in the metropolis due to the combination of two historical factors. The contingent factor has just been exemplified: the redefinition and exacerbation of sensuality in the "tropic of sins." The other factor I consider *essential* in the crystallization of Latin American machismo: the reinforcement of patriarchies. In this colony of continental dimensions, the white elite represented a fragile demographic minority, in the proportion of one white to three or four blacks, Indians, slaves, and those emancipated, besides mestizos of all shades. A famished population, exhausted by shifts of fifteen or more hours of forced labor each day, humiliated and punished with iron and fire: How could they keep this mob submissive?

Whip or stick in hand, fist or sword by the waist, an ultra-manly posture, and authoritarianism were indispensable elements for all the men who sought to live among the crowd of *negrada e tapuiada*.[43] In the enslaving colonies, there was no place for the effeminate, weaklings, cowards, *donzeloes:* delicate men, sensitive, whimperers—don't even think about it. We see the magnitude of the festivities of São João in the northeast even today—more important for family reinforcement than Christmas—noting the abundant utilization of firecrackers, some extremely violent and dangerous, such as the famous "swords" of Cruz das Almas, responsible annually for dozens of mutilations and even deaths. Such celebrations worked for our ancestors as true initiation rituals, places in which white children and adolescents were introduced to the knowledge and dominance of the use of gunpowder, raw material vital to maintaining a servile and obedient mob.

In this pioneering front of brave people, to turn one's back to another man threatened the continuity of the white conquistador's hegemony in the New World, since it was from behind that the Indians killed the careless who dared enter into the forest, from behind that the captives who revolted took the lives of their oppressors. Similar was the *fungando nas costas* (fucking from behind) of another man, about which the inquisitors tell us that the active partner, or agent, exercised his domination and maintained the stigma of the sexually passive partner.[44] And it was exactly for being in this nefarious, passive, position that a young boy in Pernambuco suffered grave discrimination and harassment, without ever knowing for sure if he was being denounced by the other in a *pega rabo* between adolescents.[45]

Let us follow the webs of this net: Domingos da Costa, *mameluco* (Portuguese-indigenous mixture), inhabitant of Olinda, twenty-nine years old, without a profession, made the following accusation. On the first Saturday of Lent in 1594,

> being 1:30 at night, dark, in the public square of the village Goiana, in front of the church, passing together with an administrator and a carpenter, they saw Francisco, a young mulatto or mestizo boy, about seventeen years old. He was in the said public square, kneeling down with feet and hands on the ground, shirted, and on top of him, laying face down over his back, behind, the carpenter's servant Pedralvares de Iguaraçu, Antônio, a white boy of the same age, also in a shirt, a chunky boy with thick eyebrows and in his forehead the signs of smallpox, from the Kingdom, and a servant of Gonçalo Gonçalvez. And together with them standing up was João Fernandes, *mameluco* boy, who was saying: *ui . . . , estes ui . . .*[46]

A week after the accusation, it is the turn of the *mameluco* himself, João Fernandes, to give his version of what he witnessed in that dawn of Lent. Queried, as customary, by the Inspector, if he had something to denounce, he responded negatively. He was then asked, "[W]ho were the ones gathered with him one night in Goiana and did they commit the nefarious sin? He responded that he saw no one do such a thing. He was then asked who those were engaged in that when he was witnessed saying: *[U]i estes, . . . ui estes,* in the public square of the church?" Then he revealed his own version of that story:

> [O]ne night in the past Lent, a year ago, when I was going to the war of Paraíba, having been in the public square of the church with Antônio, a white boy, younger than him, both [Antônio and João] started to loosen up and fight, holding each other, and Antônio told him [João] that if Francisco, Indian mestizo who stood before them, came towards them that he [Antônio] would have slapped him [Francisco], he doesn't know why, and while fighting he [João] testifies tripping said Antônio, who, while on the ground, grabbed said Francisco's feet. Then, Antônio got up and fought with Francisco and tripped him, and, laying flat on the ground, Francisco, his back turned, remained on top of said Antônio, and he [João] jumped on top and, placing one hand on the head of the said Francisco, he [João] testified that he said: *[U]i estes, ui estes,* and at that point the men arrived and the *mameluco* Domingo kicked said Antônio and made them get up.[47]

Yet a third witness is heard, confirming the previous statement, only adding that the said João Fernandes would have said, "*[U]i, ui,* what are these doing . . . [?!]," and when the white boy who was on top got up, "he saw him pull up his underwear, but he doesn't know if he raised them only because they had dropped or if they were open, and that what he witnessed is not confirmed because they didn't understand if they were doing the sin, since to him, it seemed bad to have seen them this way, but in the little time he had seen them, both were running and touching as if they were fighting."[48]

I ask the pure and unsullied reader what to make of this episode? Was it a matter of a simple prank between one from the kingdom and a *mameluco,* both seventeen years old? Or in fact, who knows what vulgar pranks could have occurred as the mestizo was already on the floor and the chunky white boy had his underwear lowered? Wasn't it maybe a game, the white first using the mestizo, while the *mameluco* voyeur waited his turn, mumbling his "*[U]i, ui,*" perhaps with the same playful tone employed by contemporary machos, especially the most contemporary generation, as they babble "*fiu, fiu*" in the attempt to seduce someone who awakens their libido? Certainly, all these erotic alternatives must have gone through the mind of the Inspector, old fox in the art of the investigative exploration of the deceitful conscience of the denouncer. "This case is nefarious and difficult to prosecute because of the secrecy and the caution with which it is committed," wrote the prosecutor of the Inspection and the bishop of Brazil in the record of another youth also arrested in Pernambuco on this same occasion.[49] More than arriving at a conclusive verdict, what interests us most in this *pega rabo de fran-*

guinhos (slang used in contemporary Pernambuco, where *frango* [chicken] is the popular equivalent to the nationally used term, *viado*) are the consequences of this episode, since they reveal the highest degree of homophobia prevalent in this land of fighting cocks.

The first reaction to such an erotic or martial hug given by the chunky white on the back of the *mameluco* was a mixture of taunting and joking: "*[U]i, ui,*" repeated the youth that accompanied them. Following this, it was the turn of the mestizo, Domingos de Casa, to manifest himself: "[H]e gave a kick to the two that were on top of each other in a nefarious and sodomitic position, and he tripped them and separated them,"[50] denouncing them to the inspector when he got the first opportunity.

In small places, even long ago, when homosexuality was the gravest of crimes, the news spread rapidly. "Domingos da Costa told that to other people of the ranch, where right away the rumors ran that they were sinning in the *nefando*." Muttering that many at times fell into verbal aggressions: "When they twit (indirectly insinuate) sodomites, do not mock them in response." This demonstrates that both partners, not just the passive, became infamous as loathsome sinners.

The one who suffered the most discrimination, however, was the youngster who was in the "succubus" position on that fateful Lenten night: "Because of that, Pedro Alvares got rid of the said servant."[51] He lost his job due to the bad fame of being a *tibira*. Furthermore, such discrimination is still practiced without punishment in our day. Where new Christians, bigamists, witches, heretics, masons, and so on have been absolved of their previous guilt, sodomites continue to be unable to work, or they are quickly dismissed when suspected or discovered in the practice of the love which dare not speak its name.[52]

THE NETWORK OF CRYPTO-SODOMITES

During the Inspection of the Holy Office of the Inquisition in Pernambuco, five men and boys were publicly defamed as sodomites: Salvador Romeiro, who had already been exiled from São Tomé for this crime; Baltazar da Lomba, who for more than twenty years was called and acted like a *tibira;* the one *fanchono das folias;* and finally the two young quarrelsome boys from Goiana, Francisco and Antônio, who were the motive of the scuffle in the case of their supposed involvement with the "wicked sin." All of them were denounced by third parties, none by any accomplice or previous rival.

Another four sodomites took the initiative and denounced themselves, certainly fearing being the targets of accusations, since according to the regulations of the Holy Office of the Inquisition, those who confessed right away, before being accused by third parties, were judged with less rigor. The first to confess was Antônio Rodrigues, a farmer from São Lourenço.

He stated that before getting married he had sinned nefariously more than twenty times with a certain Damião Gonçalves, another six times with Domingos Pires, and "had engaged in vulgar touches and committed the sin of masturbation with six or seven young boys—many more boys and many more times."[53]

The next confessant was Bastião de Morais, twenty-five years old, son of a judge of Igarassu. He said that before he crossed the Atlantic, while still in Lisbon, he slept carnally ten or twelve times with Domingos, his uncle's slave, committing *sodomias ad invicen,* an Inquisitorial euphemism for the infant-juvenile *troca-troca* (sex between boys).[54] The third to confess was Antônio Couto, from the Bishopric of Porto. Like many, he repented of the mistakes he committed while in the kingdom, in his case twenty-five years ago. For a quarter of a century, he kept secret the "nefarious touches" committed with a boy with a crooked eye and with another young boy who was the servant of a noble of Santarém.[55]

Two months after this confession, another sodomite relieved his conscience before the Inspector. João Fernandes, the twenty-year-old son of a Frenchman and a *mameluca,* said that one night, two years ago, he slept in the same hammock with Bartolomeu Pires, son of the blacksmith, at this time only eleven years of age,

> and we both had only shirts on without underwear. The said Bartolomeu began provoking him that he wanted to get on top of him, and that way proceeded to the act. The said boy threw himself on his back and he, the confessant, raising Bartolomeu's legs, threw himself over him, face down, and stuck his virile member into his inferior orifice, and this way they were joined together in the carnal nefarious and sodomitic act, effectuated and consumed, doing the ass of said Bartolomeu as he would have done in the natural orifice of a woman, polluting inside the ass.

He also told of another adventure. He was again innocently lying in his bed one night when a mulatto slave, a bearded man, began to excite him, consummating the nefarious act over the next three days, always acting as the agent.[56]

The last of this list of men who confessed their sodomitic practices was Fulgêncio Cardoso, thirty-five years old, separated from his wife, resident of Olinda.

> He said that at thirteen years of age, at his grandparents' house about three leagues from Aveiro, Bishopric of Coimbra, he and his brother, two years older, Bartolomeu Cardoso, married to the sister of his said wife, both slept in a single bed and one night it happened that feeling

each other they proceeded to such vileness that he, the confessant, threw himself on his side so that his brother stuck his vulgar virile member into his rear orifice and, inside him, he polluted this time only, and after committing the said sin, he pretended to wake up and then showed his annoyance and blamed him, the confessant, of being the solicitor and provoker of that sin, which in truth the confessant was.[57]

Here is a typical case of infant-juvenile homosexual incest.

If we add the five names accused of sodomy present in the *Livro de denunciações de Pernambuco* to these five who spontaneously confessed—it appears that, in most of these cases, homoerotic relations had occurred many years ago, in distant lands, the majority having an ocean or a few decades of separation between the "abominable sin" and their moral recovery. Some of these ex-sinners now displayed respectable alibis: they were married! In the case of the two quarrelsome boys from Goiana, it was not even certain beyond a doubt that they were really guilty. Thus, we could even conclude from these biographies that, for the well-being of everyone in Pernambuco, Divine Providence would not punish the state because of the "nefarious sin," since the sodomites were an extinct species.

Happy illusion! Let us mimic the Divine Master in the celebrations of Cana, who saved the best wine for the end of the party. Besides the *tibira* and the *fanchono das folias*, the biggest closeted sodomite of all colonial Brazilian history lived in the center of Olinda, between the most prominent Rua Nova and Rua da Conceição.[58] His name was André de Freitas Lessa. His homoerotic résumé included many accomplices with whom he had practiced more than one hundred sodomitic copulations, *molices* (mutual masturbations), *sacanagens* (licentious acts), *punhetas* (masturbations), *coxetas* (sexual act involving ejaculation between the thighs), and even a violent sodomitical assault. He confessed to thirty-one accomplices besides the partners whose names he omitted due to forgetfulness or sneakiness.

"The Lessa," as he was called, invalidated the myth that stereotypes the homosexual as a being who is delicate, frail, a sort of a third sex, as defined by Dr. Karl Ulrichs, the father of the study of homosexuality.[59] In his record, archived in the Torre do Tombo (Inquisition of Lisbon no. 8473), Lessa was described as "a tall man, a manly man, with a big mustache and valiant"—the type of physique that would cause a shudder in any gay he preys on. He was an old Christian, from Guimarães, Bishopric of Braga, son of Hierónimo Dias Lessa, a deceased shoemaker, and of Mécia de Freitas. He must have attended at least the first few grades, since he signed his confession with a nice signature, well drawn.

His confession took place on the 23 November 1593—on the last day of the "month of grace." While some sodomites were the first to confess themselves as soon as the Inspection opened, the Lessa opted for a more cunning strategy: since he had many accomplices, it was best to wait until the last moment because, with the muttering and the disloyalty that always arose as a result of these frightening judicial inquiries, he could better prepare himself as to what to say, eventually even correcting some details with his other previous partners who came to the Inquisitorial Board before him. His record does not state how long he lived in Brazil. However, it had been twelve or thirteen years since he "had first sinned in the shameful sensuality with many young boys, being always the author and provoker, having joined with virile members and with hands and soliciting and polluting each other."[60]

In his first confession, in one session alone, he cited eighteen partners with whom he had "touches and nefarious unions, alternatively, not consummating sodomy for not being able to penetrate each other. From his view they worked and sought penetration and consummation."[61] At the end of this hearing, since it was within the grace period and there was no confession nor accusation of *sodomia perfeita*—the only homoerotic act considered to be a crime—the Lessa was released, ordered to general confession with the administrator of the Company of Jesus, and ordered to bring written confirmation. This sacramental confession should have caused great distress, because he had already been committing these sins for five or six years when he fulfilled the obligation of paschal confession, consequently committing mortal sins in communing sacrilegiously, as taught by the Apostle Paul: "[W]hoever eats and drinks unrepentantly the body and blood of the Lord, eats and drinks his own condemnation."[62] Although trapped by the Inquisitorial Board, the Lessa once more disobeyed the ecclesiastic orders, stopping to see the confessor to unburden his conscience. Could it be that he had a heavy conscience for the homoerotic acts he often repeated? I bet on the negative.

After the hearing of the greatest sodomite, weeks and months went by without news. The Inspector and his auxiliary staff continued to be occupied in the daily struggle to persecute the conscience of the Pernambucans. The settlers, in turn, fearing the seriousness of the Holy Inquisitorial Office, unearthed from their memories all of the acts, words, or even omissions that could incriminate them as being in deviance from faith or morality. Six months after his confession, the Lessa suddenly lost his head and committed a homoerotic foolishness which would ruin his life. The Portuguese João Batista was the pivot of his doom.

> On the twenty-seventh of May of 1594, João Batista, an old Christian, from the island of Madeira, fifteen years old, servant of Lopo Soares, governor of this village, and resident of his house, asked for a hearing at the Board of Accusations. And he said that yesterday, at three in the afternoon, he went to find out if his boss's slippers and shoes were ready

at the house of the shoemaker called the Lessa, who lives on the ground floor of a house on the Rua da Conceição. Entering the house of the said shoemaker, he found him alone. Quickly the shoemaker took him and grabbed both of his hands and, having secured both of his hands with one of his own hands, with the other he carried him on his back and laid him face down on a hammock, used to sleep here in Brazil, kicking the front door shut. And having him face down, he got on top of him on his back and raised the leg of the loose shorts and through the said opening of the shorts stuck his vulgar virile member and reached his ass and rear orifice, pushing with his said vulgar member into the denouncer's rear orifice, moving around, wanting to penetrate it. However since the denouncer didn't allow it, he was unable to penetrate inside. And this way, on the outside of his rear orifice hole, the shoemaker was agitating and moving around with his member as it is done with women, the carnal union, until he spilled from his member, a filth that soiled his rear end with pollution. Afterwards, he released him, and the denouncer, finding himself freed, ran away quickly through the door, without the slippers or the shoes that had not been finished.[63]

Curious, and to be sure that the defenseless servant really suffered forced intercourse ("poor thing"), the Reverend Inspector provoked him to share more details of the said episode.

Taking his hands forcibly and putting himself on top of him from the back, subjugating him in a way that the accuser, because of being young, cannot resist the strength of the said shoemaker, who is a big man and strong and when he forced himself on him, the most that he did was to ask, for the love of God, let him go, and the said shoemaker paid no mind to it, telling him: Be quiet! Now we are good friends. But the accuser never agreed to the said sin and didn't scream, but he tensed up because he didn't agree to the act.[64]

Once again, the Inquisitor questioned him, suspecting that before this violent assault on chastity, possibly the servant and the shoemaker already had some intimacy. Furtado de Mendonça hit the nail right on the head!

And he asked the accuser if said shoemaker had given him yesterday or another day some money or any other thing, or if he had ever spoken affectionate or dishonest words? He responded that in earlier days whenever he went to the said shoemaker's house to find said work, the said shoemaker told him vile words and had asked him to show his nature, but the accuser paid no attention to the said words nor thought them to be malicious as he now understands it, and sometimes he would find him eating bread and bananas and other fruits with which he was invited, and the accuser, with good intentions, drank and ate.[65]

Conclusion: If they had no intimacy, they were at least buddies.

Let us remember the chronology of this nefarious imbroglio: the Lessa confessed for the first time on 23 November 1593. Six months later, on 27 May 1594, he was accused by the servant the day after he was assaulted. If the judgment of the deputy prosecutor of the Holy Office of the Inquisition had been considered then, the shoemaker would have been imprisoned *ipso facto*: "Given this *horrenda confessionem*, so that it not go unpunished and to stop such a dangerous sin that so disorderly manifests and is disseminated by the culprit in our New Republic that is so ignorant of similar offenses, while the criminal is accustomed and recalcitrant in them."[66] The action of the Inquisitorial Inspector, more astute and cautious, prevailed, for a year after the relapse of the shoemaker, his arrest order was issued by the Bailiff of the Holy Office of the Inquisition. Perhaps they expected more relapses from the big shoemaker.

On 5 June 1595, imprisoned by order of the Holy Office of the Inquisition, the Lessa was warned to complete his confession. With good intention, "he asked for paper and ink to reform his memory." Two days later, he presented a new list, adding nine more accomplices to his previous résumé of eighteen homosexual partners. Adding four others who denounced him as accomplices brought the total to thirty-one partners. It is most admirable that all of these new lovers, with whom the Lessa had committed thirty-four lustful encounters—a figure certainly understated since, with a few, "many seeds had been spilled with the hands"—had been contacted only in the last twelve months. Among these last partners, there was the "poor" João Batista, who in Lessa's list is referred to laconically: "João Batista, servant of Judge Lopo Soares, and with whom said having practiced a *connatus* (attempt of penetration), without the spilling of seed." He no longer remembered the details, since there had been so much seminal spilling, or he covered them up to diminish his guilt. Would the Lessa have known that said servant had denounced him the day following the *connatus* in the hammock?

Before returning him to the dungeon, the Inquisitors recommended to the accused that he search his memory more deeply to complete his confession. In the following week, a new hearing was held. There, he was questioned regarding why he had not gone to the general confession with the college administrator, Father Luiz de Grän,[67] as had been ordered. Cleverly, the Lessa answered that he believed that his confession before the Inquisitorial Board was equivalent to the general confession, demonstrating with this disobedience the pride of his nature. Even having his virtual executioners a few steps away from his nefarious alcove, this proud sodomite dares to disobey them and, worse, to confront them, by practicing with more than thirteen accomplices almost fifty acts, enough to lead him to the flames—flames that were not a chimera but a very close reality, since some of these records of the sodomites of Brazil have in capital letters on their front covers, "This crime deserves the death penalty" or "[T]he ordinary penalty for this crime is death." His own record is stamped, "This crime has the penalty of death."[68]

Let us see, then, in the compact format presented in table 1, the network of crypto-sodomites which existed in Olinda, in the outskirts, with whom the Lessa maintained homosexual contact from one to ten or more times. Besides being laconic, this list of thirty-one boys, with ages varying between fifteen and eighteen years, allows us to catch some regularities not only pertaining to the homoerotic preferences of the Lessa, but also of the demographic profile of the crypto-sodomites of New Lusitânia. Of the fifteen accomplices about whom information exists regarding their nationality, we have five born in Portugal, predominantly in the province of Minho,[69] from the Bishopric of Braga; two are natives from the Atlantic Islands; two are new Christians; one is English; two are *mamelucos;* and one is a mulatto.

It is evident that the shoemaker had a special inclination for white youngsters. Although black adolescents, Indians, and mestizos, either emancipated or enslaved, were much more abundant and available in the new state, Lessa himself declared that his lovers were "all white, only one *mameluco,* [and that he slept] with them in his home, close to the Church of Conceição or at the top of Rua Nova, he being the one who always assaulted and begged them, not paying only the sons of the merchants, but also swindling the others and offering them money." This is rare behavior between confessed sodomites in Brazil, since most of those implicated in the *beau vice* practiced it out of passion, getting a hard-on without the need for money.

Regarding the social categories of the shoemaker's lovers, at the top of the pyramid are two sons of merchants and one son of a farmer, three tailors, two shoemakers, and nine servants, one of them being referred to as an attendant. The predominance of domestic services in this nefarious list reflects the same tendency observed in countries of the Old World, where the rendering of sexual services was part of the tasks of the domestics. The "master of the field" Tranquilo Vannicelli, arrested by the Holy Office of the Inquisition in 1651, repeated a popular contemporary saying: "Since there are no hens that lay no eggs, there are no servants that do not serve to commit sodomy with him, because that was the service he wanted from them."[70] In those violent times, where the whip and the flames were instruments utilized by the Holy Mother Church, sexual obsession, homo or hetero, was a seigniorial privilege.

With regard to the erotic performance of these crypto-sodomitic partners of the shoemaker from the Rua da Conceição, there's a varied menu defying

Table 1 Accomplices of André de Freitas Lessa ("the Lessa")

NO.	NAME	PROFESSION	DOMICILE	ORIGIN	SEXUAL ACTS
1	Domingos	Tailor	Olinda	Viana	10
2	João			English	12
3	Francisco Abreu		Ranch, meadow		2–3
4	Hipólito	Servant	Clerical house, Olinda	*Mameluco*	2
5	Antônio Jorge	Tailor			3–4
6	Anonymous	Servant of Ant. Beiro		Mulatto	1
7	Anonymous	Shoemaker			1
8	Boy	Servant of Baltazar Leitão			1
9	Boy	Tailor		Son of tailor	2
10	Antônio Rosa	Tailor			1
11	Francisco Correa				10
12	Boy			Galician	3–4
13	Salvador	Servant			5
14	Gaspar	Servant		Lisbon	2–3
15	Francisco	Servant		Viana	2–3
16	Gaspar	His workman		Braga	2
17	Boy	Servant of Father Cabral	Olinda		2–3
18	João Batista	Servant	Olinda	Madeira Island	1
19	Diogo Enriques	Son of merchant	Olinda, São Bento	*Mameluco,* <18 years	2
20	Jorge de Sousa	Son of merchant	Rua Nova	<18 years	7
21	Salvador Barbosa	Servant		16 years	6–7
22	Young boy	Servant			4–5
23	Pereira				1
24	João	Servant of Castilian doctor		18 years	2–3
25	Rodrigo			Recently arrived in Paraíba; 15 years	2–3
26	João	Servant			1
27	Young boy			São Miguel	Many
28	Young boy	Servant			Many
29	Young boy	Servant of Judge Lopo Soares			10
30	Jorge		Below the Misericórdia		1
31	Antônio Pereira	Son of rancher		Ponte Lima	6

here another myth of straight society, which imagines that the homoerotic acts would repeat the same dichotomous limitations practiced by heterosexuals, where there's always a macho penetrator who subjugates the submissive female. Hundreds of lascivious practices of this big man reveal the great versatility of the sixteenth-century homoerotic imaginary, including "meetings of nefarious alternatives," "nefarious assaults from the back," "unions of virile members from the front," "the spilling of seed between the legs," "*pun-hetas*" (masturbations), "pollution in the hands of others," "*coxetas*" (sexual act involving ejaculation between the thighs), phallic exposure, obscene and malicious conversations, and so on. The lack of explicit reference to fellatio and to rimming repeats the behavioral pattern observed also in the Old World at this time, where the lack of bodily hygiene inhibited such orogenital intimacies, whether with the same or the opposite sex.[71] Nevertheless, we have documents confirming not only the frequent exchange of kisses and embraces between Portuguese-Brazilian sodomites of this time period, but also the practice of the above-mentioned oral sexual acts. Distinguished among the lovers of these "diabolic abominations" was the governor of Cabo Verde, D. Cristovão Cabral, thirty-three years old, to whom "his servant Gaspar Telles, twenty-five years old, thirty or forty times, put his own tongue into the rear orifice of the Governor."[72]

The Lessa, even with his superior body and manly mustache, fornicated sometimes as the active partner, and sometimes as the passive one. He engaged in masturbation, at times exciting himself and ejaculating onto others' members, or vice versa. With João Freire, the shoemaker held his member with his hands, whereas with Antônio Andrade, a married farmer, "he made him pollute himself."[73] With his thirty-one accomplices, the shoemaker from Olinda was said to have practiced sodomy with five boys, for a total of twelve acts, during seven of which he was active, and in five he was passive. So goes the famous saying: "*Tamanho não é documento!*"[74]

CONCLUSION

One aspect that warrants our attention in the record of Lessa is that, in small places such as Olinda and Recife, in an urban space so scanty, and with rigid social control exacerbated even further by the threatening presence of the Holy Tribunal, there was room in the short period of a year for a homosexual to maintain an average of one erotic meeting every ten days, contacting fourteen different lovers in twelve months. If the Lessa had not confessed twice, we would never have discovered the existence of this numerous and diversified network of crypto-sodomites that became known to posterity only because of the Inquisitorial Inspection.

How many more Lessas, with such a large group of partners, existed and were never revealed? Because they left no written documents, they are presumed nonexistent. This small record that has been serving as a channel allows us therefore to move forward and confirm what we had already discovered in seventeenth-century Portugal: the existence of a much earlier gay subculture and much more structured than the one supposed by Foucault and the social constructionists.[75]

As the first characteristic of this sodomitic subculture,[76] we could point to its clandestine nature. Just as the new Christians and practitioners of hetero-dox rituals kept secret their idiosyncratic practices, the *fanchonos* did the same, for the revelation of what went on beneath the covers or in the secrecy of the networks could lead them to the flames. Certainly they possessed dis-tinctive signs and secret symbols of self-identification, as did other crypto-minorities, as has been documented with regard to the *paedicones* (pedo-philes) of Imperial Rome,[77] the *sodomieten* (sodomites) of eighteenth-century Holland,[78] and even today in the gay ghetto.[79] Since the closeted sodo-mites self-identified and initiated courtship in colonial Brazil, unfortu-nately the documentation is neglected. We have however, some documents of the gay subculture that the Inquisitorial scribes themselves managed to record.

The young Portuguese boy Antônio Pereira, eighteen years old, from Ponte de Lima, whose father owned a ranch, "a man of honor in this land," confessed that between Christmas and Revelry of 1595 "he had six meetings with the shoemaker Lessa, who called him in the still of the night, spilling seed close to his rear orifice."[80] As Benci announced correctly: "If the streets and the alleys of the cities and villages of Brazil could talk! How many sins would be revealed that in the cover of night the day does not discover . . . and that the penalty makes them shake and frightens them from writing."[81]

Eating together before or after lovemaking—how did it occur with the Lessa and the servant João Batista? Getting drunk with smoke and *aguardi-ente*—how did it happen with the native of Maranhão, Coelho, and his *tibira*?[82] Or how did another couple of gay fisherman in seventeenth-century Paraíba balance in the same net on the veranda of a fisherman's hut in Ma-manguape in the Port of Cabidelo? Surely such things must have happened with numerous other sodomites throughout Brazil, as is widely documented in the entire Portuguese world in this same period.[83] Between one nefarious sinner and another, the sodomites of Olinda and Recife sometimes had seri-ous, tense, whispered conversations, to keep the neighbors of the wood stick houses from listening to such compromising issues.

The farmer Antônio Rodrigues told the Inspector Furtado de Mendonça that "it seemed to him that the sin of sodomy couldn't be absolved by any con-fessor. He said to his accomplices Damião Gonçalves and Domingos Pires that they should not share their sins with the confessors, until a Bull or a way to absolve themselves [appeared], which happened two years later when they received the *Bula de Crusada*."[84] This means that it was part of the subculture of the sodomites of colonial Pernambuco to omit homosexual sins from the sacramental confession—even if such omission made them guilty of another mortal sin.[85] Knowing some gays, they shared information on how to deceive ecclesiastic justice, and they used a breach instituted through the same sa-cred authority: the *Bula de Crusada*.[86]

Another aspect of the general culture of many sodomites, even of those with little sexual experience, was the knowledge that homoerotic acts could be punished by death. Bastião de Morais was fifteen years old when he possessed and was possessed by the slave Domingos, "servant of the house." Honest, ingenuous, he declared to the Inspector that "they knew very well the graveness of the sin, the said nefarious sin, and that its sentence was the burning of those who committed it."[87] Also the *mameluco* João Fernandes confirmed that the sodomites of the time were aware of the criminal status of their sexual attraction: "When he committed the said sins he already knew them to be serious and that because of them they (the sodomites) were arrested and burned."[88]

Once more the Lessa provides us with a crucial snapshot of the homophilic imaginary in colonial Pernambuco. He said to the already mentioned young Antônio Pereira that "sodomy was not a sin, but if it was planned as sin, then it was; if it wasn't planned, then it wasn't"—a casuistic practice that makes the scrupulous one the sinner and acquits the careless, retrieving in this way sodomy's "intrinsically evil" condition, as it is characterized by the current Supreme Pontiff, the most homophobic of all the post-medieval popes. This was an amoralistic pragmatism that certainly helped the crypto-sodomites to confront eventual dramas of the conscience, apart from being an extra argument, utilized by the more clever gays, to double the resistance of the more scrupulous.

Not only on the ideological level did the crypto-sodomites share a few common elements that allow us to glimpse hints of an embryonic gay subculture; as with other minorities, mainly the Jewish and the new Christians, the practitioners of the nefarious sin developed strategies to deceive the Inquisitorial Jurisdiction. Antônio Rodrigues, farmer from São Lourenço, declared in his second confession that

> after the Inspector's arrival in this state, he sent for Damião Gonçalves (with whom he had committed more than twenty nefarious acts), and both agreed to the number of times they had done said sin and about the circumstances, so that they would not find contradictions in the confessions, and what they agreed about, this is what the confessant declared in his confession. And after taking care of this matter, said Damião came to this Board and then spoke to him, the confessant, at his house and told him what he had already done at this Board.[89]

Such documents, collected only in such a short chronological period and in a small community, allow us to suggest that even among the crypto-sodomites, behavioral characteristics and a peculiar ideology were already delineated that distinguished them from the rest of the population. If this was true of the closeted sodomites, whose encounters happened in the still of

the night or in the country fields, we can conjecture on the basis of what occurred, for instance, in Lisbon during the same period that among the *fanchonos* and *tibiras* publicly defamed, identified, and accused by the rest of the
residents as sodomites the shared elements of a crystallized subculture should
have been much more evident where the expressions of an individual, his
voice, and his androgynous mannerisms were not hidden.

With this in mind, if homosexuals were publicly identified as adepts of
the love which dared not speak its name, if many homoerotics practiced
secretly but with bold frequency different libidinous performances inter-
mingled with moments of intragroup socialization, sharing camouflage
strategies to deceive the Inspectors and protect themselves from the political
persecution of the Inquisition—are not all these elements together sufficient
to convince the reader that these sodomites of colonial Brazil were more
than mere "juridical subjects," making up a peculiar subculture which self-
identified and was socially recognized as such? This subculture evidently existed long before the categorization of the "homosexual persona" by medical
science in the past century. Already in the sixteenth century, in the rustic and
small society of the Brazilian northeast, there was room for at least two types
of homosexual existence: the explicit *fanchonos* and *tibiras,* and the closeted
sodomites. Both categories behaved with a clear code of conduct, engaged in
intragroup communication, and used distinctive signs of external identification and specific strategies of social survival—the minimal and necessary
elements for the anthropological characterization of the concept of a subculture.[90]

And when the Inspector of the Holy Office of the Inquisition in Pernambuco asks more than one sodomite "if he has sinned with any woman naturally,"[91] and some respond that they have never sinned with a woman,
wouldn't such a question, and the response of these exclusive gays (occupants
of number 6 on the Kinsey scale), imply a classification of these individuals
in two distinct categories: on one side those who "sin naturally with women"
and on the other the "incorrigible sodomites," thus knocking down another
stone in the Foucauldian edifice: namely, his argument that, in former days,
the sodomite was seen solely as a relapsing sinner and juridic subject of a
crime and not as carrier of a singular nature?[92]

NOTES

1. Foucault, *The History of Sexuality,* 43. As to the validity of the use of the term *gay subculture,* see Boswell, *Christianity, Social Tolerance, and Homosexuality.*

2. Flandrin, *Le sexe et l'occident.*

3. Freyre, *Casa grande e senzala,* 341.

4. Mott, "O sexo cativo."

5. Prado, *Retrato de Brazil;* Vainfas, *Trópico dos pecados;* Mott, "A sexualidade no Brazil escravista."

6. New Lusitânia was an alternate name for the captaincy of Pernambuco. A captaincy in Portuguese America was a region ruled by a governor, who was considered a local representative of the crown.

7. Mendonça and Moreira, *Historia dos principais atos e procedimentos da Inquisição em Portugal.*

8. The *General Inquisitorial Monitor,* which mandates that every person who knows others who are guilty of the crimes of heresy and apostasy must denounce them within thirty days. In Abreu, *Confissões da Bahia,* 30–36. Only in the Regulation of 1613 is there an explicit reference to the crime of sodomy. Yet since 1547 the Holy Office of Lisbon had been taking action against sodomites. See Mott, "Justitia et misericórdia."

9. Porto, *Nos tempos do Visitador,* 25.

10. Quirino, *Os habitantes do Brazil no fim do seculo XVI,* 48.

11. Porto, *Nos tempos do Visitador,* 121.

12. Ibid., 130.

13. Brandônio, *Diálogos das grandezas do Brasil,* 27.

14. The numbers were extrapolated from the extant works. The *Segundo livro das confissões,* and the *Primer livro das ratificações de Pernambuco* are missing. The *Segundo livro das ratificações de Pernambuco, Itamaracá e Paraíba* is unedited. These numbers, relative to the accusations and confessions of Pernambuco, are subject to revisions and later additions.

15. These facts are based on my investigation of the *Livros das denunciações e confissões de Pernambuco, 1593–1595.* This work is subsequently cited as *Denunciações e confissões de Pernambuco.* Some of the documents have no specific dates; they are given when available.

16. Siqueira, *A Inquisição portuguesa e a sociedade colonial,* 228.

17. *Denunciações e confissões de Pernambuco,* 33.

18. Mott, "Pagode português."

19. Aguiar, *Evolução da pederastia,* 519.

20. Mott, *Inquisição em Sergipe,* 46.

21. *Denunciações e confissões de Pernambuco,* 27.

22. Mott, "Modelos de santidade," 104

23. Dynes, *Encyclopedia of Homosexuality,* 241.

24. Mott and Assunção, "A Gay Atheist," 8–10.

25. Schmitt and Sofer, *Sexuality and Eroticism.*

26. Mott, "A Inquisição na Paraíba," 71–96.

27. Arquivo Nacional da Torre do Tombo (Lisboa), Inquisição de Lisboa, Proc. 352, 22 April 1547 (hereafter, ANTT, IL).

28. *Denunciações e confissões de Pernambuco,* 28 November 1594, 355.

29. Mott, "Pagode português," 128.

30. Mott, *Inquisição em Sergipe,* 42.

31. ANTT, IL, Proc. 6366 (1595); all quotations in this paragraph are from this source.

32. Mott, "Justitia et misericórdia," 737.

33. *Denunciações e confissões de Pernambuco,* 9 January 1595, 392.

34. *Viado* (deer) is the generic term used to refer to male homosexuals; it is the most current and insulting expression for them in Brazil.

35. Mello e Sousa, *Inferno atlântico.*

36. Prado, *Retrato de Brazil;* Boxer, *Church Militant.*

37. Vainfas, *Trópico dos pecados,* 49–68.

38. *Denunciações e confissões de Pernambuco,* 412.

39. Ibid., 461.

40. Ibid., 420.

41. Ibid., 436.

42. Ibid., 397. Such a proverb reminds me of a popular saying in present-day Bahia (I do not know the origins of this saying): "All Baianos give small so that they don't have to give big,"

which suggests an evident tolerance for give-and-take, infant-juvenile play (boys having sex with each other), and camouflaged disapproval of homoerotism among adults.

43. These are common expressions used to refer to blacks and Amerindians.

44. Misse, *O estigma do passivo sexual*, 31.

45. This is an old expression in current use that means literally, "to catch the ass," but it should be understood as a synonym for "quarrel."

46. *Denunciações e confissões de Pernambuco*, 438.

47. Ibid., 443. The confusing and inconsistent text is caused by the Inquisitorial notary alternating pronouns.

48. Ibid., 464.

49. ANTT, IL, Proc. 5876, 12 July 1595.

50. *Denunciações e confissões de Pernambuco*, 458.

51. Ibid., 464.

52. "Preconceito contra Gays," *Jornal da Bahia*, 21 March 1985; "Empresas so aceitam homossexual que não da bandeira," *Folha de S. Paulo*, 19 January 1992; "Demitido acusa empresa de barrar homossexuais," *Folha de S. Paulo*, 18 April 1991.

53. *Denunciações e confissões de Pernambuco*, 21.

54. Ibid., 25.

55. Ibid., 40.

56. Ibid., 47.

57. Ibid., 137.

58. Closeted sodomite (*sodomita encoberto*) was the seventeenth-century Portuguese expression used as a synonym for what we today call *homossexual enrustido* (closeted homosexual), the opposite of *gay assumido*, or "out-of-the-closet gay," or of *sodomita notorio* (notorious sodomite). See Mott, "Cinco cartas de amor."

59. Kennedy, *Ulrichs*.

60. *Denunciações e confissões de Pernambuco*, 136.

61. Ibid.

62. *I Epistola de S. Paulo aos Corintios*, 11:29.

63. *Denunciações e confissões de Pernambuco*, 278.

64. Ibid.

65. Ibid.

66. ANTT, IL, Proc. 8473 (1595).

67. This priest Luiz de Grãn (1523–1608) was the second Provincial of the Jesuits in Brazil, missionary and professor of theology. See Leite, *Suma historica da Companhia de Jesus no Brazil*, 356.

68. ANTT, IL, Proc. 6366 and 6349 (1595).

69. Minho is in northern Portugal.

70. ANTT, IL, *Caderno do Nefando*, vol. 9, fol. 243, 22 July 1651.

71. Burg, *Sodomy and the Pirate Tradition*, 111.

72. ANTT, IL, Proc. 12.248 (1630).

73. ANTT, IL, Proc. 11.208 (1595).

74. Editor's note: This translates literally as "Size is not a document." It roughly corresponds to the English-language expression, "Size isn't everything."

75. See Stein, *Forms of Desire*; Boswell, "Revolutions, Universals, Categories."

76. Trumbach, "Sodomite Subculture."

77. Lima, *Inversão sexual*, 122.

78. Meer, *De wesentlijke sond van sodomie en andere vuyligheeden*, 163.

79. Pollack, "A homossexualidade masculina."

80. ANTT, IL, Proc. 5876 (1595).

81. Benci, *Economia cristã*, 118.

82. Mott, "Inquisicão no Maranhão."

83. Mott, "Pagode português," 131.
84. *Denunciações e confissões de Pernambuco*, 22.
85. Ibid., 47.
86. Rabello, "A Bula da Santa Cruzada."
87. *Denunciações e confissões de Pernambuco*, 26.
88. Ibid., 47.
89. Ibid., 21.
90. Murray, *Social Theory, Homosexual Realities*, 33.
91. ANTT, IL, Proc. 6349 and 5876 (1595).
92. André de Freitas Lessa even alleged "that he was not right in the mind, and that on full moons he would go mad and did crazy things. He was cured from this disease for five years, and the few times he committed the nefarious sin it was a full moon accident" (ANTT, IL, Proc. 8473 [1595]). Despite this excuse, he was the sodomite that received the harshest sentence in the Inspection of the Holy Office throughout Brazil: "For being so used to the horrendous and nefarious vileness of sodomy" (ibid.), he was condemned to hear his sentence in the auto-da-fé and to serve in a slave galley for ten years, forbidden to return to the state of Pernambuco, besides having to do general confession, give some spiritual penitences, and pay $198 of processing costs. After his departure to the galleys, there is no more news of this unfortunate, manly man. The majority of those condemned to the galleys died before completing the time of their sentences.

WORKS CITED

Abreu, Capistrano. *Confissões da Bahia, 1591–1592*. Rio de Janeiro: F. Briguiet e Companhia Editores, 1935.
Aguiar, Antonia A. *Evolução da pederastia e do lesbismo na Europa*. Lisbon: Universidade de Lisboa, 1926.
Benci, Jorge, S.J. *Economia cristã dos senhores no governo dos escravos*. São Paulo: Grijalbo, 1977.
Boswell, John. *Christianity, Social Tolerance, and Homosexuality: Gay People in Western Europe from the Beginning of the Christian Era to the Fourteenth Century*. Chicago: University of Chicago Press, 1980.
———. "Revolutions, Universals, Categories." *Salmagundi* 58–59 (fall 1982/winter 1983): 89–113.
Boxer, Charles R. *The Church Militant and Iberian Expansion, 1440–1770*. Baltimore: Johns Hopkins University Press, 1978.
Brandônio, Ambrosio Fernandes. *Diálogos das grandezas do Brasil*. Recife: Imprensa Universitária, 1966.
Burg, B. R. *Sodomy and the Pirate Tradition*. New York: New York University Press, 1984.
Dynes, Wayne. *Encyclopedia of Homosexuality*. New York: Garland, 1990.
Flandrin, Jean. *Le sexe et l'occident*. Paris: Editions du Seuil, 1981.
Foucault, Michel. *The History of Sexuality*. Vol. 1. *An Introduction*. New York: Vintage Books, 1978.
Freyre, Gilberto. *Casa grande e senzala*. Recife: Imprensa Oficila, 1970.
Kennedy, Hubert. *Ulrichs: Life and Works of Karl Heinrich Ulrichs, Pioneer of the Modern Gay Movement*. Boston: Alyson, 1987.
Leite, Serafim. *Suma historica da Companhia de Jesus no Brasil*. Lisbon: Junta de Investigações do Ultramar, 1965.
Lima, Estacio. *A inversão sexual*. Rio de Janeiro: Editora Guanabara, 1943.
Livros de denunciações e confissões de Pernambuco, 1593–1595. Recife: Fundarte, 1984.
Meer, Theo Van Der. *De wesentlijke sond van sodomie en andere vuyligheeden: Sodomitetenvergolvgingen in Amsterdam, 1730–1811*. Amsterdam: Tabula, 1984.
Mello e Sousa, Laura. *Inferno atlântico: Demonologia e colonização, seculo XVI–XVIII*. São Paulo: Companhia das Letras, 1993.

Mendonça, J. L., and A. J. Moreira. *Historia dos principais atos e procedimentos da Inquisição em Portugal*. Lisbon: Imprensa Nacional, 1980.

Misse, Michel. *O estigma do passivo sexual*. Rio de Janeiro: Achiame, 1979.

Mott, Luiz. "Cinco cartas de amor de um sodomita português do seculo XVII." *Resgate* 1 (1990): 90–99.

———. *A Inquisição em Sergipe*. Aracaju: Fundesc, 1989.

———. "A Inquisição na Paraíba." Paper presented to the Instituto Histórico e Geográfico da Paraíba, João Pessoa, 1989.

———. *A Inquisição no Maranhão*. S. Luiz: Universidade Federal do Maranhão, 1996.

———. "Justitia et misericórdia: A Inquisição portuguesa e a repressão ao nefando pecado de sodomia." In *Inquisição: Ensaios sobre a mentalidade, heresias, e arte*, ed. A. Novinsky and M. L. Tucci Carneiro. São Paulo: Edusp, 1992.

———. "Modelos de santidade para um clero devasso: A proposito das pinturas do Cabido de Mariana." *Revista de Historia* 9 (1989): 96–120.

———. "O sexo cativo: Alternativas eroticas dos africanos e seus descendentes no Brazil escravista." In *O sexo proibido: Virgens, gays, e escravos nas garras da Inquisição*. Campinas: Editora Papirus, 1989.

———. "Pagode português: A subcultura gay em Portugal nos tempos inquisitoriais." *Ciência e Cultura* 40, no. 2 (February 1988): 120–39.

———. "A sexualidade no Brazil escravista." *D. O. Leitura* 141 (February 1994): 6–8.

Mott, Luiz, and Aroldo Assunção. "A Gay Atheist of the Seventeenth Century." *Gala Review* 7 (1985): 8–10.

Murray, S. *Social Theory, Homosexual Realities*. New York: Gay Saber Monographs, 1984.

Pollack, Michel. "A homossexualidade masculina ou a felicidade no gueto." In *Sexualidades ocidentais*, ed. P. Aries and A. Benfin. São Paulo: Editora Brasiliense, 1985.

Porto, Costa. *Nos tempos do Visitador*. Recife: Universidade Federal de Pernambuco, 1968.

Prado, Paulo. *Retrato de Brazil*. Rio de Janeiro: Livreria José Olympio, 1972.

Quirino, Tarcizo R. *Os habitantes do Brazil no fim do seculo XVI*. Recife: Imprensa Universitaria, 1966.

Rabello, David. "A Bula da Santa Cruzada." *Revista de Historia* 117 (1984): 143–62.

Schmitt, Arno, and Jehoeda Sofer, eds. *Sexuality and Eroticism among Males in Moslem Societies*. New York: Harrington Park Press, 1991.

Siqueira, Sônia. *A Inquisição portuguesa e a sociedade colonial*. São Paulo: Atica, 1978.

Stein, Edward. *Forms of Desire: Sexual Orientation and the Social Constructionist Controversy*. New York: Routledge, 1992.

Trumbach, Randolph. "Sodomite Subculture, Sodomitical Roles, and the Gender Revolution of the Eighteenth Century: The Recent Historiography." *Eighteenth-Century Life* 9 (1985): 109–21.

Vainfas, Ronaldo. *Trópico dos pecados: Moral, sexualidade, e Inquisição no Brasil*. Rio de Janeiro: Editora Campus, 1989.

CHAPTER SEVEN

The Ashes of Desire: Homosexuality in Mid-Seventeenth-Century New Spain

SERGE GRUZINSKI

Translated by Ignacio López-Calvo

A mong the many marginalized people in New Spain's society, some had a unique place, as a silence continues to shadow their lives and existences. While many voices denounced—rightfully so—the living conditions of indigenous people, black slaves, Jews, and, more recently, women, few people wondered then or wonder now about the lives of those men who wanted and loved those of their own sex. They were the only ones who paid with their lives for that which was only a manifestation of their individuality.

In contrast with the crypto-Jews, who rejected Christianity; idolaters, who returned to their former beliefs; or blacks, who would choose the path of rebellion, all these men were doing was being themselves. Yet they were accused—and they are still being accused—of "perverting" the order of things, corrupting the social order and the order of desire. Such an accusation reminds us that, just like sanctity, perversion is a sociocultural product, not a violation of the supposed laws of "nature." Perversion is, in the first place, a category whose content varies through centuries, environments, and ethnicities. It is a category that can cover very different behaviors and that uses them to establish the dominance of the norm, to tighten its control, and to organize repression. Perhaps examining the case of New Spain will allow us to determine both what was considered a perversion in the colonial society of the seventeenth century, and how "perverts" assumed the roles imposed on them.

Even today, those men continue to be a disturbance. They do not have— like indigenous people, blacks, Jews, and even women—the opportunity to develop the usual discourses about colonial exploitation, loss of identity, or class struggle. On the contrary, they keep presenting problems. They do not have names: since the nineteenth century we have called them homosexuals, with the medical connotation that this implies; in another context, they are called *putos* (queers), using a term that was already common in the seventeenth century. During the same period, colonial authorities preferred more technical terms, such as *sodomites* or the almost metaphysical reference to the *pecado nefando* (nefarious sin). The term *perverso,* or "pervert," does not seem to be more satisfactory, either in the moralistic sense of "corrupter" or in its more modern, Freudian, and apparently scientific meaning, which postulates a supposed deviation of desire, a desire whose "normal" manifestation would obviously be heterosexual.[1] The plurality of names suffices to prove the complexity of the phenomenon that we are facing.

The history of those names becomes inseparable from a global history of sexual and affective relationships, family, women, and male chauvinism. This history is yet to be written. That is, we are not dealing with a handful of isolated and exotic deviants whose practices and sad end in the bonfire may awake some morbid curiosity, but with men whose sexual and affective liaisons must be studied within the sociocultural framework of the New Spain of the seventeenth century. This field, however, is so virgin that we will feel satisfied with gathering some preliminary data, waiting for more ambitious research to continue to increase reflection about a sector of the Mexican population that is still nowadays unacceptably despised, repressed, attacked, and killed.[2]

THE SOURCES

Among the abundant information provided by Gregorio Guijo in his diary[3] is the following, well-known account:

> Tuesday, November 6 (1658), at eleven in the morning they took out fifteen men from the Royal Prison of this Court, fourteen in order to be burned and another one, because he was a boy, received two hundred lashes and was sold to a miner for six years, all of them for committing the sin of sodomy among themselves many years before; they lived in this city where they had a home with all the commodities where they received visits and called each other by names that fallen women use in this city, as a form of adulation as well as insult, being in the city of Puebla de los Angeles.

Guijo's text, no matter how detailed it may be, did not offer an analysis that went beyond the anecdotal level, but other documents might provide the social and human dimension of the event. I found them in the Archivo General de las Indias (AGI) in Seville. An index of the letters by the viceroys of New Spain mentioned a letter dated 15 November 1658, expedited by the duke of Albuquerque, which informed Spain about the execution of fourteen people who had committed the "nefarious sin." The document, however, was not found on the indicated page.[4] It is widely known that the Spanish Crown used to keep duplicates of the documents that were received, especially when they dealt with particularly relevant matters. As a result I was able to locate in a different dossier a copy of this letter, along with another one signed by the *alcalde del crimen* (criminal magistrate), as well as a list of "those executed for committing the nefarious sin" and a summary of the judicial investigation: "Testimony of the cases against the ones charged with the nefarious sin."[5]

The content and interest of each document vary notably. The viceroy's letter outlines the case, focusing on the results of the repression. The criminal magistrate, Juan Manuel de Sotomayor, offers numerous and valuable details; whereas the "Report of the executed" provides brief yet exceptional data about 123 individuals, their names, professions, ethnic and geographic origins, and some physical features. It was too little for a serious quantitative analysis, but a lot about a minority that is usually evasive to the researcher. Finally, in the "Testimony of the cases" we find descriptive information about the sexual practices and, more generally, the habits of sociability among the accused.[6]

These sources allowed me to analyze half of the seventeenth century, the dramatic clash between the repressive colonial apparatus and the individuals who were sexually active, and, even more, a subculture on the margins of the rules in force. I must admit that it is only an inquiry, without a diachronic perspective, and that it depends greatly on the information provided by the repressive institutions themselves (the viceroy and the Royal Criminal Court). In spite of these limits, I must underscore the exceptional character of such a concentration of data, as well as the extraordinary relevance of the event as perceived by its contemporaries. According to the viceroy, the case was unprecedented: "The number of people summoned, executed, and imprisoned at the same time, for the same reason that I have never heard of before, nor is such complicity mentioned in human history."[7]

The repression of 1657–1658 was initiated by the denunciation made by a mestiza; she had seen two men having sexual relations on the outskirts of Mexico City on 27 September 1657. The denunciation sparked an unprecedented wave of repression. The criminal magistrate, Sotomayor, interrogated the woman, multiplied the investigations, and, proceeding from one denunciation to the other, he managed to arrest nineteen suspects. According to our sources, in November of 1658 fourteen men had died in the bonfire, a minor of fifteen had been condemned to six years of forced labor in the mines, and another nine cases were objects of a judicial information, while ninety-nine more suspects were wanted by the authorities. Gaps in the gathered data do not allow us to know the destiny of the last ones, except in a few cases.[8]

"WHEN CHRIST OUR LORD WAS BORN . . ."

The documents that I gathered categorize the incriminating sexual acts with the expression, *pecado nefando,* "the infamous, abominable sin." The testimony states, "Two men committing the *nefarious sin* . . . she saw in it [the room], because there was light, who were committing the *nefarious sin* . . . *to communicate nefariously.*"[9] Except for one time (the use of *sométicos,* "sodomites"), the term *sodomy* and its derivatives are never used, even though they could have been used for the sexual practices of the accused. Therefore, I consider that "nefarious sin" designates any sexual act committed between men at the same time that it connotes the forbidden, "that which cannot be said" (Latin *ne-fandus*), because it is impious and sacrilegious.

Other terms, however, reflect the official attitude toward such conduct: the viceroy's letter talks about "clumsiness, filth"; the one by Sotomayor talks about "contaminated . . . this cancer . . . so common and widespread . . . such a mortal and nefarious ailment." There are images of pestilence, rubbish, and epidemic, those of a mortal, secret, and alarming evil, which participates in the great calamities and plagues. Sotomayor adds an almost metaphysical dimension when he makes a remark in which the "policeman" mixes with the courtesan, which becomes the most implacable of all the condemnations: "When Our Lord Christ was born, all the sodomites died—as some Saints mention. I have considered it a happy omen, that this occurred at the moment when the Prince Our Lord was born[10]—whom may God protect for many years." To establish a causal relationship, or a simple correlation, between the birth of the Savior and the physical elimination of the sodomites clearly reveals the virulence of the official phobia that persecuted this sector of the population.[11]

This repulsion goes along with the confession of a stupefaction that disconcerts the high spheres of power. The viceroy believes that the case goes beyond the imagination: "[The] causes, clumsiness and circumstances of the sin are *incredible.*"[12] Lack of knowledge and, especially, lack of information translate into Sotomayor's testimony, since he admitted, without hesitation, that the success of his repression was due more to "God's Providence" than to the "judge's diligence." It is true that he himself admitted knowing something about the crime: "Twelve years ago I heard that the nefarious sin had these provinces very contaminated." Yet, it seems that a sentiment of impotence invades public officials' minds when they discover that "the circumstances of the sin are so old that many of them had been committing it for forty years, others for thirty, most of them for ten, twelve, eight. . . ."

Repulsion, ignorance, impotence, and also fear are evident here—a fear that reflects the concept of "complicity" used by the authorities, which implies an association or collusion among delinquents and is often used with reference to groups considered dangerous by the state. That is the case, for example, of idolatrous Indians or blacks believed to be planning a rebellion. Thus, lamenting the resurgence of paganism in the Marquisate at the beginning of the seventeenth century, Jacinto de la Serna mentions the discovery of a "great complicity among idolatrous Indians."[13] There are other terminological coincidences between the field of the nefarious sin and that of idolatry. Investigating the mechanisms of syncretism, another passionate extirpator of idolatries, Hernando Ruiz de Alarcón, explains, "Those who communicate a lot with Indians, especially being vile people, get easily *infected* by their customs and superstitions" (my emphasis).[14] Similarly, Gonzalo de Balsalobre talks about "contagion" among the idolaters of Oaxaca.[15] More fortunate than the sodomites, the teachers of idolatry escaped the bonfire, thus benefiting from the Church's clemency. Still, that was not the case for the Jews, who also paid, with their deaths in the bonfire, for their individuality and their supposed "complicity."[16]

The fantasies of conspiracy and epidemic blend more and more in the official discourse every time that a deviation at the group level is manifested, either on a sexual and religious basis (idolaters and Jews), or on an ethnic and social one (blacks and mulattoes). In other words, colonial authorities seem to conceive of the phenomenon of homosexuality—if we allow ourselves that anachronism—at two different levels: the individual act, considered sinful, and the group's act, when several individuals meet to commit it. Besides, the individual himself, as "a deviant, potentially dangerous person, and as a unique being, with a different nature"—namely, the homosexual as commonly defined by much scientific discourse in the nineteenth century—does not yet seem to have an equivalent in the official discourse. Of course, it should be possible to gain insight into the analysis of the authorities' position, the roots of their argumentation and motivations. One could also remember that in seventeenth-century Spain, as in the other European countries, the nefarious sin was at the same time an attack against God, nature, and the established power (the king).

Reactions and attitudes toward this problem among the population of New Spain are even more unknown. It is useful to remember that during the insurrection of 8 June 1692, many "rioters" insulted the Spaniards by calling them *mariquitas* (pansies): "Filthy Spaniards, the fleet has arrived. Go, *mariquitas*, to the drawers and buy ribbons and wigs."[17] Here we are no longer in the register of sin and sacrilege, but in that of male effeminacy, an obsession that cannot be separated from macho affirmation. But other insults were common among the people, such as the one hurled by a mestizo from Veracruz: "If your master is not Jewish or a *puto*, there are no Jews in Veracruz!" Here—as happened in the official discourse—the correlation of two excluded and persecuted minorities takes place. Yet, as in the previous case, a person (*puto*) is attacked, instead of the sexual act committed by him. Incidentally, even those who practiced the nefarious act would use the term *puto:* the mulatto Benito de Cuevas remembered that "one day before being arrested a man went to the home of the aforementioned man . . . and told him to flee because his companions had been imprisoned for being putos."[18] This foreshadowing suffices to point out the complexity of the attitudes toward sodomites and, perhaps, to distinguish at least three components: religious repudiation, social and political fear, and despisement of the very person; the act, the group, and the person, were together the targets of the repudiation, hate, exclusion, and repression.

Yet, although the whole of colonial society probably shared those reactions toward *putos*, we cannot ignore the existence, in practice and in everyday life, of margins or spaces of tolerance where more nuanced and ambiguous attitudes were expressed. I am thinking, for example, of the mestiza who surprised two men in the country, but seemed to be more curious than scandalized; of Doña Melchora de Estrada, who hosted one of the accused and his lovers; or of the owners of *pulquerías* (pulque bars), which were frequently visited by Indians "dressed as women."[19] On the other hand, the abyss that separates the low number of victims of criminal prosecution from the real population of delinquents also invites us to wonder about the degree of tolerance or secrecy that surrounded their circumstances. We must distinguish between an official and inflexible stance that, in Foucault's terms, condemns sodomy and the nefarious sin "in the same way as magic and heresy in the same context of religious profanity,"[20] and specific sensitivities, despisement, and scandal that can, nevertheless, sometimes be tolerant and even accomplice-like. Leaving behind matters that deserve a deeper analysis, let us see who those are who "commit the nefarious sin."

GEOGRAPHIC AND ETHNIC ORIGIN

Before accumulating figures, it is important to emphasize the limits of the data and calculations that follow. Obviously, 123 cases constitute a very limited basis for analysis; but the difficulty is a different one. It resides in the lack of comparable data that can give these figures their true value: not only the scarcity of information about the practice of the nefarious act, but also the absence of basic information relative to the ethnic and social demographic profile of the capital of New Spain and the city of Puebla in the mid-seventeenth century. Therefore, I limit myself to the most obvious features.

Table 2 gathers various percentages drawn from the list of the accused. An initial examination of these percentages allows us to guess at the size of all the sectors of the population in New Spain, including minorities, such as the Portuguese. Three groups reach comparable percentages: the Indians with

Table 2 Geographic and Ethnic Breakdown of the Accused

ETHNICITY	INDIVIDUALS (PERCENTAGE)	MEXICO (PERCENTAGE)	PUEBLA (PERCENTAGE)	ACAPULCO	CHOLULA	ATRISCO (ATLIXCO)
Indian	33 (26.8)	26 (31.3)	6 (16.2)	0	1	0
Mestizo	29 (23.6)	21 (25.3)	7 (18.9)	0	0	1
Black	10 (8.1)	8 (9.6)	2 (5.4)	0	0	0
Mulatto	19 (15.5)	14 (16.9)	5 (13.5)	0	0	0
Castizo[a]	1 (0.8)	1 (1.2)	0 (0)	0	0	0
Moorish	2 (1.6)	1 (1.2)	1 (2.7)	0	0	0
Portuguese	1 (0.8)	0 (0)	1 (2.7)	0	0	0
Spanish	28 (22.8)	12 (14.5)	15 (40.5)	1	0	0
Total	123	83	37	1	1	1

[a]Translator's note: In Mexico, a *castizo* was a man born in America from a mestizo and a Spanish woman, or from a Spanish man and a mestiza.

26.8 percent, the mestizos with 23.6 percent, and the Spaniards with 22.8 percent; and if we take into account the percentage of black-mulattoes, we have a fourth group, with 23.6 percent.

Let us consider now the geographic distribution of the accused. The nefarious sin, persecuted in 1657–1658, constitutes a predominantly urban phenomenon; the great majority of the accused come from Mexico City and Puebla, the two most important cities of the viceroyalty, and the two cities with the greatest proportion of Spaniards (*criollo* or peninsular). Less than a third are from Puebla, while more than two-thirds are from Mexico. The two cities, however, do not offer the same ethnic percentages.

The Indian-mestizo group is predominant in the capital of the viceroyalty, with 56.6 percent, followed by the black-mulatto group (26.5 percent); while the Spaniards represent only 14.5 percent. On the contrary, in Puebla, Spaniards are the most numerous (40.5 percent), in comparison with Indians and mestizos (35.1 percent), and blacks and mulattos (18.9 percent). In Mexico as well as in Puebla, the Indian-mestizo and black-mulatto groups keep similar relationships when compared with each other: the first group is about twice as large as the second. On the other hand, while in Mexico Indians are more numerous than mestizos, in Puebla we have the opposite situation. We must note, in addition, that the "Spanish" profile in the city of Puebla is based on the presence of a strong contingent of accused students in the data sample. Even without these students, however, the Spanish group, reduced to eight individuals, still represents a larger percentage (26.6 percent) than that of the Spaniards accused in the capital (14.5 percent). How should this data be interpreted? In the absence of trustworthy information about the ethnic percentages of the population in both cities in the mid-seventeenth century,[21] it is impossible to establish whether the incidence of the nefarious sin has to do with the ethnic origin of the accused.

The data about Puebla seem to confirm what we know about this city, which was created during the colony: it is characterized by an important Spanish and mestizo presence versus an indigenous minority. The figures relative to Mexico City are significantly more confusing. In 1644 the indigenous and Spanish populations were comparable in number; thus, it is difficult to understand why twice as many Indians as Spaniards were accused. We must not forget, however, that a police operation cannot be confused with a survey; sociopolitical considerations could have protected certain sectors and saved individuals, while perhaps linguistic and cultural barriers isolated others. I am satisfied to stress the urban nature and multiethnic character of the phenomenon described here.[22]

OCCUPATION, SOCIAL POSITION, AND ETHNIC ORIGIN

The analysis of occupation and social position poses the same obstacles and the same traps. It is even more limited, since relevant information is available for only 66 individuals out of the 123 accused. Four large categories cover three fourths of the identifiable accused: artisans; servants and slaves; those involved in food production and sale; and students. The artisanal occupations include those related to confection, tailoring, glove making, weaving, pigtail making, and shoemaking, with twenty-one persons (31.8 percent); five Spaniards and five mestizos were tailors. Further, according to the "Account of the accused . . . prisoners . . . and [those] summoned to edicts and public announcements for this case," we have servants and slaves (24.2 percent), with four slaves; seven students (10.6 percent); and those living off the production and sale of food (baker, fruit seller, chili seller, butcher, *pulquería* owner), who make up 10.6 percent. If we apply all this data to the different ethnic and racial mixtures, only one homogeneous group seems to stand out, that of the students, who are all—as expected—Spanish. On the other hand, we observe a predominance of Spaniards and mestizos among those working in confection, while mulattoes and blacks abound among the servants (ten of sixteen, or 62.5 percent), and mestizos and Indians predominate (six of seven, or 85.7 percent) in the group dedicated to food jobs. Such a percentage seems to reflect the usual profile of an urban colonial society with its well-off segments (the Spanish students); its slaves (three blacks and a mulatto);

its Indian and mestizo, mulatto, and Spanish artisans, and even some with less common professions: a puppeteer and a harp player.[23]

The representatives of the social elite, both economic and religious, are absent. In fact, we know through the testimony of Sotomayor and the archbishop of Mexico that members of the clergy also were incriminated. For them, discretion was imposed, but this did not prevent me from tracing the tracks of their sentences in the Inquisition archives.[24] In addition, the son of a town councilor from Puebla was among the incriminated. It is possible that these sectors escaped research more easily, or perhaps their names were silenced in order to diminish the scandal, so that the viceroy could affirm, "There is not in this case any man of quality or black cape, but all of them are mestizos, Indians, mulattos, blacks and all the filth of this kingdom and cities."

Either the viceroy was wrong or he was lying. But it is worth emphasizing the ease with which his pen added his social and racial prejudice to the condemnation of the sin. The reality, however, was different. Considering that the list of the accused corresponds to a chain of denunciations and, therefore, to a group of individuals who had some relationship among themselves, the nefarious sin apparently transcends social and ethnic barriers, shaping and defining an extremely original environment.

THE MANY FACES OF SIN

What was the sexual and sociocultural conduct that characterized such an environment? To answer this question, we have some clues provided by the list of the incriminated and by the details—sometimes extremely crude—revealed by the interrogations. Of course the most spectacular characters are the ones that stand out in the sources: the "effeminate ones," or "those dressed as women." In other words, the "transvestites." There are at least eight of them, including Juan de la Vega, mulatto, with the nickname of "Cotita" (Pansy); Miguel Gerónimo, mestizo, called "La Zangarriana"; Juan Correa, mestizo, with the nickname of "La Estampa" (the Print); Alonso, mestizo, "La Conchita"; Bernabé, a Spanish tailor, "La Luna" (the Moon); Sebastián Pérez, Spanish, "Las Rosas" (the Roses); Martín, an Indian with the nickname of "La Martina de los Cielos" (the Martina of the Heavens); and a black called "La Morossa" (the Slow). That is, there are three mestizos, two Spaniards, a black, an Indian, and a mulatto—6.5 percent of the incriminated (8 of 123). The scarce indigenous representation—only one Indian, "La Martina de los Cielos"—poses the question of the dissemination of "transvestism" in the indigenous environment, which remains unanswered here.

We can, however, sketch the contour of a practice inspired by female models. The gesture, the dress, the tasks performed are or are desired to be those of a woman and, sometimes, transvestites make an effort to imitate contemporary prostitutes or the beauties of the capital. Consider the nick-names used and received: "La Zangarriana . . . a nickname of a woman with lovers that lived in this city, very common. "La Estampa . . . was the name of a very beautiful lady that lived in this city." The descriptions about the female features are persistent:

> This Juan de la Vega . . . was an effeminate mulatto . . . they used to call him Cotita (which is the same as *mariquita* [pansy]) and . . . the said mulatto would move his hip and usually tied on his forehead a little cloth called "melindre" (narrow ribbon) that women use and . . . in the openings of the sleeves of a white bodice that he had, he would wear many hanging ribbons and . . . he would sit like a woman on the floor on a platform and . . . he would make tortillas and wash and cook.[25]

The mestizo Juan Correa was about seventy years old: "[H]e used to dance with these people, putting the cape he was wearing on his waist and moving his hip and complaining, saying that he was sick and that he was pregnant." Following out the logic of appropriating the model, the transves-tite pretends to be pregnant, and his mates and friends accept him as a woman, treating him as such: "the said people would give him presents and chocolates, calling him my soul, my life, and other flatteries."[26]

It seems that in order to be able to express his sexual individuality, the transvestite chooses the features and conduct that belong to the female sex in his society. It is, in fact, in the context of New Spain, as in many other loca-tions, the only culturally standardized and codified alternative that exists to masculine heterosexuality, despite the degradation and repression that this choice carries with it. In other words, transvestism constitutes a "model of misbehavior" and, for the same reason, a deviation that is easily identifiable by the other members of the community. The indigenous man may have had access to this model only if he was acculturated enough to turn into a "criollo woman," an indispensable condition if he was to integrate himself into an en-vironment that was socially and ethnically mixed, and thus answer to its tastes. Perhaps that is the reason for its representation in our source by only a single case, while there are three mestizos, and two Spaniards. It is worth adding that the model of misbehavior represented by transvestism is doubly deviant because of the inversion of roles that it implies, as well as because of the feminine reference chosen, since, as indicated, some of the nicknames (La Zangarriana, La Estampa) explicitly refer to the entourage of female prostitution, a space that is marginal itself in the society of New Spain. Be-sides the transvestites, there is no other clearly identifiable group, except for that of the boys who regularly visit Juan de la Vega, "Cotita," who seem to be prostitutes: "He was visited by some boys whom he called my soul, my life, my heart, and they would sit by him and would sleep in his dwelling."[27]

The environment was composed of the students and servants who worked in the schools of Puebla, masculine and monosexual spaces that offered a favorable ambiance for the practice of the nefarious sin. Bear in mind that in pre-industrial societies it was not easy for an individual to escape the promiscuity of everyday life, hiding his acts from his relatives and neighbors or maintaining relationships that were not the usual liaisons of alliance, friendship, or profession. Nor was it easy for a single man to survive without the help of a woman, whether she was his servant, slave, or wife. Thus, we presume that most of the accused, far from being integrated into categories or defined groups, led a double life, improvising, according to the occasion, their ways to find pleasure. Beyond a classification of "homosexuality," I want to insist on the plasticity of the conduct imposed by the need for clandestine behavior, the constant danger, and the necessary discretion. Aside from the flashy transvestites, the rest blend into the anonymous mass, unnoticed and ignored.

Yet leading a double life was a risky and harsh thing to do. The relationship with a woman could sometimes be difficult. At least, so hints Miguel de Urbina's testimony: "One day that he was with his wife, after having the carnal act with her, upset because it had not been with the man with whom he communicated nefariously, he grabbed a candle and set a figure of saint Baby Jesus that he had on an altar on fire."[28] The sexual and affective uneasiness of the Indian Miguel de Urbina took the form of a sacrilegious act that translated, in a spectacular and profoundly acculturated way (he was a "Spanish-speaking and intelligent" Indian), the difficulty of conciliating marital duties with the relationship that he kept with his lover. The clash between licit conduct and forbidden love provokes a crisis that bursts into the iconoclastic gesture. By committing it, Miguel involuntarily justifies the official condemnation that assimilates nefarious sin and heresy, as if both he and the authorities had perceived that this sexual and moral rupture could only be compared to that of heresy. Yet, as we will see later, the attitude seems to have been isolated.

THE SECRET SOCIABILITY

The environment that takes shape through our sources is characterized, above all, by an intense circulation of bodies. Therefore, Joseph Durán sleeps with Gerónimo Calbo, a mestizo who is twenty-three and is also Christoval de Victoria's lover. Gerónimo, Joseph, Simon de Cháves, Miguel Gerónimo, and Juan de la Vega are surprised together "committing the sin." During the meetings, the exchange seems to have been generalized. "In these visits they gave themselves away to each other and committed the nefarious sin with one another."[29] That is why they called Miguel Gerónimo "La Zagarriana," because she was communal to all of them.

The sources also reveal the frequency of sexual relationships: "They confessed to having committed the nefarious sin an infinity of times with many different people, indicating the place, time, hour, day, month, and year."[30] The admitted ease of the contacts is quite surprising, given the climate of repression and mortal risks that surrounded the practice of the nefarious sin. This proliferation—so contrary to the norms of a Christian society—expresses an intense search for pleasure that perhaps had very few equivalents. It also reintroduces the question of the actual threshold of tolerance that these men might have enjoyed in the capital of the viceroyalty and the city of Puebla.

On the other hand, obsessed with the "filth" of the sin, justice paid little attention to the affective and amorous dimension that these physical liaisons could have. Based on the desire for another or others, completely ignoring barriers of age, skin, or statute, this sociability is strengthened by the creation of stable relationships: Christoval de Victoria confesses being the lover of the "handsome," Gerónimo Calbo; Miguel de Urbina openly prefers his lover to his wife, whom he hates. The strength of the liaison can end up in crises and jealous scenes such as the ones that the lover of the black Nicolás de Pisa used to provoke ("there had been jealous quarrels").[31] Once again we analyze a marginal society that in some respects copies the conduct and conflicts of the heterosexual world, a clandestine environment in which deviation reproduces—although displacing them—the usual models: woman, prostitution, possession, lies, and, as described later, religiosity.

Besides the occasional relationships "in the country," far from indiscreet gazes, sexual activity took place at meetings that some people would organize in their own homes, as happened in San Juan de la Penitencia, "almost outside of the city walls," or in the neighborhood of San Pablo—normally, in secluded places. "Houses with all the commodities where they received visits" were used to meet, according to Guijo—cozy houses for friends or dates, in which older "transvestites" acted as procurers. That was the case of Juan Correa, "seventy years old, who would take the money from these visits." As we saw, Juan lived surrounded by boys who prostituted themselves. There they met on holidays, "especially on the days of Our Lady, of the Saint Apostles and other Church festivities." Not only because they were holidays, but also because they corresponded to the preferred devotion of the house owner: "Because most of them had in their oratories images of Our Lady and other previously referred to saints and, since they were going to celebrate their holidays, they invited each other." Thus, for instance, they used to meet in the home of the Indian Juan—a tanner—in order to celebrate Saint Nicholas;

they danced, slept together, "They made appointments for other visits of women in other different parts." They exchanged addresses. "They decided on other houses where they could celebrate the holidays." Youngsters, elders, transvestites, and male prostitutes had some chocolate, and some remembered the deeds and the conquests of their far-away youth, their lost beauty, and old-time pleasures. Sometimes rival lovers would fight and insult each other.[32]

Thus, the different and complementary spaces of the "nefarious" desire appear; the deserted places for furtive meetings, the holiday meetings in which one "picks up" a date, the call houses. We should also mention the dark baths, in which bodies mixed "in the hidden little rooms there are in them."[33] After arresting an Indian and a mulatto who had "committed the nefarious sin" in one of these baths, the Royal Criminal Court commented in 1687:

> The interaction of men by themselves in the baths, although it is not bad in itself, because of the circumstances that meet there—the heat, darkness, touches, movements, slaps, vapors, all together are provocative—moves, irritates, urges to carelessness and even more, given that the people who go there are of vile condition and bad habits: as a result they commit enormous sins such as sodomy.[34]

We should not forget either certain *pulquerías* in which Indians, "in order to calm their awkward appetite, dress as women at night, and sleep among them (the clients) inebriated, and provoke them into the clumsy act."[35] In addition, the forced promiscuity of the *obrajes* favored all kinds of illicit relationships, even the nefarious sin. Thus, for instance, in November 1673, seven mulatto, black, and mestizo men from Juan de Avila's *obraje* in Mixcoac, died in the bonfire.[36]

Beyond this sociability outlined by the sources, we have a sense of the existence of a subculture that has its secret geography, its network of information and informers, its language, and its codes. Think, for example, about the nicknames that designate many of these men: El Mitre Pulquero (the chief pulquería owner), Camarones (Shrimps), El Rey de Francia (the King of France), El Alazán (the Chestnut Horse), El Conejo (the Rabbit), Cascavel (the Rattle), Carita de Güevo (Egg Face). We should also remember the use of terms like *mariquita, cotita, puto, guapo* (handsome), and so on, or the anonymous intervention that informed a certain mulatto, Benito de Cuebas, about his imminent arrest. This environment escapes the networks, the institutional connections that structure the colonial society; neither the family, nor friendship, clientele, nor fraternity constitute the frameworks in which these lives develop. Hence, we can term it a "subversive" environment.

Yet, though it is undoubtedly a marginal and clandestine environment, it is not totally disconnected from the society that oppresses it. It reproduces some aspects of the semi-tolerated world of female prostitution, it integrates typically "feminine" conduct and attitudes, and it manifests a religious conformity, following the traditions and rites of Baroque devotion. In fact, through the ethnic and social plurality of its members, this environment is in permanent contact with many other different sectors of New Spanish society. Therefore, it is a privileged and even exceptional space for acculturation because of its multiplicity of connections as well as the lack of discrimination that prevails in its choices.

It is also a particularly fragile sector. We cannot ignore the limits of a sociability that is founded on a community of desire and exterior rejection. It did not resist the violence of repression, as, without torture, the first arrested people denounced all their companions, thus unchaining the infernal machine of persecution: "From the declaration of the aforementioned people, Benito Cuebas appeared as an accomplice, . . . and from the declarations and confessions of all these people, nineteen persons were apprehended. . . . They confessed to committing the nefarious sin, . . . indicating place, time, hour, day, month, and year."[37] That is how 123 suspects were discovered. We should probably attribute this unfortunate lack of solidarity to the panic that is often provoked by judicial repression and its bonfires.

THE LIFESTYLE

These men did not seem to have lived in perpetual fear, despite the spectrum of repression. Obviously, it is very difficult to attempt to perceive the way in which they assumed their individuality, the way in which they lived their "homosexual" experience. In spite of this, I believe that it is necessary to contrast testimonies that seem paradoxical. In some of them, we find the expression of a conscience of the sin along with the will to escape the temptation. This is only true, be it said, in the case of the mulatto Benito de Cuebas, who was attending mass at the cathedral and praying to Our Lady "that She take him out of the sin," at the very moment of his arrest. Whether this was opportunism (he had been warned shortly before his arrest, as noted above) or repentance, the reaction came too late and did not stop the mulatto from dying in the bonfire like the rest. Let us also remember that the explosion of anger of the Indian Miguel de Urbina expressed more the frustration of a married homosexual than the inconvenience caused by a particular desire. Yet, by committing a double transgression—sexual and iconoclastic—the Indian reveals the difficulties caused by leading a double life.

In contrast with these two cases, the other incriminated people offer a much less dramatic image. Instead of remorse, they express nostalgia, they lament no longer being able to enjoy themselves. The mestizo Juan Correa had sixty-three years of practice, as he knew the sin at the age of seven:

He was happy that the present century was ending as people did not enjoy in this one as in the past—referring to the time before the flood of the city—because this Juan de Correa said that then he used to be a pretty girl and that he dressed as a woman with other men and that they enjoyed themselves committing the nefarious sin.[38]

Therefore, before the judges who were going to send him to the bonfire, the elder evoked memories of a far-away, joyful past, prior to the great flood of 1629.[39] Others bragged about their numerous lovers: "[Christoval de Vitoria] had continuously committed the nefarious sin in this city since the time before the flood, for more than thirty years, and that he had nearly caused the whole city to be lost because of the number of people that [he] had taught to commit this sin." Through these testimonies emerges a double image of conduct that is voluntarily disseminated and presents a vindicated uniqueness, as when Juan de la Vega confesses that "he felt offended if they did not call him Cotita (Pansy)."[40]

It seems that a certain degree of narcissism substituted for the culpability inculcated by society, as well as the anguish fed by persecution and its spectacular bonfires. This same survival reaction may also explain the coexistence—in my opinion, contradictory—of the nefarious sin and Christian piety, as if the narcissistic affirmation had contributed to ignoring the Church's condemnation. We will finish by questioning the affective impact of the repression carried out against the "sodomites." How could they live with the perspective of such a horrible death? In what measure did the small number of executions (in relation to the number of people who practiced the sin) make it a reality that was too distant to be really feared? It was not too distant, however, for the victims of the repression of 1658:

> In one day The Royal Criminal Court . . . has sentenced fourteen to burn, as it was done, going out together to their death without it being necessary to torment them, because the fourteen of them were convicts and confessed, actors and receptors with each other.

> The fire penalty was executed with the fourteen of them.[41]

NOTES

1. "We qualify as perverted any sexual activity that renounced procreation in order to look for pleasure as something independent from it" (Freud, *Introduction a la Psychoanalyse*, 269).

2. A new historiographic reflection has begun to be developed about this topic in recent years; see Dover, *Greek Homosexuality*; Boswell, *Christianity, Social Tolerance, and Homosexuality*; Foucault, *Histoire de la sexualité*, vols. 2 and 3.

3. Guijo, *Diario*, 54–65.

4. AGI, México, 469.

5. AGI, México, 38, exp. 57-A, 57-B, 57-C, the viceroy's letter (exp. 57), the one by the criminal magistrate (exp. 57-A), the testimony (exp. 57-B), and a report (exp. 57-C): "Report

of the executed for committing the nefarious sin whose case was fulminated by Señor Licenciado Don Juan Manuel de Sotomayor, knight of the Order of Calatrava, of the Council of his Majesty, its magistrate of this court, that was sentenced by the Royal Criminal Court on January 4, of this year of 1658, the fourteen convicts, after confessing, and one of them confessed later, being in the chapel, and one of them, being fifteen years old, was sentenced to two hundred lashes and was sold to the mines for six years. . . . Imprisoned for this crime in the Royal Prison, whose cases are being solved. . . . They were summoned by edicts and public announcements for this reason, and most of them with two eyewitnesses, none of the summoned people were earwitnesses, that all the people included in the edicts were the following" (Fernando Fernández de la Cueva, eighth duke of Albuquerque, who was viceroy from 1653 through 1660). The Royal Criminal Court was a dependent criminal jurisdiction of the Audiencia; it was in charge of criminal matters under the direction of six criminal magistrates (Villaseñor y Sánchez, *Theatro Americano*, 37–38).

6. One might underscore the detail with which the nefarious acts are described.

7. AGI, México, 38, exp. 57.

8. Let us remember that in 1497, the Catholic kings enacted a law that made the nefarious sin equivalent to heresy and the crime of *lesa majestad* (high treason). The *Pragmatics* of Philip II (1598) established the need to condemn the suspects even without the necessary proofs. The punishment was the bonfire. Additionally, the accused were subject to degrading practices, such as the examination of their bodies by surgeons in charge of finding evidence of the crime.

9. AGI, México, 38, exp. 57-B; my emphasis.

10. He refers to the heir Prince Philip Prosper, born in 1657, the son of King Philip IV (1605–1665).

11. According to the *Malleus Maleficarum*, the famous manual for witch-hunters, he who had persevered in this sin more than thirty-three years—the time of the earthly life of Christ— lost any hope of being saved; see Institoris and Sprenger, *Marteau des sorcieres*, 176–77.

12. AGI, México, 38, exp. 57; my emphasis. Subsequent quotations in this paragraph are also from this source.

13. Serna, "Manual de ministros de indios," 74.

14. Ruiz de Alarcón, "Tratado de las supersticiones," 49.

15. "Very few locals of this place escape the contagion"; see Balsalobre, "Relación auténtica," 359. It is useful to remember that homosexuality is still considered a social disease. See, for example, Schelsky, *Sociologie de la sexualité*, 150.

16. Let us remember the autos-da-fé in 1649 and 1659, which almost exterminated the crypto-Jews of New Spain; see Liebman, *Los judíos*.

17. Sigüenza y Góngora, *Alboroto y motín*, 72.

18. AGI, México, 38, exp. 57-B.

19. Editor's note: See chapter two on Mesoamerican indigenous men who "dressed as women."

20. Foucault, *Histoire de la folie*, 101–3. For the connections between homosexuality and heresy, see Montar, "La sodomie," 1024, 1032: "In the times of the famous Imperial code of Charles V, the Carolina of 1532, sodomy . . . was mentioned among the spiritual crimes whose particular horror came from the special offense committed against God."

21. According to Charles Gibson (*Aztecs*), the indigenous population of Mexico City and of Tlatelolco was about 17,000 persons in the mid-seventeenth century. Peter Gerhard gives the figure of 7,600 indigenous tributaries for Mexico City in 1644, while the Spanish citizens numbered about 8,000 (*Guide*, 182).

22. On the sociopolitical context, see Israel, *Race, Class, and Politics*.

23. AGI, México, 38, exp. 57-C.

24. "The Inquisition Tribunal has taken measures with its prisoners, and the Bishop has imprisoned other exempt ones from his jurisdiction, as even among these this moral and nefarious illness had spread" (Sotomayor in AGI, México, 38, exp. 57-A). In a letter of 4 May 1659

the Archbishop of Mexico, Matheo Sagade Bugueiro, names three persons: a "priest named Diego de Saabedia, . . . Manuel Espinossa, presbyter, . . . Fernando Gaitán de Ayala" (AGI, México, 38, exp. 57).

25. AGI, México, 38, exp. 57-B.
26. Ibid.
27. Ibid.
28. Ibid.
29. Ibid.
30. Ibid.
31. Ibid.
32. Ibid.
33. Ibid.
34. AGI, México, 87. Letter of the Criminal Court, 12 January 1687, fols. 16r–17v, 26.
35. AGI, México, 333, Joseph Vidal de Figueroa, Canon, 1 July 1692.
36. Robles, *Diario*, 137. Editor's note: an obraje was a manufacturing plant that often used forced or coerced labor.
37. AGI, México, 38, exp. 57-A.
38. AGI, México, 38, exp. 57-B.
39. Boyer, *Gran inundación*.
40. AGI, México, 38, exp. 57-B.
41. The first quotation comes from the viceroy (AGI, México, 38, exp. 57-B). The second quotation comes from Sotomayor; see note 5 above (AGI, México, 38, exp. 57-C). In addition, according to Guijo (*Diario*, 140), on 1 October 1660 a mulatto who was twenty-seven was executed in the market of San Juan. He had been denounced by his companions.

WORKS CITED

Balsalobre, Gonzalo de. "Relación auténtica de las idolatrías . . . de los indios del obispado de Oaxaca, 1656." In *Tratado de las idolatrías supersticiones, dioses, ritos, hechicerías, y otras costumbres gentílicas de las razas aborígenes de México*. Mexico City: Navarro, 1953.

Boswell, John. *Christianity, Social Tolerance, and Homosexuality*. Chicago: University of Chicago Press, 1980.

Boyer, Richard Everett. *La gran inundación: Vida y sociedad en México (1629–1638)*. Mexico City: Secretaria de Educación Pública, 1975.

Dover, K. J. *Greek Homosexuality*. New York: Vintage Books, 1978.

Foucault, Michel. *Histoire de la folie a l'âge classique*. Paris: Gallimard, 1972.

———. *Histoire de la Sexualité*. Vol. 2. *L'usage des plaisirs*. Paris: Gallimard, 1984.

———. *Histoire de la Sexualité*. Vol. 3. *Le souci de Soi*. Paris: Gallimard, 1984.

Freud, Sigmund. *Introduction a la Psychoanalyse*. Paris, 1965.

Gerhard, Peter. *A Guide to the Historical Geography of New Spain*. Cambridge: Cambridge University Press, 1972

Gibson, Charles. *The Aztecs under Spanish Rule*. Stanford, CA: Stanford University Press, 1964.

Guijo, Gregorio M. de. *Diario, 1648–1664*. 2 volumes. Manuel Romero de Terreos, ed. Mexico City: Editorial Porrúa, 1952.

Institoris, Henry, and Jacques Sprenger. *Le Marteau des sorcieres*. Paris: Plon, 1973.

Israel, J. I. *Race, Class, and Politics in Colonial Mexico, 1610–1670*. Oxford: Oxford University Press, 1975.

Liebman, Seymour. *Los judíos de México y América Central: Fé, llamas, Inquisición*. Mexico City: Siglo XXI, 1971.

Montar, E. W. "La sodomie a l'époque moderne en Suisse Romande." *Annales* (Paris) 29 (1974): 1023–33.

Robles, Antonio de. *Diario de sucesos notables (1665–1703)*. Mexico City: Editorial Porrúa, 1964.

Ruiz de Alarcón, Hernando. "Tratado de las supersticiones y costumbres gentílicas que oy viuen entre los indios naturales desta Nueva España." In *Tratado de las idolatrías supersticiones, dioses, ritos, hechicerías, y otras costumbres gentílicas de las razas aborígenes de México*. Mexico City: Navarro, 1953.

Schelsky, Helmut. *Sociologie de la sexualité*. Paris: Idées, 1969.

Serna, Jacinto de la. "Manual de ministros de indios para el conocimiento de sus idolatrias, y extirpacion de ellas." In *Tratado de las idolatrías, supersticiones, hechicerías y otras costumbres en las razas aborígenes de México*. Mexico City: Navarro, 1953.

Sigüenza y Góngora, Carlos de. *Alboroto y motín de México del 8 de junio de 1692*. Mexico City: I. Leonard, 1932.

Villaseñor y Sánchez, José Antonio. *Theatro Americano: Descripción general de los Reynos y Provincias de la Nueva España y sus jurrisdiciones*. Mexico City: Imprenta de la Viuda de d. Joseph Bernardo de Hogal, 1746–48.

CONTRIBUTORS

DAVID HIGGS is professor of history at the University of Toronto. He edited the collection *Queer Sites: Gay Urban Histories since 1600* and is now at work on a book on the Inquisition in late colonial Brazil.

SERGE GRUZINSKI is director of research at the Centre National de la Recherche Scientifique in Paris and author of several critically acclaimed books, including *Images at War*, *The Conquest of Mexico*, and *Man-Gods in the Mexican Highlands*.

MICHAEL J. HORSWELL is assistant professor of colonial Latin American literature at Florida Atlantic University. His publications include essays on the Inca Garcilaso de la Vega, Guaman Poma de Ayala, and the topic of cultural hybridity in colonial literature. He is currently finishing a book on the transculturation of gender and sexuality in the colonial Andes.

LUIZ MOTT is professor of anthropology at the Federal University of Bahia, Brazil, and the founder and president of Grupo Gay da Bahia, Brazil's oldest gay rights organization. He is a leading human rights activist and the author of numerous books and articles about homosexuality in Brazil and Portugal, including *O lesbianismo no Brasil*, "Pagode português: a subcultura gay em Portugal nos tempos inquistoriais," *O sexo proibido: virgens, gays e escravos nas garras da inquisição*, and *Epidemic of Hate: Violations of the Human Rights of Gay Men, Lesbians, and Transvestites in Brazil*.

PETE SIGAL is associate professor of Latin American history at California State University, Los Angeles. He is the author of *From Moon Goddesses to Virgins: The Colonization of Yucatecan Maya Sexual Desire*.

WARD STAVIG is associate professor of history at the University of South Florida. He specializes in colonial indigenous social and cultural issues, especially in the Andes. He has published numerous articles, including one on a related theme, "Living in Offense of Our Lord: Indigenous Sexual Values and Marital Life in the Colonial Crucible" (*HAHR* 75, no. 4 [1995]). He is also the author of *The World of Túpac Amaru* and *Amor y violencia sexual,* and he is currently working on a project that focuses on indigenous identity in eighteenth-century rural Bolivia.

RICHARD C. TREXLER is distinguished professor of history at the State University of New York at Binghamton. Among his several monographs are *Public Life in Renaissance Florence; The Journey of the Magi: Meanings in History of a Christian Story; Sex and Conquest: Gendered Violence, Political Order, and the European Conquest of the Americas;* and *Reliving Golgotha: Profanity and Solemnity in the Passion Play of Iztapalapa, Mexico* (forthcoming).

INDEX